Adoption
and Mothering

edited by

Frances J. Latchford

DEMETER

DEMETER PRESS, BRADFORD, ONTARIO

Published by:
Demeter Press
140 Holland Street West
P. O. Box 13022
Bradford, ON L3Z 2Y5
Tel: (905) 775-9089
Email: info@demeterpress.org
Website: www.demeterpress.org

Demeter Press logo based on Skulptur "Demeter" by Maria-Luise Bodirsky
<www.keramik-atelier.bodirsky.edu>

Front Cover Design and Layout: Jan Bird
Cover Photography: Frank E. Latchford

Printed and Bound in Canada

　　　Adoption and mothering / edited by Frances J. Latchford.

Includes bibliographical references.
ISBN 978-0-9866671-5-2

　　　1. Motherhood. 2. Adoption. 3. Birthmothers. 4. Adoptive parents. 5. Foster mothers. I. Latchford, Frances Joan, 1964-

HQ759.A36 2012　　　　　306.874'3　　　　　C2012-906154-9

To my parents, Frank and Joan

Table of Contents

Acknowledgements

I want to thank Dr. Andrea O'Reilly, Editor in Chief of Demeter Press, for the opportunity, guidance, and support that made this book possible. To the book's contributors, I want to say how much I appreciate your dedication and hard work in the service of this project—it has paid off. Thank you to Suzanne Sixsmith and Luciana Ricciutelli for your patience in proofing the final copy of this work and to the creative vision of Jan Bird, who is responsible for the design of its cover. To sociologist Patti Phillips, you have helped me to think through many tangled issues. To my dear, dear friends Jackie O'Keefe and Suzie Richter, who make me laugh and cry and provide me with a thousand necessary distractions: you are my stalwart comrades who have become family. To my parents, Frank and Joan Latchford, and my siblings Vancel, Carol, Ira, Michael, Benjamin, Alphonse, and Jay: thank you for the on-going experiences of family that inspire my critical interest in its meanings and formation. To Dr. Kym Bird, your humour, encouragement, patience, and our on-going intellectual dialogue, not only fueled my desire to see this project completed, but continue to fire my imagination, my writing, and my love.

Introduction

FRANCES J. LATCHFORD

THE DOMINANT MEANING OF MOTHERHOOD that contours our social and cultural imaginations produces birthmothers and adoptive mothers as failed female subjects. These mothers do not enact *in toto* the biological *and* social practices that are expected of women as "mothers" in an evolving context that remains a bio-heteronormative patriarchy: birthmothers are deficient in the social practices of motherhood, while adoptive mothers are inadequate to the task of "natural" or biological motherhood.

Our bio-romantic notion of motherhood morally codes a dead (or mortally ill) mother as the only one who cannot be condemned for the surrender *or* relinquishment of a biological child to an adoptive mother of any kind (e.g., in/formal adoptive mothers, foster mothers, or step-mothers). This code subjects extant birthmothers to social shame and guilt, in spite of the fact that surrendering children can so often turn on coercive social forces or systems related to age, ability, race, class, the family, religion and sexuality. It popularizes cultural contempt for birthmothers that might desire, dare, and even choose to relinquish a child for reasons of self-interest, not due to coercion or socio-economic circumstance. It also renders the motives of mothers who adopt when reproduction is not an option piteous, pathological, and even pathetic; whereas, adoptive mothers for whom bio-reproduction is an option are interpreted as suspect and saccharine in what is frequently perceived as their elitism, charity, and missionary zeal.

These are cultural and institutionalized meanings with which birthmothers and adoptive mothers are often associated, and they indicate that adoption is a process of subjection through which women as "failed mothers" are constituted. From the perspective of critical adoption studies, however, these meanings can also be taken up as a sign that adoption is a productive lens through which motherhood and its narratives can be (re)examined, (re)invented, and (re)written to better represent and value women's difference as mothers.

Taken together, the concepts of adoption and mothering throw normative meanings of motherhood into question; they elicit paradoxes that concern our abilities to think about what it means to be a mother. Adoption troubles westernized concepts of motherhood because, first and foremost, these concepts assume a naturalized view of the social practice of mothering *as* a causal effect of women's reproductive biology. Coupled with the phenomenon of adoption, the notion of "mother" is troubled explicitly because adoption magnifies the ways in which mothering, for a sizable number of women, is solely a social practice *or* a biological situation and not both. Although twin concepts, in that mothering is embedded in the meaning of adoption to an important degree, these concepts are also antithetical. Whether we speak of it as open or closed, formal or informal, transracial and/or transnational, or in terms of fostering and step-parenting, adoption is conceived, primarily and inevitably, as a kind of lack that is transposable with the identity of women who either fail at, or reject outright, the bio-social project of naturalized motherhood. Adoption, it is commonly assumed, is the result of the adoptive mother's lack with respect to biological reproduction, the birthmother's, or first mother's, lack of service as the primary caregiver to her biological child, and the lack that these two kinds of mothers are thought to bequeath to the adopted child.[1] There are, of course, adoptive mothers who have biological children and birthmothers who engage in the social aspects of mothering by virtue of open adoption and even reunion, but these mothers are not the mothers who dominate the popular imagination when the subject of mothering is conjoined with that of adoption.

Adoption and Mothering is an interdisciplinary collection of scholarly essays that elucidate, critique, expand and challenge Western meanings of motherhood from the vantage point of adoption. Its authors traverse questions of adoption and mothering from myriad critical perspectives rooted in the humanities and social sciences: as a group, they enlist various forms of feminism, conflict theory, cultural theory, poststructural and postcolonial theories, psychoanalysis and symbolic interactionist theory, and queer and disability theories. Its authors' relationships to adoption and mothering are also diverse, in that they are birthmothers, adoptive mothers, the adult children of these mothers, and/or persons poised to become mothers through adoption.

What is most unique about this edition with respect to adoption studies is that it is concerned exclusively with mothers and mothering: it addresses critical issues concerning birthmothers and adoptive mothers and it confronts the ways in which these mothers are commonly portrayed in adoption debate and discourse. Its focus on mothers and mothering contains and specializes its analyses of adoption as a phenomenon that is provocative and challenging with respect to our ideals and the realities of being mothers, women, and family members. Together, its articles fashion a new and nuanced dialogue between Canadian and American scholars whose relations to adoption and mothering are varied and complex in light of their experiences of adoption as either an institution, locus of power, discourse, mode of knowledge, choice and/or lifestyle.

This book is not an adoption primer. It is not modeled on books like the *Handbook of Adoption*, edited by Rafael A. Javier *et al*, in that it does not primarily target researchers, practitioners, and students in adoption psychology, social work, and social science. Of course, it is my hope the book will be interesting to this constituency, but it is nonetheless designed as a critical dialogue about and/or between birthmothers and adoptive mothers, one that will be engaging to anyone who thinks mothering, adoption, and family studies must be revisited and rethought from various perspectives in critical studies that are feminist, postcolonial, psychoanalytic, queer and/or concern disability.

This book is also distinct from many other adoption readers in that it does not focus on all members of the adoption triad, nor attempt to give a broad, comprehensive overview of historical and contemporary debates in adoption research. Instead, it looks directly at mothers and at how meanings of adoption complicate meanings of motherhood and family. There are, to be sure, many wonderful compendiums and monographs in print that address birthmothers and adoptive mothers; popular books such as *The Adoption Reader*, edited by Susan Wadia-Ells, *The Girls Who Went Away*, by Ann Fessler, or *I Wish for You A Beautiful Life*, edited by Sarah K. Dorow are books that speak directly to mothers in the context of adoption primarily through personal narratives, histories and/or letters. *Adoption and Mothering*, conversely, is a book of scholarly essays that, in the main, are written by authors whose research in the humanities and social sciences is driven by a personal interest in critical questions surrounding adoption and mothering. This is what informs their theoretical, social, and political analyses of what it means to be a birthmother and/or adoptive mother; their stake in these issues serves, not merely as an object of their study, but as one among many interpretive lenses through which the experience, subjectivity and/or social location of birthmothers and adoptive mothers can be explored, characterized, and theorized.

This book is also unique in that it includes chapters from both sides of a divide maintained by so many adoption readers and anthologies between the social sciences and the humanities. Sally Haslanger and Charlotte Witt's excellent edition, *Adoption Matters*, for instance, is a book of scholarly interdisciplinary essays that take up various adoption issues from the perspective of social, political and legal philosophy, but it does not extend beyond the humanities. Conversely, *Adoption*, edited by Anthony Douglas and Terry Philpot, is a multifaceted collection that is broad in subject matter and style, including the voices of lay birthparents, adoptees and adoptive parents in and amongst the work of policy makers, practitioners and academics, but it does not effectively step outside the social sciences. *Adoption and Mothering* mixes up the disciplines and gives birth to a hybrid with articles from a range of disciplines that will capture the attention of researchers and students in the humanities and social sciences, as well as readers who are generally knowledgeable about adoption.

This book begins where the story of adoption and mothering begins, with birthmothers themselves, and then moves on to essays that focus on adoptive mothers. It investigates the debate, discourse, and politics of adoption that both surrounds these mothers and impacts contemporary notions of motherhood as biological and non-biological kin. Its essays offer critical perspectives on adoption and mothering that challenge institutionalized ideas, assumptions, pathologies, and psychologies that are used to interpret birthmothers and adoptive mothers. Its authors interrogate questions of race, gender, disability, class and sexuality as they relate to the experience, identity, and the subjectivity of "mothers" who are marked by the institution of adoption. It pursues historical and contemporary themes, language, law, and practices that concern mothering in closed and open adoption systems, and in transracial and transnational adoption. It critically explores the expectations, scrutiny, and liminality that birthmothers and adoptive mothers often face. It looks at imperatives that mothers be the keepers of culture, potential adversaries, and borderland mothers. In effect, it creates a productive and exciting dialogue about and between birthmothers and adoptive mothers that I suspect will challenge its readers and traditional notions of motherhood.

Karen March's "Denial of Self: Birthmothers, Non-disclosure Adoption Laws, and the Silence of Others," is the first essay in the collection and it allies key concerns in feminism, adoption studies and mothering studies through interview research with birthmothers. A sociologist, March focuses on how "a woman's sense of self can be affected deeply by how others respond to her motherhood"; she applies a "symbolic interactionist" perspective, wherein she regards the "self as a social process" that

4

is "formed in interaction with others." In this light, she considers how the social operation of motherhood as a "master status" in conjunction with "motherhood negation," a process that is mediated through demands of secrecy and/or the treatment of the birthmother's pregnancy and relinquishment as a "non-event," diminishes birthmothers' abilities to present and experience the self in all of its complexity. At the hands of family members, partners and friends who allot no social meaning or value to their unique experiences of motherhood, March shows how birthmothers are led to assume "non-mother" identities.

Nicole Pietsch's essay, "Good Mothers, Bad Mothers, Not-Mothers: Privilege, Race and Gender and the Invention of the Birthmother," which can be said to speak to the work of March on some fronts, considers further processes of differentiation that affect birthmothers. Pietsch applies a feminist poststructuralist analysis to examine the birthmother's invention through hegemonic binary constructs of race-specific motherhood. She argues these constructs lead to privileged and marginalized femininities that impact "diversely-located expectant mothers" differently in North American adoption discourse and practice. She illuminates how "birthmothers," in relation to a racialized hierarchy of "good mothers," "bad mothers," and "not mothers," emerge as a corollary to "constructs of White femininity [that] continue to inform our expectations of legitimate, capable motherhood."

Katherine Sieger's, "A Birthmother's Identity: [M]other Living on the Border of (Non)Motherhood," approaches birthmother identities as fluid, multiple, and hybrid, especially in the context of open adoption. She resituates the question of birthmother subjectivity in the context of "border identity theory," as proposed originally by intersectional feminist Gloria Anzaldúa. In response to adoption research that "focuses mainly on how understanding the birthmother benefits the adoption community (i.e., adoptive parents and adoption workers)," Sieger's project reframes past inquiries that are concerned with, but not concerned for, birthmothers. She argues birthmother identity is not fixed, but "simultaneous," because it occurs "on the border of (non)motherhood." In doing so, Sieger poses a new and important question: "how does understanding birthmother identities benefit birthmothers themselves?"

Kate Livingston's essay, "The Birthmother Dilemma: Resisting Feminist Exclusions in the Study of Adoption," turns the critical lens of feminism, in the context of adoption studies, back on itself. She takes a self-reflexive and interdisciplinary feminist approach, one that utilizes postcolonial insights, and arrives at a constructive critique of various feminisms in adoption studies that leave birthmothers out in the cold. A key observation Livingston makes is that "feminist adoption scholarship is structured by a binary opposition that occurs between essentialism and social construction, one that threatens to efface birthmothers in new feminist definitions of the family." This binary, she argues, "produce[s] irreconcilable challenges for birthmothers," ones that lead to what she calls "the 'birthmother dilemma;' the situation wherein birthmothers find they must simultaneously undermine and embrace normative constructions of family in order to be acknowledged by adoption studies." Livingston's ultimate aim is to encourage feminists to more readily challenge this binary wherever it occurs in adoption theory and to circumvent it with new feminist theories of family that prevent any further marginalization of birthmothers in life and theory.

"Reckless Abandon: The Politics of Victimization and Agency in Birthmother Narratives" is my contribution to this book and it is written from the perspective of queer feminism, psychoanalysis and poststructuralism. In it, I investigate how birthmother discourse that relies on naturalized views of motherhood operates in a manner that effaces the reality of some birthmothers' agency, which I argue has profound implications for women with respect to the choice *to be, or not to be* mothers. I show how and why this discourse, which operates as a basis for the right to access the child, casts birthmothers as fundamentally traumatized women that must come to terms with their biological motherhood. I also contend the phenomenon of relinquishment is too often associated with the idea that, due to systemic oppression and social circumstance, birthmothers essentially lack agency, because no woman, unless crazy or compelled, *chooses* to relinquish a child. My aim is to interrogate the bio-essentialism of birthmother discourse, its relationship to gender, and the effacement of women who do *choose* to relinquish, even as they may also choose open adoption or to search; it is to show how important questions about women's subjectivity, freedom and equality are elicited through a more critical understanding of this discourse and its effects.

Turning attention now to issues that face adoptive mothers, in "Re-Thinking Motherhood and Kinship in International Adoption," Sarah Wall addresses paternalistic bias and pathologization in adoption research and practice that targets mothers who adopt transnationally. She does so based on her experience of international adoption; she shows how adoptive mothers' knowledge of their children and families is often dismissed as suspect, false, or as a kind of "denial." Her work is unique in the context of this collection because it is a feminist autoethnography; as an adoptive mother, who also happens to be a feminist sociologist, Wall expressly validates the personal experience of adoptive mothers as a legitimate scholarly basis from which to critique the dominant "story of international adoption" that "too easily becomes one about otherness, disruption, and risk." She argues that this story or bias—on the part of adoption experts, for instance—occurs too readily "because of the ways in which Western society privileges biological kinship." Her intriguing response to this bias is that while adoptive mothers' ties "are not genetic," their experience, nonetheless, "is fully embodied."

Amy E. Traver conducts a feminist, sociological study that "interweaves literature on ethnicity and mothering" to reveal how the "*ethnic* efforts" of American adoptive mothers of children from China can "best be understood as White, middle-class *mothering* strategies." In "Mothering Chineseness: Celebrating Ethnicity with White American Mothers of Children Adopted from China," she "examines the central role *adoptive mothers* play in the cultural celebrations" of "their children's ethno-cultural heritage." Based on interview data, she assesses what motivates white adoptive mothers' celebratory practices, at least, in part: these mothers "often identify with their children's ethno-cultural heritage to make visible and maintain their maternal relationships." Traver's findings are fascinating in that they imply these mothers' celebratory cultural practices are not aimed solely at securing the transnational or transracial identity of the adopted child, but their own identities as "mothers." In effect, she argues these mothers enlist "ethnic performance" as a strategy both to "attach or identify themselves with their children" and to secure their social positions as "mothers" in a white, middle-class American context that is hostile toward "intra-family difference."

Jenny Heijun Wills dialogues with Traver across disciplines, in "Narrating Multiculturalism in Asian Adoption Fiction," in that white Western mothers who transnationally adopt Asian children are the subject of her work also. She enlists feminism, postcolonialism, literary criticism, and cultural studies to discuss narratives by which adoptive mothers are produced in contemporary fiction by and about Asian adoptees in the Western context. The centrepiece of her analysis is best articulated by Wills herself: "[i]f the biological mother is a metonym for an adoptee's lost Asian culture in these novels, I suspect the adoptive mother is a metonym for the Western colonization and consumption of transracial and transnational adoptees." Wills acknowledges transcultural adoptive mothers can participate in "asianphiliac" or neo-liberal Orientalist mothering, for instance, where they capitulate uncritically to "adoptee psychology that calls for cultural preservation, and impose performances of race and ethnicity onto their reluctant children." However, she also argues the idea that the inclination for these adoptive mothers to do so is one among three narrative brushes that is used in Asian adoption fiction to paint overarching cultural portraits of these mothers, a phenomenon she thinks needs to be addressed for its own negative implications.

Judith Martin and Gail Trimberger's "Adoptive Mothering: A Transracial Adoptee's Viewpoint" challenges us to rethink the frameworks through which research on adoptive mothering is typically conducted. They note, "most research on adoptive mothering tends to focus on caretaking responsibilities and measures success by assessing how well the emotional and physical needs of children have been met." They also observe that too frequently it is "the autobiographical materials of adoptive mothers" that are used to examine the outcomes of transracial adoption. To countervail both of these trends, Martin and Trimberger reframe the meaning of success creatively as a question that should measure the "empowerment" of the adoptive mother, and they do so based on the autobiography of a transracially adopted child. They analyse Jaiya John's *Black Baby, White Hands: A View from the Crib* through the feminist lens of "Andrea O'Reilly's mothering paradigm" to arrive at a new praxis for meanings of success, ones derived through study of "the role of authority, agency, autonomy, and authenticity in adoptive mothering."

Elisha Marr's "Are You My Mother? How Transracial Adoption Provides Insight into Who Can Be a Mother and Who Can Be Mothered" treats transracial adoption as "a unique opportunity to better understand how the structural forces of race and class shape mothering in contemporary society." She interrogates transracial adoptive mothering as a nexus wherein the inner workings of race and class hierarchies can be studied, better understood, and ultimately thwarted. The purpose that drives her "conflict theory" analysis of current transracial adoption research, both ethnographic and empirical, is "to seek an understanding of why certain mothers have the opportunity to adopt as well as why certain children are more likely to be adopted." She explores this question to illustrate how white adoptive mothers' "micro-level decisions" can implicate them in "macro-level political, organizational, and cultural forces" of race and class. Marr's study exposes how these forces work through adoptive mothering as a race/class system or apparatus that further marginalizes women of colour with respect to becoming adoptive mothers. She also argues that it undermines black children's access to being adopted and mothered at all.

Alice Home's social work study, "Knowing You Made a Difference: Mothering Adopted Children with Hidden Disabilities," contributes to feminist adoption and mothering studies by bringing attention to adoptive mothers of children with disabilities. She demonstrates that, typically, these mothers "are portrayed as doubly deviant" in adoption research by means of what she refers to as the "'good Mum' stereotype." As she explains, this entails that where women are known to adopt children with disabilities, they are treated systemically as anomalies—they are regarded as either "saints" or "weird" or both—and this has lead to a fundamental neglect in adoption research, which fails to take seriously either their needs or experiences as mothers. As Home notes, the tendency of social work adoption research is that it too narrowly "focus[es] on placement and early adjustment issues rather than on supporting" mothers who adopt children with disabilities. Through her study of the "rewards and challenges" reported by adoptive mothers of "children with ADHD and related disabilities," Home presents a more nuanced and multi-faceted account of these mothers' lives and experiences with their children.

In "Lesbian Adoption: Transcending the Boundaries of Motherhood," April Sharkey examines the ways "in which the bio-normativity that impacts adoptive families and the heteronormativity that impacts lesbian families converge." From a feminist perspective that is informed by queer theory and lesbian and gay studies, one that builds on social science research that focuses on lesbian mothers, Sharkey argues that "lesbian couples' *adoption practices* cannot help but disrupt the *bio*-heterosexual matrix, because adoption is as much a disruption of bio-heteronormativity as lesbianism or queerness is with respect to heterosexuality alone." Sharkey's work, in one sense, is a response to a perception that as lesbians increasingly become mothers, they are also co-opted by mainstream ideals of motherhood and womanhood. More than this, though, her primary focus is to show more plainly how lesbian mothers' reliance on different kinds of adoption plays a key role in what makes their families transgressive even if they have acquired marriage and adoption rights, and even when they attempt to mimic bio-normativity through the combined use of New Reproductive Technologies and adoption.

For reasons that range from shared interests in a child, to questions of women's rights to information, child access, and/or parental autonomy, birthmothers' and adoptive mothers' interests often appear to be at odds. Richard Uhrlaub and Nikki McCaslin examine how cultural, legal and linguistic influences in adoption history create the social and political conditions for what they refer to as "adversarial motherhood." In "Culture, Law and Language: Adversarial Motherhood in Adoption," Uhrlaub and McCaslin show how, in the United States, ideological trends of the mid-twentieth century infiltrate the institution of adoption and create the opposition of birthmothers and adoptive mothers. They show

how the effective social positioning of these mothers as antagonistic rivals occurs through notions of motherhood fitness that "evolved out of a combination of eugenic influences, the motive to remove the stigma of illegitimacy from children, and the desire to stabilize adoptive families." The authors show how suspicions with which birthmothers and adoptive mothers may approach each other today, even in the context of open adoption, can be traced historically to these ideologies, as well as to the prior codification of adoption secrecy and shame.

As this brief introduction suggests, this rich and wide-ranging group of essays takes up some of the most important issues confronting scholars in adoption and mothering studies today. It also addresses the contemporary experience and concerns of people personally affected by adoption. I suspect you will find these works not only informative, but highly engaging, provocative and compelling.

[1]While "first mothers" is one term used by women who have surrendered children, this collection primarily uses the term birthmother because it is the term authors chose to use in their contributions to the book.

WORKS CITED

Dorow, Sara K., Ed. *I Wish for You A Beautiful Life: Letters from the Korean Birth Mothers of Ae Ran Won to Their Children.* St Paul: Yeoung & Yeomh Book Company, 2009. Print.

Douglas, Anthony and Terry Philpot, Eds. *Adoption: Changing Families, Changing Times.* London: Routledge, 2003. Print.

Fessler, Ann. *The Girls Who Went Away: The Hidden History of Women Who Surrendered Children for Adoption in the Decades Before Roe v. Wade.* New York: Penguin Books, 2007. Print.

Haslanger, Sally, and Charlotte K. Witt, Eds. *Adoption Matters: Philosophical and Feminist Essays.* Ithaca: Cornell University Press, 2005. Print.

Javier, Rafael A., Amanda L. Baden, Frank A. Biafora and Alina Camacho-Gingerich, Eds. *Handbook of Adoption: Implications for Researchers, Practitioners, and Families.* London: Sage Publications, 2007. Print.

Wadia-Ells, Susan, Ed., *The Adoption Reader: Birth Mothers, Adoptive Mothers, and Adopted Daughters Tell Their Stories.* Seattle: Seal Press, 1995. Print.

1.
Denial of Self

Birthmothers, Non-disclosure Adoption Laws, and the Silence of Others

KAREN MARCH

DURING THE MID-TWENTIETH CENTURY, North American legislators instituted non-disclosure laws that sealed adoption records and kept the identity of adoption triad members, that is, adoptive parents, adopted persons and birthparents, confidential. In part, this practice was designed to protect women from the public shame arising from an out-of-wedlock birth. Under non-disclosure, "a woman could have a baby in secrecy, place the baby for adoption, return to her family, and continue on with her life 'as if' nothing had happened" (Garber 2).

Follow-up studies of birthmothers, that is, women who place their biological children for adoption, challenge the "as if" scenario. Despite the passage of time since the adoption, birthmothers continue to think about and worry over their placed children (Farrar; Fessler). Many express unresolved grief from their loss and latent guilt over their placement decision (Fravel et al.; Inglis). Lack of information on their child's current life situation reinforce feelings of low self-esteem, unworthiness, and underlying depression associated with their pregnancy and placement experiences (Deykin, Campbell and Patti; Pachecho and Eme). These effects are intensified by the anxiety of keeping their birthmother identity a secret from others (Triseliotis, Feast and Kyle).

In this article, I examine data taken from in-depth interviews with 33 birthmothers who had experienced contact with their adult placed children. The women described an adoption process in which significant others treated their maternity as a "non-event." This lack of recognition made it difficult for them to perceive themselves as mothers who were justified in grieving for the loss of their child to adoption. It contributed also to their sense of uncertainty over when, and with whom, they could discuss their motherhood. Specifically, the birthmothers in my study interpreted the silence of their significant others as a signal to comply with the "as if" scenario that is offered by non-disclosure adoption laws.

11

They decided to continue on with their lives and pretend that nothing had happened.

The birthmothers I interviewed described their participation in the "as if" scenario as "living a lie." They experienced a sense of being fraudulent when they hid their birthmother identity and felt duplicitous for denying their placed child's existence. Contact requests from their adult placed children, however, nullified the legal secrecy of non-disclosure. Specifically, their acceptance of contact involved the public acknowledgement of a placed child whose physical presence could not be denied. In this way, the acceptance of contact with their adult placed children gave birthmothers a sense of self-authenticity. It destroyed the social context of silence surrounding their motherhood and presented them with opportunities to express their birthmother identity openly, thereby enabling them to incorporate it more appropriately as a part of "self."

Drawing upon a symbolic interactionist framework of analysis, I define the "self" as a social process formed in interaction with others. Additionally, I conceptualize motherhood as a "master status" for women, that is, "a status so central to a person's identity that it overshadows all other statuses he or she may have" (Shaffir and Kleinknecht 270). Within Western culture, motherhood is considered the core component of women's identity (Hertz). Young girls are socialized to become mothers (Fox; McMahon) and childless women are stigmatized socially for their failure to reproduce (Miall 1987, 1986). Single mothers, lesbian mothers, immigrant mothers and welfare mothers all encounter distinctive social sanctions for not meeting all of their children's needs (Little; Nelson). As Sharon Hays notes, therefore, a woman's sense of self can be affected deeply by how others respond to her motherhood.

BIRTHMOTHER CHARACTERISTICS

The data presented in this manuscript on the silencing process experienced by birthmothers stem from an in-depth interview study conducted in 2000 with a sample of 33 birthmothers residing in northeastern Ontario. Participants were accessed through self-help search organizations, advertisements in local newspapers and by word-of-mouth. For example, after conducting a lecture in a family course, one of the students in the class approached me and suggested I interview her mother. Another interview was arranged after my husband discussed my research at work and a woman identified herself as a birthmother. Consequently, the interview data may exhibit the type of bias that is created by volunteers who offer responses they think the researcher desires. However, the accounts provided by my sample resemble birthmother accounts found in studies that use other methods such as randomly sampling adoption reunion registry files, approaching social service agencies for contact names or involving participants of a previously constructed adoption research project (i.e., Fravel et al.; Triseliotis et al.). My experience as a researcher of adoption search and contact,[1] and my knowledge of adoption literature, also provide a methodological triangulation between the data obtained in these interviews, others' research findings and my own previous work in the field that supports my confidence in the data results.

Kerry Daly and Michael Sobol describe the typical birthmother in Canada as "Caucasian, single, Protestant, between 15 and 19 years of age, attending high school and living at home with her parents" (5). All of the women in this study are Caucasian. Thirteen (40 percent) are Protestant and twenty (60 percent) are Roman Catholic. At the time of placement, almost two-thirds (21; 64 percent) were between the ages of 15 and 19, three (9 percent) were aged 14, and nine (27 percent) were over the age of 20. Three-quarters (75 percent) lived at home and were attending high school when they became pregnant. Over half (17; 52 percent) went to maternity homes and eight (24 percent) lived with extended family until their child was born. Eight (24 percent) were self-supporting and lived on their own.

The women's post-placement experiences in my study resemble those found for other birthmothers (i.e., Deykin et al.; Triseliotis et al.). Over one-third (12; 36 percent) did not return to school and only a minority (9; 27 percent) completed college or university. Thirteen (40 percent) gave their occupation as housewife, waitress or secretary. Five (15 percent) never married, eighteen (55 percent) were married and eight (24 percent) were divorced. Three (9 percent) had married the birthfather but two had divorced him. Nearly three-quarters of the sample (24; 73 percent) had subsequent children. Three (9 percent) had placed a second child for adoption.

The sample in this study is distinctive in that it represents four decades of treatment philosophies and changing public attitudes toward adoption. Two (6 percent) women had placed in 1945, seven (21 percent) in the 1950s, 18 (55 percent) in the 1960s, five (15 percent) in the 1970s and one (3 percent) in the 1980s. Thus, for example, women who placed before the 1950s were more likely to be viewed as "immoral sexual deviants," women who placed in the 1950s and 1960s tended to be treated as "neurotic or psychologically disturbed," and women who placed after the 1970s are generally regarded as "immature and reckless" (Farrar; Fessler; Inglis; Kunzel).

The time pattern and proportion of placement observed in this sample is also representative of the placement pattern found in Ontario for those same decades. According to Daly and Sobol, the largest percentage of adoption placements occurred in the mid-1960s and the smallest percentages occurred before the 1950s and after the 1970s. Previous to the Second World War, it was generally believed that compelling women to keep their babies would ensure they would "sin no more" and adoption placement was rarely condoned (Kunzel). In contrast, the largest percentage of adoptions occurred during the mid-1960s (Daly and Sobol). This time period represents the change of attitudes occurring during the 1950s and 1960s when the perception of unmarried mothers as neurotic and, therefore, incapable of caring for their children meant that few unmarried mothers were supported in keeping their babies (Rains; Fessler). Similarly, after the 1970s when women's sexuality became more socially acceptable, and contraception was made available to unmarried women and financial aid was more easily accessed by single mothers, the proportion of placements dropped significantly (Daly and Sobol; Fravel et al.).

At the time of first contact with their older placed children, the ages of the women in this sample ranged from 27 to 75 with a modal age of 44. At the time of interview, their ages ranged from 33 to 80 with a modal age of 51. Contact relationships occur when a relationship is formed between a biological relative and an adult adopted person who had been placed at birth. Due to the legality of non-disclosure, neither party has had knowledge of the other's identity since the adoption occurred. For the purpose of this study, the adopted adult had searched for and contacted a birthmother who was now trying to maintain a relationship with her birthchild. The contact relationships for this sample spanned 1-12 years with almost half (16; 48 percent) of the women reporting contact relationships of more than six years.

SELF, IDENTITY AND THE REFLECTED APPRAISALS OF OTHERS

Central to my theoretical understanding of the relationship between secrecy and the denial of women's motherhood is George Herbert Mead's concept of self. Mead believed the self emerges when the infant begins to reflect upon and identify itself as a unique object, one that is separate from other objects in its environment and, as such, is deserving of special treatment. Infants achieve this sense of self-awareness through the use of language and symbols, an ability they acquire through their social interactions with others. According to Mead, as infants begin "taking the role of the other," they start to visualize the self as others see them (362-364). It is through this process of viewing the self from the standpoint of others that self-consciousness emerges. Specifically, infants begin to internalize the labels, descriptions, and attitudes of others as a part of self. In this way, an infant's interpretation and evaluation of its treatment by others is central to the development of self.

Mead refers to those individuals who are the most influential in the infant's development of self as "significant others" (157-158). Significant others tend to be individuals who have primary contact with the infant such as parents, siblings and primary caregivers. As infants mature and their social world enlarges, the range of significant others expands. For example, friends, teachers, neighbours or media personalities may also serve as significant others. Significant others are important because children model themselves on the basis of their perceptions of a significant other's response. They form identities consistent with those perceptions. For instance, if a significant other tells a child she is beautiful, the child may internalize this message, perceive her "self" as beautiful and form the identity of "beautiful child." If a significant other labels certain behaviour as "bad" behaviour, a child who performs this behaviour may identify self as "bad."

Gradually, children gain the capacity to view and evaluate their own behaviour from many perspectives at the same time. They create a "generalized other composed of the symbols and meanings shared by their society" (Hewitt 121). They also begin to identify the self from this position. For example, children may use the generalized other to assess their social status or where they stand relative to the given group(s) to which they belong.

"Possession of a self" means individuals think of the self, view the self, and act toward the self as a separate object with particular social characteristics, behavioural traits and peculiarities of action. Depending upon their perceptions of others' responses, individuals may keep, alter or reject the symbols and meanings that are applied to them, change their perceptions of self, and/or reconstruct their social identities. In effect, neither self nor identity is static. Different significant others and different social contexts may elicit different meanings and different perceptions of the self by the self.

The birthmothers in my study described how significant others, especially parents, treated their maternity as a "non-event." This behaviour contributed to their performance of the "as if" scenario originally demanded by adoption non-disclosure laws. The women experienced a sense of being fraudulent when they hid their motherhood from others, which led to a perceived experience of self as living a lie. For them, denial of their birthmother identity meant denying a core part of self. In contrast, contact with their placed children offered them a more socially acceptable context for revealing their birthmother identity and the ability to merge this identity more appropriately with other parts of self. From this perspective, contact engendered a sense of self-authenticity. The following discussion outlines this process through a description of participants' experiences of (1) motherhood negation, (2) living a lie, and (3) telling others. For the purpose of confidentiality, pseudonyms are used with quoted material.

MOTHERHOOD NEGATION

In the context of this study, few birthfathers were involved actively in the adoption process. Four of the self-supporting birthmothers had received proposals from the birthfather but, believing that pregnancy was not a strong basis for marriage, they declined. Several birthmothers reported abandonment, much like Grace who explains, "I told him I was pregnant and he just walked away." Given their youth, a majority of birthmothers told their parents about their pregnancies, and then parents severed relationships between their daughters and birthfathers and initiated the adoption process for them. As Evelyn noted, "I was only 16. There was no asking me, 'What do you want?' They completely took over. I guess I was willing to let them. Except inside, I wasn't. I had done the worst thing a girl could do to her family. So, I didn't have any control or choice. I told my mother. My father never ever spoke to me about it. They decided I'd be sent away. Not that I asked to. It was just understood I would go."

This was the point at which motherhood negation began. Over half of the women were sent to maternity homes so others would not learn about their pregnancies. A small minority (8) were self-supporting and lived alone. The remainder went to live with relatives in another town. Unlike maternity home residents who were protected by institutional walls, birthmothers who were either self-supporting or transplanted to relatives' homes engaged in identity concealment tactics. For example, Irene replied, "I was sent to another city to my godmother's. I could only go out at night with a long coat on. I had to wear dark glasses and a wig. To disguise myself so no would recognize me. I could only go out for a few minutes for a walk or to the doctor. My family had a good name. I could not spoil that." Comparatively, Carol who had been self-supporting remarked, "I left my job. It was hard. I basically went into hiding. I stayed in my place and didn't go out. I was too ashamed and afraid of people seeing me."

Most of the birthmothers viewed their confinement as a form of protection from personal shame and a safeguard of their family's reputation. Few realized the full implications of motherhood negation until their hospitalization just prior to giving birth. Far away from home and family, the majority laboured alone and delivered their babies with the aid of impassive medical staff. Many were isolated in rooms separate from other mothers. Six were not allowed to see their baby after delivery. A noticeable number reported experiencing a sense of disapproval from hospital personnel or other patients and their visitors. To quote Jan:

> *I was only 15. I was put in this room by myself. They left me alone. When the time came, the nurses kept telling me to push. I said I didn't think I could do it. There was no sympathy. Only, "Well, you just have to do it. What did you expect was going to happen here?" Then, they wouldn't bring her to me in the room. I had to go down to the nursery and look at her through the glass. She was in a corner by herself separate from the other babies. People would look at me with a look like they knew. They would flick their eyes away fast so I wouldn't see them. The last day they took me into a room and said "Identify your daughter." It was like an order. Then, it was downstairs to my parents, over to the office to sign the adoption papers ... and the long drive home.*

All of the birthmothers left the hospital without their babies. Nonetheless, many were surprised by the lack of interest demonstrated by others toward their children's birth, especially, from parents who had sanctioned adoption. Some raised the topic but were told, "That chapter's closed, we're not discussing this ever again." The majority reported things much like Alice, who says, "My parents drove me to the home. Both came to the hospital to pick me up after he was born. But, they never saw him. From that point on, it was never mentioned again. Ever! It was as if it never happened."

Demoralized by their confinement and hospital experiences, the women in this study viewed their parents' silences as an indication that they, too, should manage their birthmother identities in silence. Indeed, very few birthmothers turned to other family members as an outlet for discussing either their motherhood experiences or grief over losing their children to adoption. Nor did their family members raise these topics with them. For example, Liz claimed, "The silence was so strong. My sister had a child and placed it too. We never discussed it. Our situation was the same but we never talked about it. It was something that was not discussed. She was sent away to a maternity home. When she came back, we didn't talk. It just wasn't talked about. Looking back, we could have shared so much."

Non-family members further contributed to this silencing process through their disregard of the birthmother's abrupt absence and sudden reappearance. Almost every woman in the study described how friends and neighbours greeted her return "without a single word as if nothing had happened." Birthmothers who went back to high school said they were "treated just like I had been away sick even though everybody likely knew." Similar to Pam, birthmothers who had been self-supporting claimed, "I had to leave my job. They hired me back afterwards. Likely, the other people at work also knew. I had disappeared and came back later for no reason. But, no one said anything to me about it. I went back to work and went on with my life."

LIVING A LIE

The birthmothers I interviewed had internalized motherhood negation through a series of social acts such as being sent away, identity concealment, hospital isolation and the treatment of their children's births as non-events. The unequivocal silence exhibited by significant others, especially parents, supported this negation of the self as mother. Having lost access to their placed children, the women saw little choice but to follow the scenario offered by non-disclosure adoption laws and, thus, continued on with their lives "as if" nothing had happened.

Adhering to an "as if" scenario was not easy. Although the women had internalized what I call, the "self-concept of motherhood negation," they were not prepared for the arbitrary ways in which their birthmother identities intruded upon their everyday lives. Nor were they prepared for the ways in which keeping their motherhood secret would exacerbate their sense of loss. To quote Beth: "I didn't know it would be so hard. It's like having a part of you cut off, not feeling completely whole. There was this hole there that, even when I had my other children, that hole stayed. Even when people ask you how many children you have. You can't tell the truth. Do I say three children? Because I had three but I didn't. It's very hard to give up that part of yourself."

According to Beth, part of secrecy meant "you can't tell the truth." In this way, non-disclosure adoption laws added an element of self-deceit to the social process of motherhood negation. Alice provided a more explicit description of this dilemma when she remarked:

It was a lie. There are times when it's not a question of keeping a secret, it's just participating in a situation, "Oh yeah, I remember the labour." And, you can't talk about it. Then, you become conscious of denying that it ever occurred. For example, I had the hardest time when I had to fill in forms for my job and, I am not given to lying, but how do I explain a six-month gap in my life? Or, when I had to fill in a form at the doctor's office and it asks if you have any children, I didn't know what to fill in. I thought, "Can I lie to a doctor?" He can look at my body. He can see I've had a child. But, do I have any children? Did I give birth? Yes, I did, but I don't have children. Depending which way I said it, yes, it was denial. But, worse than that, it was an outright lie.

As Alice noted, medical appointments caused particular anxiety. Many women said they had worried whether keeping their birthmother identity a secret might affect either their own health or the health of their subsequent children. Others had questioned whether the doctor would know they were lying and penalize them in some way for not being truthful. Despite these concerns, few birthmothers discussed their pregnancies with medical staff until after they had been contacted by their adult placed children. The negation of motherhood internalized by the women in this study, along with a perception of the demand of secrecy rooted in non-disclosure adoption laws, created a common sense of uncertainty with regard to whom one's birthmother identity should be revealed and under what conditions.

A noticeable number of birthmothers in my study also described how the demand that they keep their first pregnancies secret marred their subsequent mothering experiences. Thus, Kathy said, "I didn't enjoy the pregnancy with my son. I didn't get involved with it. It was treated like this was my first child and it wasn't. But, the second pregnancy...which was really my third, I could relax and enjoy it. I could acknowledge I had been pregnant before. I didn't feel phony or a fake."

This sense of being "a fake" was salient for women who presented a self that was childless. For instance, Susan replied, "It was hard. In a work situation when people start talking about when they were pregnant. Or, you'd go to baby showers. They would say, 'Oh, you don't understand giving birth. You don't know the scenario.' I'd want to say, 'Yes, I do. I've been there too.' That's where the lies come in. Where you don't tell people. To a certain extent, you are living incognito. I wanted to say, 'I've lived it!' But, I couldn't. It was a secret. I had promised."

TELLING OTHERS

The women I interviewed lost access to a significant part of self through the process of motherhood negation. They experienced the "as if" scenario as "living a lie," "being fake" or "feeling phony." Despite these experiences and their effects, the majority of women concealed their birthmother identities until they were contacted by their adult placed children. Before contact, the process of motherhood negation, the silence of significant others, and the secrecy required by non-disclosure adoption laws all reinforced the perception that the identity of birthmother was a shameful part of self. To quote Beth, "A lot of it was because it had to be a secret. What kind of person are you to give away a child? What kind of person were you that you got pregnant without being married? It was the beginning of the seventies when women who did this were shameful. I was one of them."

The majority of women in this study were so ashamed of being birthmothers that, prior to contact, the only persons they told about the adoptions were potential husbands. Similar to Jan or Alice, most said, "I told him because I thought he should know who he was getting involved with," or "I was going into marriage and I couldn't hide something that important." Four women told subsequent children "as part of their sex education" or "to make sure if she ever came back into my life that it wouldn't be a surprise." Six told close friends.

For the birthmothers in my study, telling others was part of the contact process. Some were so excited by initial contact they revealed their birthmother identities without considering how others might respond. For example, Liz replied:

> *I was at work when the letter came. My husband called and he read it to me over the phone. I remember getting off of the phone, laughing and crying. I actually punched the wall. And, I had to tell somebody. I remember before it was this bad secret I had. But, I just had to tell somebody. I was bursting. So, I called one of the supervisors in and told her. She hugged me and was so thrilled. I was shocked. I told some others. And, they were thrilled. Two of the women I work with were adoptive parents and they were so happy. Even they were delighted for me. And, it was such an awakening that it wasn't so awful. I had expected some disapproval but everybody was so thrilled. Nothing had changed. It was still the same story. But, it was acceptable now. I had a happy ending.*

Most were more cautious than Liz, however, especially in telling their subsequent children. As Ann recalled, "It took time. I found it difficult to tell my sons. But, the oldest, he just laughed and said he had never imagined something like that from me. The other one said, 'What did you think I was going to do, say you weren't my mother?' They were happy for me. And, both have accepted her as part of my life."

Once they realized contact was likely to be long-term, a noticeable number of women organized large-scale "telling" activities. Several described experiences like Brook's, "I sent out birth announcements. There were members of my family that didn't know. It was a shock for them. But, I didn't care. It was time the secret came out." Comparatively, Diane observed:

Just after I met her, I phoned all of my friends and I said I'm having a party for a special thing. So, anyway, I sort of had a birthday party for her without her being there. I didn't want to parade her around. I just wanted to tell my friends so that when she was down, they would have all known. I had pictures of her by then. We just celebrated the fact. They were all excited for me. None of them seemed to be shocked. They were just pleased that it turned out ... that, we had made contact. Some were surprised because they had known me for over twenty years and knew nothing. But, everyone was happy for me. Even when I told my dad, he said, "I'm so pleased for you."

Often, "telling" leads to revelations of a common identity on the part of other birthmothers. Thus, Ann noted, "I had a good friend and I called her. It was difficult to say at first because in my generation you didn't talk about it. It was never mentioned to anyone. Finally I came out with it and she said, 'Well, I'm in the same boat.' It was surprising. We had known each other for so many years and never said a thing." Comparatively, Martha replied, "Most people are positive. They will say, 'Gee, if it happened to me, I would do the same thing.' And, some will admit that they did it too. Like I think it happens more than a lot of people are aware of."

The women in my study found that the social affirmation gained from telling others eased their sense of shame over being a birthmother. Additionally, the more social affirmation demonstrated by others toward their status as birthmothers, the more likely they were to express their birthmother identity. The more they expressed their birthmother identity, the more it became integrated as an acceptable part of self. To quote Cynthia:

Now I am totally open. I introduce her as my daughter. She introduces me as her birth mother. When you tell people ... some become quite emotional. I've seen tears in some women's eyes when I tell them. They know. They know what it was like back then. Back then, it was a shameful thing. I didn't tell anyone. I practically went into hiding. It was frowned upon. I didn't tell anyone after. Now, we have found each other, I can be open. I am complete.

CONCLUSION

The 33 women in my study describe how the social process of mother-hood negation, the silence of significant others, and the secrecy required by non-disclosure adoption laws intensified a deep sense of shame with respect to being a birthmother. In light of this social and internalized shame, it was reasonable for these women to defer to the "as if" scenario and keep their birth-mother identities hidden. They did not realize, however, that an acceptance of the "as if" scenario also entailed a presentation of self as a non-mother in a social world in which motherhood occupies a major part of the ideal woman's everyday life. Specifically, the pre-dominance of motherhood as a sign of social status amongst women meant birthmothers were frequently placed in situations in which they had to deny both their motherhood and their birth child's existence. At such times, their sense of self involved feelings of duplicity and the experience of life as a sham.

Each of the women took significant risks with the self when they accepted contact from their adult placed children. Contact meant exposing their shameful birth-mother identities, making decisions to integrate their placed children into their lives, and public explanations. Over time, however, these women met more and more people who accepted their birthmother identities, which further validated this part of self. They became less fearful of having their motherhood judged and more comfortable discussing the circumstances of a placed child's adoption. For the birthmothers in my study, contact eliminated the lying involved in maintaining the "as if" scenario and any sense of phoniness created by this deception. They experienced a sense of self-authenticity because they could present an open sense of self in all of its complexity. Liz described this contact outcome best when she said:

I was a pretense all of my life. Because I had to hide so much, I guess. I presented a picture to the world that wasn't me. Before

I met S., I think it made me less able to get totally comfortable
with people because there was part of me that I had to hide and
that became part of who I was. This sheltered person not letting
anyone get too close to you in case they found out the truth. After
meeting S., I blossomed. I'm much more comfortable being me.
I love being me. Before, a part of me was not developed. Now,
I like who I am. I like being me.

[1]See March, *The Stranger*; March, *Perception*; March, *The Dilemma*;
March, *Who Do I*; March, *Perceptions of*; and March and Miall.

WORKS CITED

Daly, Kerry and Michael Sobol. *Adoption in Canada.* Guelph, Canada: University of Guelph Press, 1993. Print.

Deykin, Eva Y., Lynn Campbell and Patricia Patti. "The Post Adoption Experience of Surrendering Parents." *American Journal of Orthopsychiatry* 49.2 (1984): 271-280. Print.

Farrar, Patricia D. "Abject Mothers: Women Separated from Their Babies Lost to Adoption." *Unbecoming Mothers: The Social Production of Maternal Absence.* Ed. Diana L. Gustafson. New York: Haworth Press, 2005. 51-72. Print.

Fessler, Ann. *The Girls who Went Away: The Hidden History of Women who Surrendered Children for Adoption in the Decades before Roe v. Wade.* New York: Penguin Press, 2006. Print.

Fox, Bonnie. *Family Patterns, Gender Relations.* Don Mills: Oxford University Press, 2001. Print.

Fravel, Dianne, Ruth McRoy and Hal Grotevant. "Birthmother Perceptions of the Psychologically Present Adopted Child: Adoption Openness and Boundary Ambiguity." *Family Relations: Interdisciplinary Journal of Applied Family Studies* 49.4 (2000): 425-434. Print.

Garber, Ralph. *Disclosure of Adoption Information.* Report of the Special Commissioner to the Honourable John Sweeney, Minister of Community and Social Services, Government of Ontario, 1985. Print.

Hays, Sharon. *The Cultural Contradictions of Motherhood.* New Haven: Yale University Press, 1996. Print.

Hertz, Rosanna. *Single by Chance, Mothers by Choice: How Women are Choosing Parenthood without Marriage and Creating the New American Family.* New York: Oxford University Press, 2006. Print.

Hewitt, John P. *Self and Society: A Symbolic Interactionist Social Psy-*

chology. Boston: Allyn and Bacon. 1987. Print.

Inglis, Kate. *Living Mistakes: Mothers Who Have Relinquished Babies for Adoption*. Chicago: Chicago Review Press, 1984. Print.

Kunzel, Regina G. *Fallen Women, Problem Girls: Unmarried Mothers and the Professionalization of Social Work, 1890-1945*. New Haven: Yale University Press, 1993. Print.

Little, Margaret Jane Hillyard. *No Car, No Radio, No Liquor Permit: The Moral Regulation of Single Mothers in Ontario, 1920-1997*. Toronto: Oxford University Press, 1998. Print.

March, Karen. *The Stranger Who Bore Me: Adoptee-Birth Mother Relationships*. Toronto: University of Toronto Press, 1995. Print.

March, Karen. "Perception of Adoption as Social Stigma: Motivation for Search and Reunion." *Journal of Marriage and the Family* 57 (1995): 653-659. Print.

March, Karen. "The Dilemma of Adoption Reunion: Establishing Open Communication Between Adoptees and their Birth Mothers." *Family Relations* 46 (1997): 99-105. Print.

March, Karen. "Who Do I Look Like? Gaining a Sense of Self-Authenticity through the Physical Reflections of Others." *Symbolic Interaction* 23 (2000): 359-374. Print.

March, Karen. "Perceptions of Motherhood through the Lens of Adoption." *Doing Ethnography: Studying Everyday Life*. Eds. Dorothy Pawluch, William Shaffir and Charlene Miall. Toronto: Canadian Scholar's Press, 2005. 238-247. Print.

March, Karen and Charlene Miall. "Reinforcing the Motherhood Ideal: Public Perceptions of Biological Mothers who Make an Adoption Plan." *Canadian Review of Sociology and Anthropology* 43 (2006): 367-385. Print.

McMahon, Martha. *Engendering Motherhood: Identity and Self-Transformation in Women's Lives*. New York: Guilford Press, 1995. Print.

Mead, George Herbert. *Mind, Self, and Society*. Chicago: University of Chicago Press, 1934. Print.

Miall, Charlene. "The Stigma of Adoptive Parent Status: Perceptions of Community Attitudes toward Adoption and the Experience of Informal Social Sanctioning." *Family Relations* 36 (1987): 34-39. Print.

Miall, Charlene. "The Stigma of Involuntary Childlessness." *Social Problems* 33 (1986): 268-282. Print.

Nelson, Margaret K. *The Social Economy of Single Motherhood: Raising Children in Rural America*. New York: Routledge, 2005. Print.

Pacheco, Frances and Robert Eme. "An Outcome Study of Reunion Between Adoptees and Biological Parents." *Child Welfare* 72 (1993):

53-64. Print.

Rains, Prudence M. "Moral Reinstatement: The Characteristics of Maternity Homes." *American Behavioral Scientist* 14 (1970): 219-236. Print.

Shaffir, William and Stephen Kleinknecht. "Coping with Electoral Defeat: A Study of Involuntary Role Exit." *Doing Ethnography: Studying Everyday Life*. Eds. Dorothy Pawluch, William Shaffir and Charlene Miall. Toronto: Canadian Scholar's Press, 2005. 260-272. Print.

Solinger, Rickie. *Beggars and Choosers: How the Politics of Choice Shapes Adoption, Abortion and Welfare in the United States*. New York: Hill and Wang, 2001. Print.

Triseliotis, John, Julia Feast and Fiona Kyle. *The Adoption Triangle Revisited: A Study of Adoption, Search and Reunion Experiences*. London: British Association of Adoption and Fostering, 2005. Print.

2.
Good Mothers, Bad Mothers, Not-Mothers

Privilege, Race and Gender and the Invention of the Birthmother

NICOLE PIETSCH

POPULAR RHETORIC PORTRAYS MOTHERHOOD as a universally desired and valuable female experience: "women live their lives against a background of personal and cultural assumptions that all women are or want to be mothers, and that for women motherhood is proof of adulthood" (Bailey et al. 102). But just like the nuances of womanhood itself, the value of a woman's pregnancy, offspring and her admission into motherhood is not static. Concepts of socially-responsible reproduction and one's right of entry into motherhood are socially-situated. In effect, the experience of motherhood is dependent upon a woman's ability to meet the requirements of hegemonic femininity. This in turn shapes the social practice we know as adoption.

Adoption is a system contingent upon notions of and values accorded to social location. Adoption as a contemporary practice usually aims to reposition a child from a marginalized social location to a more privileged one. It also intends to relieve marginalized women from under-resourced motherhood, while awarding the privilege of mothering to women who, ostensibly, have more resources. Class inequality is a significant factor in the practice of adoption: as adoption critic B. K. Rothman states, "thirty-two-year-old attorneys living in wealthy suburbs do not give up their children to nineteen-year-old factory workers living in small towns" (cited in Edwards and Williams 161).

Yet while sex and class are *explicit* in adoption rhetoric, other social categories—race, age, and one's capacity to endorse and enact hetero-patriarchal norms, for example—are *implicit* and necessarily *intersecting* with notions of class and sex. Patrick Hopkins notes that the behaviours expected of members of specific social categories are prescriptive: activities and behaviours that are oppositional to what is expected of one's social category can result in "serious reaction" from those whose personal and political identity is deeply invested in traditional binary categories defining privilege and marginalization (98).

Much in line with Hopkins's concept, contemporary adoption discourse indeed embodies the "problem of who meets the ... ideal of femininity and who is cast out from its bounds" (Ringrose 413). The woman who meets "the requirements of hegemonic femininity—i.e., White, middle-class, heterosexual, able-bodied" is expected to enact and endorse the values of her hegemonic culture (Batacharya 184). On the other hand, racialized women have been treated and depicted "as though they exist outside of [femininity's] boundaries" (Cole and Zucker 2). In this, racialized mothers, both historically and today, represent a permanent "colonized identity in a space that is designed for the good White mother" (Mullings 32). Patricia Hill Collins' extensive writing on the subject corresponds, noting that racist images of Black womanhood "place African-American women in an untenable position" in which their capacity and agency as mothers is either challenged or negated (79).

These racialized constructs of women informed a dominant adoption discourse that originated in North America following the Second World War, and continue to shape notions of motherhood today. During the postwar years of 1945-1965, North Americans became fixated on "social problems" that threatened to challenge hegemonic (that is, White-identified) constructs of gender and family. One of these problems was an increase in pregnancies amongst unmarried White and Black females. But constructs of femininity invariably affect both social policy on adoption and adoption trends: in 1960, "when approximately 70 percent of white illegitimate babies were adopted, [only] about 5 percent of such non-white babies were placed" for adoption (Solinger, *Wake Up* 203). And while the popularity of adoption as a viable alternative to unpartnered motherhood has certainly declined since the immediate postwar years, the socially-located phenomenon concerning which mothers relinquish their infants and which do not remains: studies throughout the 1980s and 1990s show that North American birthmothers are still typically young, White, and generally belonging to a higher socioeconomic class than White or racialized young women who choose to parent (Edwards and Williams 162).

This essay aims to address the relationship between privileged constructs of femininity, marginalized constructs of femininity and how these notions, including the interlocking aspects of oppressions operant within them, work to assemble binary categories of motherhood in North America. This essay takes a feminist poststructuralist approach to identify historical constructs of hegemonic womanhood, the implications such constructs have on diversely-located expectant mothers, and how these constructs have informed adoption practices and discourse. A poststructuralist framework also identifies historical values that contribute to race-specific, including White-specific, constructs of motherhood. Through this work, I illustrate how constructs of White femininity continue to inform our expectations of legitimate, capable motherhood—including who may claim membership to this motherhood and who cannot. I examine the interdependent positions of White hegemonic femininity and motherhood ("good mothers"), Other (including racialized)-identified femininity and motherhood ("bad mothers"), and the "different than and less than full mother[s]" ("not-mothers") that these binary categories necessarily create (Lynn 3; Solinger, *Wake Up* 95).

I argue that mothers who challenge or resist bounded categories of race and gender performance are constructed as "not-mothers." I explore the birthmother—the White female who transgresses White female norms of purity, passivity, and heterosexual marriage and becomes a manifestation of North America's historical and "cultural construction of the white unwed mother who ought to disappear" (Solinger, *Wake Up* 95, 111). I also explore the image of the Black mammy who, in post-slavery North America, "serve[d] the needs of the [White] nation" through domestic service as a nanny, babysitter or wet-nurse, yet was denied any decision-making or power within her mothering roles (Mullings 38, 35). Like the birthmother of the immediate postwar years, the mammy functioned as a politicized "transitional object" during a specific period of North American history highly concerned with maintaining differences between Whites and Blacks, the possibility of re-balancing of political privilege between Whites and Blacks, and the intersecting notions of race and sex that these concerns necessarily created (Wallace-Sanders 3).

Hopkins theorizes that social privilege is most consistently accorded to individuals who comply with "a binary system—[of] man and woman," and their associated binary-gendered traits (97). I agree and, in this essay, extend Hopkins's theory to identify White-defined binary notions of race as they have characterized (and continue to characterize) social constructions of hegemonic motherhood and single motherhood. "Birthmother" is not simply the title for a woman who has relinquished a child for adoption. Similar to other social constructs of marginalized motherhoods, I suggest the birthmother is a socio-political position of invented intermediate Otherness, created via the prescriptive tenets of hegemonic White femininity, White motherhood, and racist constructs of Black motherhood.

GOOD MOTHERS

In order to be a good mother, one must first be a real and valuable woman. In Elizabeth R. Cole and Alyssa N. Zucker's "Black and White Women's Perspectives on Femininity," the authors describe a socially-constructed "prescriptive set of normative feminine behaviors" and attributes that are culturally valued and expected of women: these include, amongst others, "beauty, demeanour … sexuality, and (White) race" (1). Features of dominant femininity, the authors argue—as well as "the typically White upper-middle class women who can achieve it"—are "conspicuously valued within mainstream [North] American culture" (1). Inevitably, these standards create "a normative yardstick for all femininities in which [non-white] women are relegated to the bottom of the gender hierarchy" (1). For both White and racialized women, a parallel pattern of valuing and devaluing women's mother-hood and mothering capacity follows.

In *Pregnancy and Power: A Short History of Reproductive Politics in America*, Rickie Solinger points out that one concept that separated enslaved Black women from White women (and, therein, Black mothers from White mothers) in late-eighteenth-century North America was the idea of chastity. Women who could, or were perceived to, suppress their sexual impulses, as well as successfully evade the impulses of others, were awarded higher social and political status (52).

The privilege of both the appearance and reality of chastity was not easily afforded to Black women who faced the daily realities of slavery, which entailed state-mandated tolerance of sexual violence perpetrated against Black women, the ongoing threat of sexual violence, and a greater lack of sexual agency. It was also not so easily afforded to working class women. In this, chastity was an ideological and political mechanism that functioned to differentiate subordinated women from privileged women. Chastity, as well as its relational and behavioural tenets—for example, refraining from sexual activity, minimized contact with the opposite sex, and avowal to virginity until marriage—retained great value in White society. Sexual availability and accessibility, on the other hand, signi-fied an inferior and subordinated womanhood. In effect, chastity and Whiteness intertwined to construct a hegemonic femininity necessarily contingent upon class and racial privilege. Chaste White women were therein constructed as:

> relieved of the dangerous lustiness of the body. And being relieved, they were free to become moral mothers, intellectual persons....

In white America in this era, white female chastity could stand for the self-ownership of free white women. (Solinger, *Pregnancy* 52-53)

The gendered notion of chastity effectively separated White womanhood ideologically, socially, and politically from racialized womanhood. The resultant contrasting constructs of Black womanhood represent White male interests in defining Black sexuality and fertility; yet moreover, such constructs also represent White women's interests in defining (and maintaining) White female privilege. As Patrick Hopkins notes, social identity is a dynamic of achieving the appropriate gender performance, as well as avoiding oppositional others: "What it means to have a particular identity depends on what it means not to have some other identity" (98). For White women both historically and today, the social privilege afforded to them is dependent upon their ongoing ability to enact and endorse sexual and fertility behaviours—for example, abstention from pursuing or conceding to sexual activity, and only engaging in sexual relations and reproducing within the confines of marriage—associated with White femininity.

Within this historical framework, Black women "prior to slavery, during slavery and even today have been used to describe and represent the *worst* of femininity," female sexuality and motherhood (Hillman 21). Delores Mullings notes that, like femininity, notions of "good" motherhood are "based on the values of White middle-class women" (Mullings 32). Women who are understood as those who really "deserve to have children" tend to exemplify or reproduce behaviours or values associated with the social construct of the good White mother (Wood 50). At the same time, women perceived as good mothers typically sit in socially-located positions of privileged womanhood as well:

the good mother, against whom all others are measured, has the following characteristics: The *good* mother is heterosexual, married, and monogamous. She is White and native born. She is not economically self-sufficient, which means, given the persistent gender gap in earnings, largely economically dependent on her income-earning husband. (Goodwin and Huppatz 5-6)

The good mother is the precise amalgamation of feminized privilege (i.e., White race, heterosexual identity, married, and presumably middle-class), and acquiescence to dominant patriarchal subordination. True White motherhood, therein, is defined not only by what it *is* (i.e., heterosexual, married, and monogamous) but also what it *isn't* (i.e., attributes opposite of the former—a sexual identity other than heterosexual, unpartnered, or with multiple partners). To perform as an appropriate mother, one necessarily participates in certain predictable behaviours, and avoids behaviours associated with the Other.

As we have seen, the good mother is implicitly gendered and raced via binary systems of gender and race. Accordingly, the good mother is one side of two in the binary social construction "motherhood."

BAD MOTHERS

Notions of goodness and badness, like notions of the feminine and the unfeminine, are interdependent. Racist depictions of Black women as unattractive, aggressive, sexually promiscuous and bad mothers, for example, stand in direct contrast to hegemonic representations of femininity which award White women a naturalized higher social and political status (Cole and Zucker).

Within motherhood discourses, racialized mothers are usually presumed to subvert dominant behaviours and values that are associated with (and expected of) White mothers:

> As an African Canadian woman, I am expected to be an unpartnered mother and I am expected to mother [only] Black or Black-biracial children. (Mullings 37)

> The social problem discourse of teen pregnancy is itself racialized.... The stereotypical Urban girl is assumed to be poor, of color, out of control ... at risk and at fault. She embodies the problem of teenage pregnancy. (Brubaker 530)

In accordance, social commentary and policy around motherhood, in particular single motherhood, has been greatly influenced by the construct of (and value accorded to) White femininity—as well as the oppositional attributes associated with racist constructs of racialized femininity. Within a culture where hegemonic femininity and motherhood hinges on criteria associated with Whiteness, Black mothers in general are perceived as *women who defy White ideals* of feminized sexuality, heteronormative gender roles, and family through their motherhood:

> The Black matriarchy thesis argues that African-American women who failed to fulfill their traditional "womanly" duties

at home contributed to social problems.... As overly-aggressive, unfeminine women, Black matriarchs allegedly emasculated their lovers and husbands. These men, understandably, either deserted their partners or refused to marry the mothers of their children. (Collins 75)

The image of the matriarch contrasts sharply (and precisely) with images of privileged White femininity, and "is central to intersecting oppressions of class, gender and race" (Collins 75). Black women also bear Black or bi-racial children, which defies White supremacist ideals of reproduction and, by extension, the (White) re-population of the state. Black females who become mothers while young, poor, unmarried or otherwise unsupported by a male partner appear to reaffirm the image of deviant women who defy White norms of acceptable femininity, family and motherhood. And White women who fail to fulfill social requirements for at least the image of chastity and heteronormative sexuality characterize a subordinate or Othered version of femininity.

How has White-dominated North America interpreted these two populations? Rickie Solinger's *Wake Up Little Suzy* compares state responses to Black and White single mothers in the postwar years—a time in which, between 1940 and 1957 alone, the percent of women of childbearing age who had babies out of wedlock tripled (13). Solinger notes that Black single mothers of the post-war period were rejected by social policy and social services that either refused or limited service to pregnant applicants based on their social location as single Black females. White women, on the contrary, were encouraged to seek social service-based support (for example, counselling) or community-based "treatment" (for example, residence at a maternity home) in response to single pregnancy (87, 95). During this period, Black women were far less likely to be permitted entrance to maternity homes (51). The function of such maternity homes was not simply to provide the mother shelter for the duration of her pregnancy; moreover, for single, pregnant women, the homes became training schools for females who had violated norms of White femininity through illegitimate pregnancy. Indeed, Solinger notes: "most homes offered courses or workshops in the feminine arts of grooming, glamour, charm, beauty, cooking, handwork, and flower arranging before they offered courses with vocational or educational content" (50). Maternity homes also functioned to support the postwar adoption system as a whole. The intention of maternity homes—and as we will see, of an adoption arrangement during this period—was largely to facilitate a woman's rehabilitation into appropriate (that is, White) femininity.

But where the criterion for hegemonic femininity and motherhood is Whiteness, women of color are necessarily ineligible. A Black woman could not be rehabilitated into appropriate White womanhood because she did not occupy this social location to begin with, nor could she in the future. Moreover, as a woman of color, she was presumed to be biologically incapable of achieving White socio-sexual mores.

Even today, Black women continue to face racist stereotypes that depict them as socially and sexually *unqualified* to realize activities or behaviours associated with White womanhood. These notions transmit prescriptive and "distinctive messages about ... female sexuality" in diversely-located women that are necessarily oppositional to White female sexuality (Collins 84). Constructs of Black women, for example, reflect sexist and racist myths from the slavery era such as the "jezebel stereotype, where Black women are perceived as sexual temptresses" with an "irresponsible hypersexuality" (Donovan 724; Solinger, *Wake Up* 42). Images of aboriginal women are also relative to White womanhood: throughout colonial history in countries such as Australia and Canada, aboriginal women were seen as markedly sexual, in contrast to the passive, prudish Victorian woman (Pinnuck and Dowling 54).

In this, the Black single mother violated cultural values of hegemonic White femininity by both who she *was* (a racialized woman) and what she *did* (engage in sexual relations outside of marriage and become pregnant):

> Black unwed mothers were guilty of being without a man, thus in some sense independent, or at least 'on the loose' in a way that violated gender norms.... They were guilty of being extra-maritally sexual, again a violation of gender norms, but were also guilty of being mothers, the ultimate gender role fulfillment. (Solinger, *Wake Up* 52)

Cultural perception of unpartnered, unmarried Black mothers appears to affirm their motherhood as real—but then stigmatizes it as bad and punishes them for it. In this discourse, Black motherhood is strategically differentiated from White motherhood. During the postwar years, indeed "the prevailing definition of white single pregnancy as a psychological rather than sexual phenomenon was bolstered by the definition of black single pregnancy, in distinction, as [a] purely sexual [phenomenon]" (Solinger, *Wake Up* 43). Here once again, notions of chastity and sexuality function to distinguish White womanhood from racialized womanhood. The Black-White distinction represents a White-dominant society's interest in delineating and maintaining White privilege via sexist, race-specific constructs of motherhood.

As we have seen, the bad mother is the second side of two in the binary social construction "motherhood." Clearly, differently-raced notions of femininity and motherhood are not valued equally.

NOT-MOTHERS

The bad mother and the good mother are the two disparate sides of the raced and gendered social construction "motherhood." But what if a woman mothers from a social location, social or sexual performance, or some combination of the two, that amounts to a place of "intolerable ambiguity" (Grosz 64)? Of course, mothers who defy bounded categories of binary race and gender exist.

In her work "Mothering White Children: An Africana Canadian Woman's Experience," Delores Mullings describes her experience as a Black woman mothering White children in her role as a foster mother. As a woman of color, Mullings is expected by White female professionals and her White-dominant community to mother only Black or bi-racial children. In mothering White children, Mullings finds that her motherhood status is routinely challenged, or deemed as not legitimate: to the privileged women "who harbour [stereotyped] notions of Black mothers," Mullings notes, "I am a non-entity and ultimately invisible" (36). Mullings conveys the predicament of the mother who resists or confounds bounded categories of social location; for example, a marginalized *woman*, operating as a mother within a privileged community (that of White children in her care, and the observing professional community). In response, she is constructed as a not-mother—a woman performing some aspects of mothering role or duties, who must be stripped of agency or right to make decisions about the children in her care.

Birthmothers, within dominant adoption discourse, are another example of women who defy binary categories of raced and gendered motherhood. It is important to recognize that this dominant discourse originated during a particular period in North American history that was highly invested in maintaining binary categories of gender and race. During the immediate postwar years, heteronormative marriage, children and families were heralded as examples of North American postwar success. Differentiated gender roles, including dominant (that is, White) expectations of femininity, were part of this idealized postwar North America. The same period, however, saw an explosion of out-of-wedlock pregnancies and births in both White and Black populations of women.

How did North Americans understand these populations of mothers? How did they integrate—and differentiate—these women within the context of the postwar culture and values? I suggest that the anxieties of this time period informed a dominant adoption discourse implicitly more concerned with White women and their capacity to meet ideals of White femininity than about parenting capacity and children. It was during the immediate postwar period that adoption's mandate shifted from the care of marginalized children, to "secur[ing] patriarchy and white supremacy by way of ...'protection' (meaning control) of white girls and women," and the simultaneous exclusion of Black girls and women (Brubaker 530). Although historically-situated, this dominant discourse continues to pervade adoption systems and social constructs of mothers today.

Dominant adoption discourse from the postwar period separated Black unwed mothers physically, ideologically and politically from White unwed mothers. Black unwed mothers were understood as *real* mothers, albeit "bad" mothers who transgressed White feminine ideals of womanhood and motherhood, and raised Black children who were not valued by White-dominant society. The White unmarried expectant mother generated concerns that were different than those presented by Black mothers. White females certainly met the criteria for hegemonic womanhood and motherhood—yet having transgressed norms of White purity, passivity, and heterosexual marriage, they exhibited behaviours associated with White-identified constructs of *racialized* femininity. The White unmarried pregnant woman opposes White values, and her body stands as evidence of purported "larger social problems," such as the precariousness of White chastity, the subversion of innocent White girlhood, and the necessity of compulsory heteronormative marriage for White mothers (Lynn 5). In this, the White un-partnered pregnant woman of postwar North America became an amalgam: "an ambiguous being whose existence imperil[ed] categories and oppositions dominant in social life" (Grosz 57). White single pregnant women exhibited the very embodiment of *crossing-over* foundational cultural gender and race boundaries.

To allow a coalescing of these categories creates a socio-political crisis wherein identity is fluid—and normalized hierarchies therein become immaterial. How could privilege continue to be defined and maintained as a benefit owed to Whites only if White women were, ideologically, no different than Black women? The dominant discourse on adoption and birthmothers was constructed and operationalized from this specific cultural anxiety.

The postwar adoption mandate held that an adoption arrangement functions as a "safety valve" to release the White single woman from motherhood, thereby restoring her status as a woman of White-defined privilege and performance: "through adoption, the unwed mother could put the mistake—the baby *qua* baby and the proof of nonmarital sexual experience—behind her" (Solinger, *Wake Up* 155, 153). In this, the White birthmother became a transitional object of privileged femininity: neither "good mother" nor "bad mother," but something in between. By the late 1940s, adoption as a social practice and social service policy had largely institutionalized the unfeasibility of White womanhood alongside single motherhood, thereby reaffirming hegemonic White motherhood: "for the first time, it took more than a baby to make a white girl or woman into a mother," and under the postwar adoption mandate, "by definition, an unmarried mother who kept her child lacked the maturity to mother it" (Solinger, *Wake Up* 153, 155).

In dominant adoption discourse the birthmother remains constructed as, physically and politically, *occupying an ambiguous, intermediate place* of motherhood and not-motherhood:

> Some women can make a baby but can't make a family...When a woman gives birth to a baby, and realizes that she can't be a real mother to that child, for whatever reason, she may decide to place it for adoption. (Rolfe 2)

> The girl's task was simply and straightforward to be a mother by relinquishing the child. (Solinger, *Wake Up* 158)

Here, the birthmother is defined as literally a transitional object: she gives birth, and then physically moves on without the child. As a White woman who fails to meet the ideals of White femininity she is also, ideologically and politically, a transitional object: "a symbol of reconciliation and redemption" for the fallen woman of privilege "seeking to establish ... her pedigree" (Wallace-Sanders 5). Within dominant adoption discourse, the birthmother role supports the differentiation of single White pregnant women from single Black pregnant women. The construct of the birthmother also supports binary and racialized images of femininity—as well as White supremacist constructs of White motherhood as good, and Black motherhood as bad. Indeed, pregnant White women and girls of the postwar period "learned this core lesson: that they were different from the black girls they glimpsed pushing baby buggies outside" (Solinger, *Pregnancy* 153). The salient message within the dominant adoption discourse was that Black girls and women were not like White girls and women; and, accordingly, White girls and women were not like Black girls and women.

Another "not-mother" created out of a specific historical moment concerned with binary categories of race and gender is the construct of the Black mammy. Like the birthmother of the postwar adoption mandate, the mammy performs some aspect of mothering duties, however, she has no power as a mother or guardian of children. The mammy is typically depicted as content with this marginalized role, which suggests that she is also content with (and complicit in) her powerlessness.

The mammy, too, functioned as "a transitional object" during a specific period of North American history that was concerned with the re-balancing of political privilege between races (Wallace-Sanders 3). During and directly following the American Civil War, the mammy emerged as an embodied construct of intermediately Othered motherhood, positioned within White households, and providing domestic service to Whites. The mammy is typically depicted as mothering White children with more care than her own children, and her domestic work—in particular her special mothering service to White children—functions to define the significant bounds of social privilege: that is, who receives mothering services, compared to who provides this service work.

Further, the mammy's mothering role is to nurture White children ("good"), but she cannot meet the criterion for "White saintly motherhood" ("bad"); she is, by workplace definition, mothering, however she cannot be the "real" mother to White children. Mammy's intermediate position is immutable and important, and this is made clear by the subordinate rank she achieves within the whole: regardless of her workload, extensive mothering duties and "regardless of her status in the family, she remains a mere servant" (Mullings 35).

Although abolition proposed an America where racial privilege is eliminated, White supremacist animosity and resistance toward the possibility of racial de-stratification is ever-present in mammy's constructed image:

> The mammy's body serves as a tendon between the races, connecting the muscle of African American slave labor with the skeletal power structure of white southern aristocracy.... The mammy body produced the milk that made white southerners more *purely white* and therefore more genteel than their less affluent counterparts. (Wallace-Sanders 3, 5)

The construct of the mammy, like that of the birthmother, is no accident. Her role, instead, is a strategic position of invented political intermediary. Mammy functions within the post-slavery period, within the White household, and in Southern nostalgia to simultaneously *reaffirm* racial inequality, and *render it invisible*: the White-defined image of the "faithful, obedient" mammy makes "slave status more innocuous or benign" (Mullings 35; Wallace-Sanders 5). Moreover, like the White birthmother, the mammy is constructed as understanding her place within the socio-political hierarchy of race, accepting this place, and then enacting it without protest.

It is interesting that the Black mammy and the White birthmother were borne out of periods that were highly concerned with clear hierarchies of gender and race. The privileged classes of these historical moments were invested in seeing (and preserving) the maintenance of status quo hierarchies. Within them, the mammy and birthmother functioned to endorse binary categories of race and gender by way of being *positioned outside of them* as not-mothers.

CONCLUSION

Between 1945 and 1965, out-of-wedlock pregnancies increased exponentially in populations of Black and White women in North America. This phenomenon, alongside other social factors explored in this paper, resulted in 80 percent more children adopted in the early postwar years than in the years before and during the war. The majority of these adoptions involved White infants born to White unmarried mothers, and adopted by White families (Solinger, *Wake Up* 154).

While this essay remarks upon adoption practice and rhetoric from a specific historical timeframe, I believe that the popularity of the postwar adoption mandate, the mandate's adherence to already-entrenched essentialist notions of race and gender, and the sheer number of women and children it affected makes it the *dominant discourse* that permeates adoption practices and notions of unwed mothers even today. I extend that this dominant adoption discourse endorses systemic racism *amongst all mothers*, via an implicit motherhood discourse that posits racialized womanhood and motherhood as necessarily divergent from White womanhood and motherhood.

I am struck by contemporary adoption discourses which continue to frame birthmothers as organically intermediate, invisible or deficient mothers (see Wood's "Fertile Territory: The Moral Agenda of Intrauterine Plot Devices," and Edwards and Williams' "Adopting Change: Birth Mothers in Maternity Homes Today"). This framing, I believe, echoes nostalgic adoption practices, which access constructs of White femininity and reaffirm these constructs as integral to good motherhood. This framing also functions to diminish the organic mothering capacity of marginalized (m)Others who mother in and amongst privileged populations, or mother children of privileged social locations. What does this over-arching discourse establish for 'good' motherhood—for all motherhoods? As Solinger asks, "Do we want educational qualifications, age, ethnic, racial, marital, financial qualifications" for mothers (Solinger, *Wake Up* 245)? Is mothering about succeeding in being the right kind of feminized woman (as the postwar adoption mandate suggests), or is it about successful parenting?

Historical gender and race-based constructs such as the Black mammy, the White birthmother, and the postwar adoption mandate illustrate that contemporary motherhood is not without context. When considering mothers, in particular marginalized mothers, we must acknowledge that "social hierarchy is inevitably at play" in and amongst *all* motherhoods (Batacharya 185). The notion that reproductive choice is equally accessible to all women, including the case of women "choosing" adoption, proves to be highly dependent on the woman's social location—and how that particular social location defines true motherhood.

"Such as living with the uncertainty that I'll never find the words to say which would completely explain" (Green): the author respectfully acknowledges D. Mullings, R.V. and M.R. for their considerable influence in achieving this work.

WORKS CITED

Bailey, N, G. Brown, G. Letherby and C. Wilson. "'The Baby Brigade': Teenage Mothers and Sexuality." Ed. Andrea O'Reilly. Toronto: York University. *Journal of the Association for Research on Mothering: Mothering, Sex & Sexuality* 4.1(2002): 101-110. Print.

Batacharya, S. "A Fair Trial: Race and the Retrial of Kelly Ellard." *Canadian Woman Studies* 25.1,2 (2006): 181-189. Print.

Brubaker, S. "Denied, Embracing and Resisting Medicalization: African American Teen Mothers' Perceptions of Formal Pregnancy and Childbirth Care." *Gender & Society* 21.4 (2007): 528-552. Print.

Cole, E. R. and A. N. Zucker. "Black and White Women's Perspectives on Femininity." *Cultural Diversity and Ethnic Minority Psychology* 13 (2007): 1-9. Print.

Collins, P. H. *Black Feminist Thought: Knowledge, Consciousness, and the Politics of Empowerment.* New York: Routledge, 2000. Print.

Donovan, R. "To Blame or Not to Blame: Influences of Target Race and Observer Sex on Rape Blame Attribution." *Journal of Interpersonal Violence* 22.6 (2007): 722-736. Print.

Edwards, C. E. and C. L. Williams. "Adopting Change: Birth Mothers in Maternity Homes Today." *Gender and Society* 14.1 (2000): 160-182. Print.

Goodwin, S. and K. Huppatz. "The Good Mother in Theory and Research." Eds. Susan Goodwin and Kate Huppatz. *The Good Mother: Contemporary Motherhoods in Australia.* Australia: Sydney University Press, 2010. 1-24. Print.

Green, D. "Sleeping Sickness." *Bring Me Your Love.* CD. Prod. Dan Achen and Dallas Green. Dine Alone Records. Hamilton, ON: Catherine North Studios, 2008.

Grosz, E. "Intolerable Ambiguity: Freaks as/at the Limit." Ed. Rosemarie Garland Thomas. *Freakery: Cultural Spectacles of the Extraordinary Body.* New York: New York University Press, 1996. Print. 55-66.

Hillman, P. L. *Negotiating the Dominant Script: Middle-Class Black Girls Tell Their Story.* Diss. Faculty of Arts & Sciences of American University, Washington, DC, 1999. Print.

Hopkins, P. "Gender Treachery: Homophobia, Masculinity, and Threatened Identities." *Rethinking Masculinities: Philosophical Explorations in Light of Feminism.* Eds. Larry May and Patrick Hopkins. Second Edition. Maryland: Rowman and Littlefield Publishers, Inc., 1996. 95-115. Print.

Lynn, K. "Canadian Council of Birthmothers: Mothers Without Their Children." Paper presented at Mothers Without their Children Conference, Association for Research on Mothering, York University, Toronto, Canada, 5 May 2001. Print.

Mullings, D. V. "Mothering White Children: An Africana Canadian Woman's Experience." Ed. Andrea O'Reilly. *Journal of the Association for Research on Mothering: Mothering, Race, Ethnicity, Culture and Class* 9.2 (2007): 31-39. Print.

Pinnuck, F. and S. Dowling. "The Gendered and Racialized Space within Australian Prisons." Ed. Toni Lester. *Gender Nonconformity, Race and Sexuality: Charting the Connections.* Madison: University of Wisconsin Press, 2002. 44-61. Print.

Ringrose, J. "A New Universal Mean Girl: Examining the Discursive Construction and Social Regulation of a New Feminine Pathology." *Feminism and Psychology* 16.4 (2006): 405-424. Print.

Rolfe, D. "Adoption: Solution or Sentence?" Mothers Without Their

Children Conference, Association for Research on Mothering. Toronto: York University, 5 May 2001. Print.

Solinger, R. *Wake Up Little Susie: Single Pregnancy and Race before Roe v. Wade*. New York: Routledge, 2000. Print.

Solinger, R. *Pregnancy and Power: A Short History of Reproductive Politics in America*. New York: New York University Press, 2005. Print.

Wallace-Sanders, K. *Mammy: A Century of Race, Gender and Southern Memory*. United States of America: University of Michigan Press, 2008. Print.

Wood, S. "Fertile Territory: The Moral Agenda of Intrauterine Plot Devices." *Bitch: A Feminist Response to Pop Culture* 26 (2004): 49-55. Print.

3.
A Birthmother's Identity

[M]other Living on the Border of (Non)Motherhood[1]

KATHERINE SIEGER

A WOMAN WHO CHOOSES TO PLACE HER CHILD for adoption enters into a world of ambivalence and unconventionality immediately upon making this choice. She is neither a mother nor a non-mother: she is a birthmother. The institution of motherhood, which Adrienne Rich defines as the patriarchal control of women's power within motherhood, makes no space for birthmothers or what they can offer beyond birthing. It does not allow for "part-time" mothering, mentor mothering, ambivalent mothering, long-distance mothering, or even "imagined" mothering, all of which are roles birthmothers in open adoptions may perform, however fluidly, at any given time. Although many birthmothers have experiences that are maternal, they are nearly invisible as such within the institution of motherhood; they are disregarded generally as it relates to "real" or "good" mothering.[2] At best, the institution of motherhood grants birthmothers a place as "other" mothers.

There has been little scholarly research done to understand the difficult and fluctuating identities of birthmothers. Past research focuses mainly on how understanding the birthmother benefits the adoption community (i.e. adoptive parents and adoption workers), arguably to provide more control over what has become a consumer-driven trade.[3] But how does understanding birthmother identities benefit birthmothers themselves? In this paper, I explore the idea of a simultaneous birthmother identity wherein she is both a mother and non-mother, and I discuss the implications of this hybrid identity for the patriarchal institution of motherhood. I explore the possibilities of situating this identity within the framework of "border identity theory," as outlined by Gloria Anzaldúa's (1999) *La Mestiza*. I have chosen this framework because it provides an analogy for the experiences of alienation and isolation that come from living on the border of (non)motherhood, and it demonstrates how the binary structure of "good" mother versus "bad" mother narratives deny many women real recognition within the confines of the meaning of motherhood. Ultimately, I argue that a birthmother's experience of maternity within open adoption is a fusion of both motherhood and non-motherhood, which thrusts her into a hybrid identity of [M]other.

In order to assess the prevalent experience of border identities within the birthmother experience, I focus on three specific themes: pregnancy and birth, placement and separation, and ongoing contact with the child. These themes represent experiences of motherhood that are valued by the institution of motherhood and provoke ambivalent feelings in the birthmother who engages in open adoption, insofar as she is both in and outside of motherhood. My analysis is based on narratives from secondary sources of women who placed their children in open adoptions. I focus on the stories of six birthmothers. These women fit the demographic of infant adoption placers—they are young (i.e., they placed during adolescence to early adulthood), unmarried, and white (Chandra et al.; Moore and Davidson; CWIG 2005b; EBD Adoption Institute). One narrative is Patricia Dischler's memoir, *Because I Loved You*. The remaining five occur in personal interviews carried out by Alice Grace Joosse based on her dissertation entitled, *The Birthmother's Experience of Open Adoption*.[4] I focus on this study because the availability of works that depict birthmothers' experiences of open adoption are still very limited. This is due to the relative newness of open adoption and the fact that many experiences of this kind are still "in process." In addition to these works, I include my own experience when relevant.[5] I am a birthmother in an open adoption relationship with my son. I have often felt as though I lived on the border of "motherhood," which is why I am particularly drawn to the theoretical notion of border identities to explore birthmothers' positions. I also fit the demographic of the other women I discuss here in terms of age, race, and marital status at the time of placement, in that we all come from societies that advocate the normative patriarchal family.[6]

INSTITUTION OF MOTHERHOOD: CONSTRUCTING [M]OTHERS

Adrienne Rich's groundbreaking book, *Of Woman Born*, gave voice to the millions of mothers who felt inadequate, demeaned, and rejected by the demands of motherhood. It brought forth two very important distinctions regarding the social and cultural realities of mothering; one involves motherhood as experience, or "the potential relationship of any woman to her powers of reproduction and to children" (13), and the other refers to motherhood as an "institution, which aims at ensuring that that potential—and all women—shall remain under male control"

(13). It is in light of these distinctions that a woman who chooses to place her child in an open adoption can be understood to have a hybrid experience as a mother.

The institution of motherhood demands that to be a "good" mother, a woman's biology must be in good working order, she must be young and healthy, married and heterosexual, financially secure, selfless and exclusively available to her offspring (Rich; Ruddick; Hays; Gustafson). As experience, motherhood has fewer requirements and celebrates the essence of "mothering." Andrea O'Reilly explains that, "the word 'mothering' refers to women's experiences of mothering that are female-defined and centered and potentially empowering to women" (2004a: 2). These experiences bring women the opportunity to mother against the institution of motherhood in order to break the cycle of patriarchy that historically controls maternal power (Rich; Hays; Yngvesson; O'Reilly 2004b). Many of these experiences occur in and through the maternal care that adults give to children. Sara Ruddick further maps out the potential of experiential motherhood with her theory of maternal thinking. The essential components of maternal thinking include: offering a child preservative love, fostering a child's growth, and training the child to become an independent adult (18-19). Maternal thinking, therefore, is not necessarily contingent on biology or proximity, or other rigid demands made by the institution of motherhood. Rather, it requires actively solving real or potential threats to one's child (both in the present and future) and acting in a manner that diverts such threats.

Acts of maternal thinking arise from actively engaging experiences of motherhood. For example, when a young woman plans to place her infant in a safe home that has more to offer than she currently does, she is actively planning for her child's life and future. She is making a life decision to preserve her child and provide him/her with opportunities to grow into a healthy adult. With open adoption, this is taken one step further; she ensures her child will have knowledge of their biology, ethnicity, ancestry and other histories that are valued by individuals and families. She is taking on a responsibility wherein she is prepared to make herself available to provide her child with this information. This type of maternal thinking exposes her to experiences of motherhood that are unlike any other because open adoption creates an opportunity for birthmothers to experience motherhood in more than just a biological sense. It is, thus, biology *and* a continued relationship that leads birthmothers to develop an identity that is on the Borderlands of (non) motherhood, an identity that borders the un/acceptable and good/bad dichotomies of mothering.

When individuals experience multiple worlds, cultures, races, languages, traditions, and authorities at one time, they may feel contradictions within their identity. When they do not or cannot identify with one group, they may question who they are, what they represent, and how they "fit in." Author Maria de los Angeles Torres argues that identity is a process of socialization that "requires continuous negotiation among the individual, the community, and the society at large" (373). It is a process that is crucial to the individual's ability to decipher how society perceives her, and how she sees herself within society. In *Borderlands/ La Frontera*, Gloria Anzaldúa explores the complexities of Borderland experiences for Chicanas. Anzaldúa is of Aztec, Mexican, and American blood; her heritage is a rich and complex history of ownership, war, displacement, conquest, triumph, and defeat, and it has filled her life with physical and emotional borders that she must navigate (25). As a Chicana, Anzaldúa's mixed blood means she remains in a Borderland in which she has to deal with being an outcast within Mexican and American culture. Due to contradictions of mind, body, and social experience, she faces borders not only physically, but culturally, racially, and psychically. She explains this struggle as she writes, "I have so internalized the Borderland conflict that sometimes I feel like one cancels out the other and we are zero, nothing, no one" (85). Her pain and ambivalence occurs out of an internal feeling of displacement that is due to the ongoing cultural clashes she experiences.

Anzaldúa manages her life in the Borderlands by embracing *la Mestiza* (mixed blood) identity. Through the *Mestizaje* method she claims to embrace all things different, manage duality, and encourage fluidity between normatively incongruent spaces, consciousnesses, and cultures. One of the key aspects of Anzaldúa's *Mestiza* identity is her refusal to live within the dichotomies of the dominant culture (Torres, L.; Sandoval; Anzaldúa; Saldivar-Hull; Torres, M.). Refusing to deny any part of herself, Anzaldúa, as a Chicana woman, enters a new place; she creates a homeland of her own, one that encompasses all that she is, including her contradictions: "...if going home is denied me then I will have to stand and claim my space, making a new culture—*una cultura mestizo*—with my own lumber, my own bricks and mortar and my own feminist architecture" (44).

Birthmothers have much to learn from Anzaldúa because their experiences of motherhood, which are in opposition to the institution of motherhood, also make them feel as though they live in a Borderland. Like Anzaldúa, they are situated *in between*, as both mother and non-mother, and this gives rise to a similar sense of hybrid identity that I will call [M]other. Thus, just as Anzaldúa's *Mestiza* brought her a safe home, birthmothers can arguably find solace in the embrace of a [M]other identity.

The juxtaposition of birthmothers' experiences of maternal thinking, against the demands of the institution of motherhood, places these women in the position of the "other" mother, leaving the standards of the institution of motherhood intact. This "othering" works as a mechanism to further control women's positions within motherhood. However, this othering relies on these "other" mothers' ignorance of the power they have to disrupt patriarchy. In other words, the construction of birthmothers as "bad" mothers allows us to see the ways in which "good" mothers have been socially constructed to aid the patriarchal institution of motherhood; birthmothers act as the foil against which the good mother is defined. Therefore, I suggest that the power of these "other" mothers lies in an embrace of their status as [M]other. The power of this identity, akin to Anzaldúa's *Mestiza*, is that it signifies that the woman who has placed a child, will not, *cannot*, be separated from the aspects of her identity that are and remain *mother*.

BIRTHMOTHER AS [M]OTHER

Birthmothers in open adoptions create a very specific problem for the institution of motherhood: they are women who have become pregnant in a manner which clearly defies the institution of motherhood. Yet, through adoption, they also have the opportunity to become "good little girls" and postpone joining the institution of motherhood until a more "appropriate" time. However, the choice of open adoption demands that they remain in their child's life. Ultimately, this choice places them both in and outside the institution of motherhood. Birthmothers in open adoptions defy the institution of motherhood in three specific ways: they demand legitimacy with respect to an illegitimate pregnancy; they refuse to be rendered abject; and they demand to be seen as a mother of their child.[7] This defiance enables the birthmother to have a fuller experience of motherhood, while she is simultaneously rejected by the institution of motherhood. Her refusal, through open adoption, to deny herself a greater share in the experiences of motherhood gives rise to her identity as [M]other.

Demanding Legitimacy With Respect to an Illegitimate Pregnancy

Nicole Pietsch argues that an illegitimate pregnancy can be defined in two ways: the mother is unwed, or the pregnancy is unlawful or illogical.[8] Furthermore, the social connotation of illegitimacy is that any woman experiencing a pregnancy out of wedlock is perceived to be irresponsible and unconventional (65-66). The spectre of illegitimacy, therefore, would appear in part to be negated by a birthmother's choice of open adoption: open adoption *requires* a woman's active participation, as mother, in both a physical and legal sense that grants her a real degree of responsibility. Such responsibility works against this understanding of illegitimacy. The act of planning an adoption shows that the woman is taking on a maternal responsibility because she both offers immediate preservative love and ensures her child is protected and cared for in the future. Furthermore, to do this, birthmothers actively engage in maternal thinking.

Although maternal work and thinking usually starts while a birthmother is pregnant and planning an adoption, she is frequently disregarded nonetheless as a "real" mother due to her "illegitimate" state. Alice Grace Joosse recounts the story of Sheila, a young woman who was planning an open adoption for her newborn son, who was scorned while in a maternity ward: "…I would go into the room where there were a bunch of moms with their babies, and I would hang out there too, and they would look at me like I had the plague, and they would say, 'How could you do [adoption]?' and I said 'Well sorry, that's just the way it works. It's my decision…'" (62-63). Sheila's place as a mother was inconceivable to the other women on several levels. First of all, she was young (18 years old) and single, both of which are circumstances that are still unacceptable to the normative family. Secondly, Sheila had been outspoken about her plans to place her son for adoption, so the surrounding mothers understood she would soon be without her son, and in their eyes this negated any rights or privileges she had to motherhood. By "publicly" claiming a right to her choice *and* her status as a mother, Sheila makes the others very uncomfortable. She also finds herself in a Borderland: occupying the identity of "mother," which she feels herself to be, while at the same time she is treated as "other" by the mothers who refuse to recognize her as such. She finds herself in a dual space that, as Anzaldúa puts it, is "a vague and undetermined place created by the emotional residue of an unnatural boundary" (25). For birthmothers, open adoption becomes an unnatural boundary that potentially reconstitutes the "land" or standard of "good" mothering in every family.

The birthmother's struggle with being branded "illegitimate" heightens her Borderland experience and hinders her ability to fully embrace motherhood. She may question whether or not she should allow herself to love and bond with her baby. Indeed, many birthmothers reason "why love my baby as a mother when I will not remain the mother?"

> *I didn't get attached, because I knew I couldn't, I just knew I couldn't, because then you wouldn't be able to go through with [the adoption plan].* Sheila (Joosse 55)

> *Once I decided on adoption ... I said, "you know what, I'm not going to get too attached, I'm just gonna leave it...." I didn't want to get the attachment.* Heather (Joosse 79)

Both Heather and Sheila appear to be aware of societal standards that demand a child have only *one* mother to whom it is attached—the adoptive mother. As bonding with a newborn represents a significant initiation into motherhood, and may come naturally to many women shortly after giving birth, they find themselves on the Borderlands forced to decide whether or not bonding is something their impending identity as a birthmother allows them to embrace.

This Borderland experience is pronounced more conscientiously for Taylor as she wrestles with truly wanting to bond with her son and wondering what those bonds will mean within an open adoption: "...after he was born I felt I couldn't stop myself from bonding ... but then why should I because I'm going to have a relationship with him" (Joosse 145). The continued contact of an open adoption allows Taylor to reason that her attachment to her son would not pose a problem in the future. In some sense, the anticipation of open adoption would not allow Taylor to view the boundaries of maternal bonding as exclusively for the adoptive mother, as Heather and Sheila had. However, Taylor continues to grapple with her potential bonding when it comes to breast feeding and acknowledges that, "...As much as I wanted to, I think I was afraid; I think it was just another way to bond, another bond to break..." (Joosse 146). She recognizes that although attaching to her son is acceptable considering the relationship she plans to have with him, it would ultimately transform once the adoption took place. This meant many bonds she made (especially through breast feeding) would be bonds she would have to break.

The struggle Taylor experiences, however, not only demonstrates the pain and ambivalence that can and does occur in open adoption, it also depicts the difficulties of finding where within motherhood she belongs. As with Heather and Sheila, Taylor is aware of what is expected of a "good" mother. An inability to fully comply with the standards of the institution of motherhood (i.e. take on the bonding, or completely reject it) leaves these women straddled and wondering if they are inside or outside "real" motherhood and what they must do to "fit in." So although each of these birthmothers may remain uncomfortable granting themselves the status of "mother" in relation to their child, they do assert a bond, to some degree, through their open adoption. Therefore, even though there is a social expectation that with adoption a birthmother should cut her maternal connection to her child, this expectation does not have to end in the complete loss of a maternal identity. Just like the Chicana who is asked, "Are you American, or not?" the birthmother who is pressured to make a choice as to whether or not she is a mother need not do so, nor pretend to do so. To expect a birthmother to "assimilate" the lifestyle of a childless woman when she is connected to her child is just as unreasonable as asking a Chicana to assimilate to American culture when Mexican culture is a part of her everyday life. To do either is to ask someone to deny her lived, albeit complicated, identity and history and thus, erase a part of themselves.

Refusing to be Abject

The various experiences of motherhood that birthmothers have during adoption placement and separation from their baby show a refusal to be abject. My use of abjection here pertains to Julia Kristeva's investigation of that which simultaneously intrigues and repels; it is an unnamable, unspeakable self-experience that is neither subject nor object. In "Abject Mothers," Patricia Farrar looks at birthmothers who have lost their children through closed adoption and their positions as the abject. Using Kristeva in her analysis, Farrar views the process of adoption and relinquishment, which encompasses the pregnancy and the birthmother experience, as sites of abjection due to the harsh demand for secrecy. Farrar theorizes that in coping with the loss of self as mother, birthmothers try "to preserve [a] private sense of self as 'mother,' while presenting a projected self as 'other' or non-mother" (66). If the birthmother's experience, as Farrar contends, verges on the abject, or is that of the outcast because she is and is not mother, the adoption of a Borderland identity is arguably her best defense. It allows her to sit comfortably and openly, as opposed to secretly, with the duality of her experience.

The birthmother in open adoption, therefore, is well-placed to resist the threat of abject experience. Her openness denies the secrecy that otherwise demands the suppression of maternal memories: it encourages an honest representation of the painful journey that is open adoption (Yngvesson; Gritter; Wegar). She can refuse abjection by embracing open adoption as a family form, because neither her grief over relinquishment, nor her desire to retain a maternal identity needs to be denied. While birthparent grief, as James L. Gritter advises, should be confronted fully to make adoption a healthy experience for those involved, there is no imperative to do it in secret. Indeed, family members in open adoption will necessarily share in the journey and grief a birthmother faces (120). There are no secrets about birthmother grief when the adoptive parents come to pick up their new baby:

> *Ed and Maureen [adoptive parents] came in ... I was giving him [my newborn son] kisses and holding him, and got him all bundled up and put him in the car seat .... We all cried; they were crying, and I was crying.... It was hard....* Jill (Joosse 182)

Nor are there secrets when family and friends participate in a Placement Ceremony for the adoption:

> *We had an entrustment ceremony ... I think that helped a lot; I'm glad we did that, just as sort of a sense of closure. It gave me permission to grieve, and gave them permission to parent ... that next week, I was a mess ... I remember sobbing hysterically in my bed ... I was just feeling lonely.* Taylor (Joosse 149)[9]

Like Taylor, I had a small ceremony before my placement was legalized. I was apprehensive about too many people being involved, so it was just the adoptive parents, our son, and myself. It was a very emotional experience for the adoptive parents and myself. I remember feeling very vulnerable having them see how much pain I was in, but at the same time relieved they were deeply saddened by my grief. After the ceremony, I was very confident in my adoption decision and although I could not deny my maternal love for my son, I did withdraw all maternal acts. From that point on, for me and for him, his adoptive mother was *the* mother.[10]

My refusal to be abject is evident in the fact that I had my ceremony videotaped. It was very important to me to have "proof" that I loved my son. This was critical for me for several reasons. First, I was nervous his parents would not keep their commitment to open adoption and we would lose contact. If this happened, and my son came to find me one day, I wanted to be able to show him the video and say, "See, I did love you and placing you was the hardest thing I have ever done in my life." Secondly, I think somewhere in the back of my head I wanted to have the option of wallowing in misery whenever I didn't feel "maternal." Reviewing the video might help me to remember the feeling of love I had for my son and, thereby, affirm my maternity. Finally, I thought that were anyone to ever insinuate that placing a child for adoption was "easy" or unloving, this video would prove otherwise. My need for "proof" is significant when thinking about abjection and the erasure of birthmothers. As Farrar's work thoroughly demonstrates, historically a society's reaction to adoption has meant eliminating the existence of birthmothers and rejecting any possibility of their maternity. My knowledge of this history made me determined to *not* be forgotten as a mother.

Birthmothers of open adoption can use various strategies, just as I did, both to deal with their grief and to embrace the new "birthmother" identity. As Anzaldúa insists, the pain and grief of Borderland experiences must be confronted and lead to something productive. When an individual is able to face the pain of being split in two, it "transforms living in the Borderlands from a nightmare into a numinous experience. It is always a path/state to something else" (95). Therefore, as a birthmother works through her grief, she is also navigating the conflicting spaces of mother/non-mother. By refusing to be pushed into a state of abjection by society, she can take conflicting messages and experiences and transform her despair as a [M]other. Rarely in open adoption is the struggle to embrace [m]otherhood a process that can be erased, hidden, or denied. Consequently, the veracity of birthmother experiences can be used to negate abjection by refusing to deny the experiences, even when it means embracing the pain.

Demanding To Be Seen as a Mother to her Child

For some birthmothers, acknowledging a role as "mother" may only entail the recognition of a biological contribution to the child's life, while for others it can involve role-modeling and maternal participation in the child's life. Either way, it involves the birthmother demanding respect for her place as *a* mother; a birthmother may not be the only mother, but she is *a* mother. Demanding a space within her child's life, in whatever capacity, is perhaps the most defiant and empowering action a birthmother can take in an open adoption. As noted earlier, granting a child two mothers is not something the institution of motherhood normally accepts. But open adoption means the child is aware of adoption and the "other" mother. Although it could be argued that all adopted children (who know themselves as such) acknowledge the existence of another mother, the birthmother's participation in open adoption means not only that she *exists*, but also that she is *present* as another mother. This presence may take different forms, depending on the open adoption arrangement and it varies in intensity at different times. Nonetheless, it is a presence; one that allows the birthmother to impart maternal values to her child, as well as a maternal identity. However, this is not to say her presence is always accepted or acknowledged easily.

Birthmothers of open adoption have to negotiate their relationships in the adoptive family. Like any relationship, negotiations are continually revisited as individuals grow and circumstances change. Growing through change is difficult for many birthmothers, regardless of whether it is the birthmother or adoptive family that desires modifications to contact patterns. The birthmother stories I reviewed for this paper demonstrate nervousness, fear, and ambivalence about changes in contact. Modifications can be particularly challenging if and when a birthmother feels the need to get on with her life. Jill remarks of her son, "I'm just busy, and I'm trying to live my own life, and he's part of it, but I don't need to be there all the time to know that he's part of my life" (Joosse 187). Although fluctuations in contact can pose difficulties, it is manageable, as Jill suggests, because just as a child does not need to be ever-present for a mother to know they are a part of his/her life, a mother does not need to be ever-present for a child to know they are a part of her life. Indeed, this is evidenced in the fact that children today already manage a variety of formal and informal familial relationships, for instance because of divorce or because they live with a grandmother, an aunt, a step-parent, even an older sibling. In this way, open adoption is yet another example of the reworking of normative family values.

Still, it is not always easy. For as much as birthmothers are willing to negotiate the amount of contact they have with their children, there is often little they can do to ensure contact actually continues. Open adoptions are not legally binding agreements; they are made in good faith and depend on it to work (CWIG 2005a).[11] The fact that the adoptive family essentially "calls the shots" when it comes to maintaining contact highlights their identity as the accepted "family" within the institution of motherhood. The adoptive parents' control of the relationship allows them to manage the family's appearance within a society that advocates normative standards of family.

The fear of losing contact with a child is often the greatest fear held by birthmothers. It leaves them wanting and needing to know that their child is safe, healthy, and happy. This fear and the need to know is directly connected to a birthmother's sense of self and identity. If a birthmother is constantly living as both mother and non-mother, a change in contact with her child disrupts the spaces she creates as [M]other, spaces that allow her to manage her multiplicity. Disruptions in these spaces can elicit fears of powerlessness and eradication. Kaitlyn expresses the paralyzing effects of disruption: "We haven't talked for quite a while ... [so I'm thinking] 'Do they not want to talk to me anymore?' I'm thinking like, ' ...can't you even return my calls and say we don't want to talk to you anymore; go to hell. So that *I* can hang up on you...'" [emphasis added] (Joosse 125). The residue of such a break in contact has the potential to rupture the hybrid mother identity. A disruption in what was initially an open adoption may render the birthmother a non-mother, the one thing she *cannot* accept. This fear is echoed in Kaitlyn's response and demonstrates the inability many birthmothers have to seamlessly accept changes in contact with the adoptive family. It also highlights the potential power adoptive parents have to erase the "other" mother, especially if they stop contact before the child has real and conscious memories of the birthmother.

EMPOWERMENT OF THE [M]OTHER

The relative newness of open adoption puts birthmothers in a unique position: collectively they are in the process of creating their history; having no "home" of their own, particularly within motherhood, they are better able to build an identity that encompasses all that they are. Just as the Chicana can find a home in the Borderlands as *la Mestiza*, an identity which embraces her duality, so, too, can a birthmother find solace as a [M]other. Through the discussion and stories I explore here, I would suggest that many birthmothers are already re-writing history as [M]others.

Within the "good" mother narrative, the birthmother's maternal work, thinking, and value is not accepted or recognized as such. Her maternal contributions are typically regarded and rejected as kinds of part-time, ambivalent, long-distance and/or absent mothering. Fighting this rejection and the label of "bad" mother is tiresome. It pushes the birthmother into the Borderlands where she is both mother and non-mother. The birthmother's fight against the "good" mother/"bad" mother dichotomy, a fight demanded by her continued and open relationship with her child, necessarily brings her to the place of [M]other.

The birthmother's ability to work through her contradictory experiences of motherhood is often very difficult. It is painful to feel split in two, to feel like an outcast in a space you believe you have a right to inhabit, a right rooted in normative ideals of family that are based upon biological connection. Although there are many reasons a birthmother can feel ambivalent towards her child and their open relationship, the rigidity of the "good" mother narrative is bound to play a key role in the production of this ambivalence. The hybrid identity of [M]other

disrupts patriarchal motherhood and thwarts the pain of this ambivalence because it reveals that a woman's position as "mother" is rarely, if
ever, fixed. The birthmother demonstrates that motherhood is and can
be fluid, something the institution of motherhood denies; she is able to
perform as both a mother and non-mother simultaneously or in different
spaces. This picture of the hybrid [M]other is messy. It also destabilizes
the institution of motherhood because women can no longer be pinned
down neatly and exclusively as either *good* or *bad* mothers. [M]others
blur the binary construction of motherhood. They also undermine the
unattainable and idealistic demand that mothers be utterly altruistic. They
allow for a new narrative, one that accepts the possibility that a mother
could willingly "give her baby away," experience little or no bonding,
live a great distance from her child, and/or be removed from the daily
responsibilities of childcare, while at the same time exercising a maternal
bond that she and her child value.

[1]Portions of this paper are taken from a Masters Research Project by
the same title.

[2]In this paper, "birthmothers" refers to women who have voluntarily
placed their children in open adoption and are participating in an ongoing
relationship with that child. Not all mothers, birthmothers included, have
a deep "maternal" connection or bond to their children; nonetheless,
their maternal participation in a child's life can have value.

[3]The idea of adoption as a market or trade and babies as a commodity
of capitalism, is discussed by Solinger; Zamostny et al.; Gritter; Carp;
Roberts; and Rothman, among others. Though the scope of this issue
is beyond the parameters of this paper, it is worth noting the industry's
approach, which constructs women as "suppliers" and the babies they
"produce" as commodities, perpetuates both the institution of motherhood and adoption as raced and classed institutions.

[4]I utilize Joosse's dissertation, in particular, because it seeks to understand
birthmothers' experiences of open adoption using qualitative research
methods that place a value on each birthmother's story told in her own
words. Joosse's interviews demonstrate the multiplicity of birthmothers'
experiences.

[5]Whether my experiences are explicitly detailed in the text or not, my
position as a birthmother has strongly influenced my work.

[6]The demographics to which I am referring are Australian, Canadian,
and American contexts that are rich in British, Anglo, Eurocentric, and
Christian notions of the normative family.

[7]Although the legal system of the United States no longer refers to chil-dren as "illegitimate" or "bastard," the value judgment of illegitimacy can still affect the mother. This is due to the fact that sealed birth records completely erase the birthmother (although the duration of sealed records varies by jurisdiction). In the eyes of the law, the adoptive mother is the only legitimate mother, a distinction that gives rise to the social stigma of illegitimacy where the birthmother is concerned.

[8]Pietsch uses the term "illogical" in regard to an action that is "contrary to law." This implies, historically, any pregnancy that occurs out of wedlock suggests that, "[i]deologically, [the mother] is non-conformist and lawless: functionally, she is morally, socially and sexually aberrant" (66). This definition helps to demonstrate the normative values of "good" motherhood.

[9]Some members of the triad choose to participate in a placement ceremony or "entrustment ceremony" as a way to honor each other and to create a safe place to acknowledge grief.

[10]The state I was living in required a court appearance in order for me to relinquish my rights; my son was legally my responsibility until then. He was in my care for three weeks and then foster care for two weeks. His parents had regular visits with him during these five weeks. Our cer-emony was held while he was in foster care. The ceremony, and the break of foster care itself, helped me let go of my role as maternal caregiver.

[11]Currently, there are 22 American states that have some form of legally binding post-adoption agreements; the specificities of the agreements depend on the type of adoption taking place (i.e., infant, step-parent, relative, foster care, etc.) and the parties involved. No state allows a post-adoption agreement to be enforced in a way that would reverse the adoptive placement (CWIG).

WORKS CITED

Anzaldúa, Gloria. *Borderlands/la Frontera*. 2nd ed. San Francisco: Aunt Lute Books, 1999. Print.

Carp, E. Wayne. *Family Matters: Secrecy and Disclosure in the History of Adoption* Cambridge, Mass.: Harvard University Press, 1998. Print.

Chandra, A., J. Abma, P. Maza, and C. Bachrach. "Adoption, Adoption Seeking, and Relinquishment for Adoption in the United States." *Advance Data* 306 (from Vital and Health Statistics of the Centers for Disease Control and Prevention) National Center for Health Sta-tistics, U.S. Department of Health and Human Services, 1999. Web. 31 October 2006.

Child Welfare Information Gateway (CWIG). "Postadoption Contact Agreements Between Birth and Adoptive Families." *State Statute Series*, 2005a. Web 18 February 2006.

Child Welfare Information Gateway (CWIG). "Voluntary Relinquishment for Adoption." *Numbers and Trends*, 2005b. Web. 18 February 2006.

Dischler, Patricia. *Because I Loved You: A Birthmothers View of Open Adoption*. Madison, WI: Goblin Fern Press, 2006. Print.

Evan B. Donaldson Adoption Institute (EBD). *Safeguarding the Rights and Well-Being of Birthparents in the Adoption Process*. New York: Evan B. Donaldson Adoption Institute, 2006. Print.

Farrar, Patricia D. "Abject Mothers: Women Separated from Their Babies Lost to Adoption." *Unbecoming Mothers: The Social Production of Maternal Absence*. Ed. D. L. Gustafson. New York: Haworth Clinical Practice Press, 2005. 51-72. Print.

Gritter, James L. and Child Welfare League of America. *Lifegivers: Framing the Birthparent Experience in Open Adoption*. Washington, DC: CWLA Press, 2000. Print.

Gustafson, Diana L. *Unbecoming Mothers: The Social Production of Maternal Absence*. New York: Haworth Clinical Practice Press, 2005. Print.

Hays, Sharon. *The Cultural Contradictions of Motherhood*. New Haven: Yale University Press, 1996. Print.

Joosse, Alice Grace. *The Birthmother's Experience of Open Adoption: An Interpretive Inquiry*. Diss. University of Alberta. ProQuest Digital Dissertations, 2004. Web. 18 March 2006.

Moore, N. B. and J. K. Davidson. "A Profile of Adoption Placers: Perceptions of Pregnant Teens During the Decision–Making Process." *Adoption Quarterly* 6.2 (2002): 29-41. Print.

O'Reilly, Andrea. *From Motherhood to Mothering: The Legacy of Adrienne Rich's Of Woman Born*. Albany, NY: SUNY, 2004a. Print.

O'Reilly, Andrea. "We Were Conspirators: Outlaws from the Institution of Motherhood." *Mother Outlaws: Theories and Practices of Empowered Mothering*. Ed. A. O'Reilly. Toronto: Women's Press, 2004b. 95-104. Print.

Pietsch, Nicole. "Un/titled: Constructions of Illegitimate Motherhood as Gender Insurrection." *Mother Matters: Motherhood as Discourse and Practice*. Ed. A. O'Reilly. Toronto: Association for Research on Mothering, 2004. 88-100. Print.

Rich, Adrienne Cecile. *Of Woman Born: Motherhood as Experience and Institution*. 10th Anniversary ed. New York: Norton, 1986. Print.

Roberts, Dorothy. *Killing the Black Body: Race, Reproduction, and the*

Meaning of Liberty. New York: Vintage Books, 1997. Print.

Rothman, Barbara Katz. *Recreating Motherhood: Ideology and Technology in a Patriarchal Society*. New York: Norton, 1989. Print.

Ruddick, Sara. *Maternal Thinking: Toward a Politics of Peace*. New York: Ballantine Books, 1989. Print.

Saldivar-Hull, Sonia. "Introduction to the Second Edition." *Borderlands/ la Frontera*. 2nd ed. Ed. Gloria Anzaldúa. San Francisco: Aunt Lute Books, 1999. 1-15. Print.

Sandoval, Chéla. "Mestizaje as Method: Feminists-of-Color Challenge the Cannon." *Living Chicana Theory: Series in Chicana/Latina Studies*. Ed. Carla Mari Trujillo. Berkeley: Third Woman Press, 1998. 352-370. Print.

Solinger, Rickie. *Pregnancy and Power: A Short History of Reproductive Politics in America*. New York: New York University Press, 2005. Print.

Torres, Lourdes. "The Construction of the Self in U.S. Latina Autobiographies." *Third World Women and the Politics of Feminism*. Eds. C. Mohanty, A. Russo, and L. Torres. Bloomington: Indiana University Press, 1991. 271-287. Print.

Torres, Maria de los Angeles. "Transnational Political and Cultural Identities: Crossing Theoretical Borders." *Latino/a Thought: Culture, Politics, and Society*. Eds. F. H. Vázquez and R. D. Torres. Lanham, MD: Rowman & Littlefield, 2003. 491-510. Print.

Torres, Monica. "'Doing Mestizaje': When Epistemology Becomes Ethics." *Entre Mundos/Among Worlds: New Perspectives on Gloria Anzaldúa*. Ed. Ana Louise Keating. New York: Palgrave, 2005. 195-204. Print.

Wegar, Katarina. "Adoption, Family Ideology, and Social Stigma: Bias in Community Attitudes, Adoption Research, and Practice." *Family Relations* 49.4 (2000): 363-369. Print.

Yngvesson, Barbara. "Negotiating Motherhood: Identity and Difference in 'Open' Adoptions." *Law & Society Review* 31.1 (1997): 31-80. Print.

Zamostny, Kathy P., K. O'Brien, A. Baden and M. Wiley. "The Practice of Adoption: History, Trends, and Social Context." *The Counseling Psychologist* 5.31 (2003): 651-678. Print.

4.
The Birthmother Dilemma

Resisting Feminist Exclusions in the Study of Adoption

KATE LIVINGSTON

A S A BIRTHMOTHER, AN ACTIVIST, AND A SCHOLAR, I've observed with increasing fascination the unprecedented visibility of adoption narratives in American culture.[1] Adoption storylines have saturated the media landscape, signaling new possibilities for exploring the experiences of birthparents in adoption. Popular search and reunion shows such as *The Locator* and *Find My Family* portray adoption as a life-long experience, disrupting the deeply entrenched cultural assumption that birthmothers' experiences with adoption end at placement. The MTV television program *16 & Pregnant* and the film *Juno* (2007) position birthparents as protagonists, whereas the recent film *Mother and Child* (2010) narrates multiple interconnections that occur out of adoptive and birth relationships. In 2011, celebrity media giant Oprah Winfrey announced that her mother placed her younger sister for adoption and presented us with one of the most high-profile birth family reunions in recent memory. These representations of adoption make culturally recognizable an experience that historically has been invisible to the general public; the proliferation of adoption narratives in the media gives us a cultural point of reference for renewing public dialogue on adoption and birthmotherhood. Inasmuch as these representations point to "how far we've come" in acknowledging the existence of birthmothers, the discussions they provoke should be ones that interrogate the extent to which these representations still traffic in negative adoption stereotypes, (re)create exclusions, and fail to let birthmothers account for their experiences on their own terms.

In parallel with these public discourses on birthmothers, the inter-disciplinarity of critical adoption studies is producing a growing body of literature that attends to these new dialogues and examines the social, political, historical and economic contexts from which they emerge. Adding to a rich history of activist writing and memoir, scholars throughout the academy (many with personal connections to adoption) theorize diverse interconnections between the study of adoption in disciplines such as literature, law, history, cultural studies, philosophy, media studies, arts and the social sciences. Perhaps unsurprisingly, feminists from these disciplines have emerged at the vanguard of this developing field, bringing a wide range of theories to bear on the study of adoption. Notably, feminists have re-imagined kinship within and outside of heteronormative constructions of the family and have examined adoption as a raced, classed and gendered practice that is implicated in the production of heteronormativity. Through this kind of inquiry, feminist adoption scholarship has carved out a space for the articulation of those who are deemed to be "outside" of the normative family: adoptees, adoptive parents, birthparents, single mothers, fictive kin, transnational, transracial and queer individuals and families, to name just a few.

Like the proliferation of adoption narratives in the media, feminist adoption scholarship provides us with new and meaningful ways to theorize birthmotherhood. On a personal level, such scholarship has pushed my engagement with adoption beyond my individual experience and challenged me to account for feminist questions of identity and difference in the development of my activist and scholarly work. Likewise, feminist theoretical interventions have been critical in pushing the boundaries of adoption studies towards a more expansive inquiry into the politics of family life. However productive they may be, these feminist interventions frequently fail to acknowledge the unique material stakes that birthmothers often have relative to these important conversations about family life. As we engage with important developments that feminist theory has made in the field of adoption studies, we must continue to (re)examine the kinds of exclusions that persist in feminist adoption scholarship. Just as we use a feminist lens to complicate the narratives of adoption in media, so, too, must we turn our critique inward and work to address the limitations of academic narratives in our scholastic communities, particularly with respect to birthmothers.

As a part of that project, this essay explores several ways in which scholars use feminisms to theorize adoption and further examines the extent to which birthmothers are situated, uniquely, relative to these discussions. It focuses primarily on the ways in which adoption scholars tend to use feminist analyses of essentialism to critique adoption policy and practice. I argue that these frameworks, while critically important to the study of adoption, also produce irreconcilable challenges for birthmothers. It examines what I call the "birthmother dilemma;" the situation wherein birthmothers find they must simultaneously undermine and embrace normative constructions of family in order to be acknowledged by adoption studies and in "real life" more generally.[2] This unfortunate paradox in which birthmothers are situated is rooted in long-standing feminist debates over essentialism and social construction, which, this paper contends, do not sufficiently account for the experiences of birthmothers. It argues that feminist adoption scholarship is structured by a binary opposition that occurs between essentialism and social construction, one which threatens to efface birthmothers in new feminist definitions of the family. Finally, it suggests that feminist considerations of adoption must explicitly attend to the precarious position of birthmothers relative to these discussions in order to resist the exclusion of birthmothers in adoption scholarship, policy and practice.

Feminist conversations about everything from subjectivity to social movements are, in many ways, fundamentally structured around the question of identity and the articulation of difference. Issues of "difference" in feminist theory typically turn on the tension between essentialist and constructionist understandings of identity. As a result of the influence of feminist scholarship, much work in critical adoption studies now explores the productive tensions that emerge from feminist debates on essentialism and social construction; this framework of inquiry has begun to structure the ways in which adoption—as experience, practice, relationship, and politics—is theorized within the field. For the purposes of situating my claims within what is a larger feminist dialogue, I briefly examine some of the many ways in which feminist theory is framed by essentialist and social constructionist debates.

Whereas essentialist notions of identity reduce individuals to an immutable and constitutive quality, constructionist frameworks interrogate notions of identity as the historical production of difference through "representation, social and material practices, laws of discourse and ideological effects" (Fuss 2). Feminist theorists from many disciplines have largely critiqued essentialist notions of identity, pointing to the myriad ways in which essentialism flattens out differences, creates political exclusions and reinforces hierarchical relations of power. As a matter of illustration, feminist political theorists have engaged this debate in critiques of liberalism to explore the ways in which the construction of an allegedly neutral, free, rational and individual subject in liberal political theory obscures race, class, gender and sexual differences (i.e., Pateman, *The Sexual Contract*; Hirschmann; Winnubst). For women, people of colour and property-less workers, political agency depends on the ability to eschew difference and assert an approximate sameness with the essential liberal subject, a subject revealed in feminist critique to implicitly reflect white male experience (Winnubst 22). Feminist theorists of colour have similarly negotiated the limits of essentialism and often argue that the deployment of "women" as a political category assumes a monolithic experience of women's oppression and ignores the specificity of intersecting oppressions faced by women of colour, sexual minorities and the working class (i.e., Combahee River Collective; Lorde; Crenshaw; Harris). As a challenge to essentialism, feminist poststructuralist and queer theories advocate for the deconstruction and denaturalization of identity categories positing instead subjectivities that are fluid, multiple and unstable (Richardson). A major point of contestation within feminist theory, however, is the extent to which the deconstruction of identity categories impacts our ability to name oppressions rooted in group differences. Consequently, some feminists debate whether queer and poststructuralist theories deconstruct identity categories at the expense of attention to women's lived, material oppressions and foreclose the deployment of identities as strategic frameworks for political mobilization (MacKinnon). Postcolonial feminist theorist Gayatri Spivak negotiates this tension by theorizing a "strategic" deployment of essentialism for political purposes. Still others have attempted to theorize an anti-essentialist construct of identity as one imbedded with discursive and material histories that reflect relationships among people and social institutions rather than real essences (Harris; hooks). For feminists, what is at stake in these discussions is the ability to articulate difference and eschew normativity while retaining possibilities for understanding subjectivity and forming a politic. While this brief discussion certainly does not exhaust the list of feminist theorists who engage with these questions, it illustrates how essentialism operates as a central problematic that frames feminist inquiries.

As one of many fields in which the feminist question of essentialism is relevant, critical adoption studies is similarly occupied with many of these same tensions. Many feminist considerations of adoption explore the ways in which dominant heteronormative discourses of the family essentialize bio-genetic kinship as normal and "natural" while positing adoptive kinship as comparatively unnatural and constructed. Feminists have long argued that heteronormative bias (i.e., the bias toward privileging heterosexual familial, kinship and intimate arrangements) in law and public policy, which emerges from constructions of the "natural" family, has produced devastating effects that marginalize and exclude non-normative individuals and families (Lind). As such, feminist discourse on adoption has often centered on a presumed conflict between full recognition for the adoptive family and the heteronormative biological family as a "natural" and essential unit of association.

In *Making Babies, Making Families,* feminist political theorist Mary Shanley synthesizes feminist objections that target bio/genetic essentialisms within dominant constructions of the family. She examines the politics of open and transracial adoption, surrogacy, gamete transfer, and same-sex parenting and theorizes the impact of these developing practices on normative constructions of the family. Drawing from feminist theoretical perspectives, she argues that traditional notions of the family have rooted personal identity and authenticity in biological relationships; "natural" families are comprised of heterosexual, two-parent unions that create biological children through "coital procreation" (1). Within this "natural" family ideology, such families represent the fulfillment of the natural sexual order, the stability of which is considered the foundation of all social order in liberal political theory (i.e., Pateman, *The Sexual Contract*; Shanley). She rightly notes that "natural" family ideology is confounded by the practice of adoption; adoption legally dissolves "natural" biological ties and replaces them with comparatively "unnatural" families that are socially constructed (Shanley 15).

Shanley argues that approaches to adoption in the U.S. have been shaped by the popular presumption of a mutually exclusive relationship between adoption and the ideological primacy of the "natural" biological family. Twentieth-century American adoption practices, particularly during the mid-century, sought to create adoptive families that could "pass" as biological families, a model that Shanley and others call the "as-if family" (Yngvesson 43; Shanley 12). Many scholars have discussed the numerous ways in which adoption policy and practice underscores the "natural" two-parent family configuration by foreclosing the possibility that children can have legally and/or socially recognized relationships with multiple mothers and fathers (Shanley 32). Race-matching in adoptive placements, closed adoption and sealed birth records are but a few of the mechanisms within adoption law and practice that demanded the performance of heteronormativity on the part of birth and adoptive families in the service of bio-genetic privilege (Solinger; Bartholet; Yngvesson; Shanley; Fogg-Davis; Allen). Through secrecy in adoption, unwed mothers could obscure their sexual/social illegitimacy and get a second chance at creating a normative family in the future (Willke and Willke; Shanley). Similarly, adoptive families could maintain the illusion of the "as if" family, avert the stigma of infertility and avoid presumptions that their family form was somehow "second best."

Shanley's analysis contextualizes a popular imperative in critical adoption studies—the deconstruction of bio/genetic ties as "natural" and essential—and illuminates the ways in which many feminist interventions in adoption are predicated upon the fundamental opposition between essentialism and social construction. Emerging from poststructuralist thought, many feminist interventions consider normative social and legal constructions of the family to be based upon the false assumption that adoptive families are constructed imitations of the "natural" family (Yngvesson; Shanley; Smith; Leighton; Brettschneider). As a remedy, popular feminist and queer approaches deconstruct gender, race and sexual normativity by positing "biology" as a social construct, which is in contrast to biology's popular configuration as an essential and immutable quality (Butler; Haslanger; Leighton; Witt; Brettschneider). Consequently, adoptive and biological families are uniformly legitimated; "natural" families simply do not exist. In de-naturalizing biological family connections, families once marginalized as non-normative can function as legitimate in a diverse field of family formations.

By illustrating the social-construction of all families, adoption is imagined as a libratory practice, one that, at its best, provides necessary care for children and undermines heteronormative, patriarchal privilege by extending the family "franchise" toward greater inclusivity. While many theorists have acknowledged the ways in which experiences of adoption are structured by gender, sexual, economic and racial inequalities, others imply that adoption's potential might outweigh its inherent limitations (Bartholet, *Nobody's Children*; Allen). As the institution of adoption has progressively expanded in light of these feminist critiques, visible practices like open and transracial adoption have emerged to further challenge traditional boundaries of kinship with respect to gender, sexuality and race. Feminist theorists have argued that practices of international, transracial and same-sex parent adoptions make visible the "constructed" nature of adoptive families and they further refuse the performance of the "as if" family as one that benefits adoptive kinship (Bartholet, *Family Bonds*; Shanley; Fogg-Davis; Brettschneider).[3] Unlike practices of secrecy (i.e., closed adoption) that imply new family ties can be forged only if the birth family is rendered invisible and inaccessible, feminists contend that visible adoption practices illuminate the possibility of multiple mothers within the family and thereby subvert the normative two-parent configuration. In contrast to the binary model of closed adoption (which considers adoptive and birth families as mutually exclusive), visible adoption practices suggest a child can have multiple sources of family identity and that subjectivity can be co-constituted through these different fields of experience (Yngvesson; Shanley).

While the feminist deconstruction of bio-genetic ties unmasks heteronormative privilege in dominant family ideologies and enables the social and legal recognition of adoptive kinship, birthmothers remain precariously situated relative to these interventions. Feminists have noted that birthmothers represent an internal contradiction within dominant constructions of motherhood and family. On one hand, women who choose adoption are understood to have divorced their reproductive capacity from the natural imperative of caretaking, which marks them as unnatural and deviant in heteronormative constructions of the family. On the other hand, dominant discourses on adoption often posit birthmothers as the epitome of self-sacrificial motherhood; they are women guided by an essential maternal obligation to recognize their own insufficiencies and "gift" their children a "better" life by placing them with adoptive families. While feminist theoretical interventions have successfully illuminated this contradiction, I argue that this paradox creates a rupture in *both* normative constructions of the family and feminist critiques of the heteronormative family model. Insofar as biological connections are conflated with normativity and privilege, birthmothers render incoherent traditional constructs of the "natural" family *and* feminist critiques of adoption. They do so because their role or relationship is simultaneously biological and non-normative. Despite their claim to "biology," birthmothers, like adoptive families, are decidedly marginalized by dominant constructions of a natural family order that presumes biology and care go hand in hand. Birthmothers cannot appeal to heteronormative biological privilege because they fail to achieve the feminine, maternal ideal of care.

That birthmothers trouble the normative coherence of the "natural" in dominant family ideologies can, of course, be seen as a validation of feminist critiques of adoption. It is not my intention to invalidate conceptual gains made through feminist interventions; rather, it is to think about the ways in which birthmothers are situated within critical discourses that rely on a fundamental dualism between the "essential" and "constructed" or the "natural" and "non-normative." Even as feminists deconstruct this binary, the binary continues to frame the terms of the debate. In the anthology *Outsiders Within: Writing on Transracial Adoption*, adoptee theorists of colour point to this dualism's operation within transracial adoption discourses. Anti-essentialist "colorblind ideologies" in adoption deny the importance of race in the lives of transracial adoptees who live in a discursive world that essentializes race, nation, culture and communities of origin as central to identity formation (Trenka et al. 4-5). Within this dualism, the experience of race is either considered essential and all-important to an adoptee's identity or it is considered constructed and inconsequential. These adoptee theorists argue that the lived realities of transracial adoptees remain unaccounted for as the experiences of adoptees of colour are reflected in *both and neither* of these frameworks of identity. Simply put, the subjective experiences of transracial adoptees are decidedly more complex than the discursive binary can accommodate.

Given the logic of *Outsiders Within*, how do we address the interests of birthmothers in the midst of an adoption debate that primarily pits heteronormative biological ties against the legitimacy of socially construct-ed adoptive ties, a dichotomy which, at best, renders the birthmother's location precarious and, at worst, invisible? What consequences do the limits of this debate yield for birthmothers?

While feminist interventions that deconstruct the natural family benefit some non-normative families (single parent, queer and adoptive families, etc.), birthmothers remain caught between dominant adoption discourse and critical feminist accounts of adoption. As a scholar in the field of critical adoption studies, a birthmother in an open adoption, and the facilitator of a large birthmother support group, I've observed birthmothers struggle to realize—within social and legal contexts framed by dominant family ideologies—the possibility of new family forms which are proposed by feminist accounts of adoption. For example, while feminist interventions posit that the marginalization of adoptive families and birth families is shared relative to heteronormative family constructs, adoptive families, by and large, ignore the ways in which feminism legitimizes not only adoptive kinship connections but those of birthmothers as well. Some birthmothers enjoy relationships with adoptees and adoptive parents that arguably realize feminist possibilities in adoption, but many adoptive families deliberately maintain distance (literal and/or psychological) from birthmothers, which heeds the call of dominant discourses that posit birthmothers as a threat to the stability and legitimacy of adoptive kinship.

While open adoption is discussed as a successful feminist intervention that disrupts normative constructions of the family, birthmothers in open adoptions experience the tensions between dominant frameworks and critical feminist accounts of adoption rather acutely. Feminist discourses on liberal freedoms, reproductive self-determination and "choice" have underwritten a contemporary shift toward openness and visibility in adoption practice (Solinger, *Beggars*). While many feminists argued that "real" choices in adoption still remain contingent on normative racial, economic, and sexual privilege,[4] new forms of choice have emerged in the institution of adoption, both in the way some women experience adoption as birthmothers and the way others create new families through adoption. Birthmothers may "choose" post-placement contact with the adoptive family; adoptive families can "choose" visible practices like open and transracial adoption. Openness has yielded a progressive destabilization of heteronormative models of the family, yet the discourse of "choice" that underwrites many feminist justifications of openness remain paradoxically complicit with heteronormativity, particularly where birthmothers are concerned. Some feminists argue that the valuation of freedom and choice in adoption implies that birthmothers and adoptive families should be free to choose not only practices of visibility and inclusion, but ones that entail anonymity and autonomy through closed adoption (Allen). Effectively, feminist "choice" discourse implies a right to engage in both openness and new forms of closed adoption, because such choice is presumed necessary to confer women's agency and subjectivity. In other words, new birthmothers continue to be subsumed by the juggernaut of heteronormativity that closed adoption accommodates, but this is presumed to reflect women's agency rather than the kinds of coercion faced by birthmothers of previous generations.

In this context, even birthmothers who have "elected" visibility and inclusion through open adoption face the constant threat that adoptive families can reclaim normativity for themselves by calling upon social and legal mechanisms rooted in heteronormative privilege to justify birthmother exclusion. In part, this is because feminist redefinitions of the family have yet to be fully institutionalized in adoption law and practice and, thus, they often rely on informal agreements that can be dissolved easily. For example, few American states offer legally enforceable post-adoption contract agreements. In my own state, the legal recognition of open adoption is explicitly prohibited, which means my child's adoptive parents, with whom I participate in an informal open adoption, can discontinue contact with me at any time for any reason.

However innovative feminist interventions are on a theoretical level, birthmothers negotiate a social and legal reality that is decidedly hostile to their claims of legitimacy. In this context, a birthmother's most salient claim to legitimacy continues to lie in the biological relationship that she shares with her child. Within structures of family that privilege biology, birthmothers often rely on the perceived "naturalness" of their biological relations to justify their social inclusion within contemporary constructions of motherhood. For example, activist writings on the part of birthmothers and adoptees alike often deploy naturalized notions of biological connection to articulate a claim to political rights, access and recognition.

While a birthmother's essential, identity-based claim to "natural" motherhood has significant currency in liberal, political, Western contexts, a birthmother's simultaneous positioning as non-normative and unnatural in relation to dominant constructions of family subjects her to an ideological dilemma. To achieve inclusion, birthmothers must advocate for an alternative construction of the heteronormative family, one that is not predicated on the "naturalness" of a two-parent configuration, wherein a "mother" typically assumes the primary caregiver's role. Without dismantling or, at least, expanding the dominant, heteronormative, biological family model, there is no room to legitimate birthmothers whose children are integrated into adoptive families, because adoptive families must mirror a normative model to secure their own ties too. In order to make themselves visible, therefore, birthmothers face a crucial dilemma: they must strategically ground their legitimacy in nature/biology and, at the same time, challenge the hegemony of the natural family to expand the two-parent configuration of family that denies them meaningful access to their children.

The "birthmother dilemma" is an effect of dominant adoption discourses and feminist responses to them, both of which are framed by the fundamental opposition between essential and socially-constructed understandings of motherhood and kinship. Within this oppositional framework, the complex realities of birthmothers' experiences are obscured. They are left with few ways to articulate and validate experiences of motherhood on their own terms, and when they do, their accounts of motherhood are too often ignored. Take, for example, a woman in my support group who was refused a glimpse of her son at the maternity hospital at which she gave birth many decades ago. Feminist theories that trace the desire to find her son (a yearning that has spanned 50 years) to an essentialist imperative of maternal care, one which is socially constructed, is little consolation in the face of a material experience that is profound, painful, and a defining feature of her subjectivity. Is it a productive intervention to qualify her understanding of biological connection as a political, historical and cultural production? For the women of my group in open adoptions who have no legal right to see their children but for the good graces of adoptive parents, on what grounds do they advocate for themselves in the face of broken promises? What phenomenon brings these women to my group—a phenomenon that connects some women to children they have never even seen? It is not my intention to suggest that this phenomenon is, in fact, rooted in some sort of biological essentialism. Rather, I'm suggesting that in light of birthmothers' material realities, the essential/constructed dualism within dominant adoption discourses and feminist critiques of adoption presents birthmothers with untenable choices. Do we articulate ourselves as "natural," biological mothers at the risk of shoring up the heteronormative family forms that exclude us? Do we stress the constructed nature of kinship and give up our most salient claim to legal and social recognition in the current socio-political climate? Either choice produces our exclusion and fails to account for the complexity of our subjective experiences, our relationships, and our place in the larger social fabric of family life.

The feminist process of re-envisioning the family offers a unique opportunity for redressing structural inequalities and exclusions that marginalize birthmothers and non-normative families. However, popular feminist approaches to the study of adoption fall short of their own promise because they largely fail to include birthmothers as a critical part of the family as it is re-envisioned. An important part of bringing feminist theory to bear on the study of adoption is to challenge the marginalization of birthmothers within dominant heteronormative discourses and feminist considerations of adoption. As a part of this project, feminists must examine the ways in which their critiques inadvertently participate in fundamental oppositions that implicitly re-inscribe their new definitions of the family with exclusions that continue to marginalize birthmothers. For example, some feminists working in the field of care theory argue for the redefinition of "family," "away from certain familial structures … toward intimate relationships of care and dependency" (Levy 73). On this basis, families are legitimated by interconnected relationships of care and dependence, rather than delineated by bio-genetic ties. By conceptualizing families as relationships of intimate care, these feminist definitions of family expand beyond a normative biological configuration to include non-normative families such as adoptive and queer families and "fictive kin," or those persons who participate in caretaking, but are neither biologically nor legally related (Levy 69). Feminists who look to challenge the marginalization of birthmothers should consider whether these definitions of "care work," which are intended as interventions with respect to normative family models, nonetheless preclude birthmothers from being included in the family. For instance, the woman in my group enjoys no social relationship that might count as care work because she has never seen her child; thus, she has little claim to being deemed "family" on the basis of a care work model. The question with which we are left, therefore, is how do new feminist interventions that stress the socially constructed nature of kinship begin to address the plight of birthmothers, who have been prevented or discouraged from participating in care work? Feminists must look toward the precarious position of birthmothers to make sure the definitions of care work being deployed sufficiently account for birthmothers' material realities and do not recreate their exclusion.

Feminists must more rigorously trouble the strict opposition between essentialism and constructionism that is embedded in many feminist considerations of difference. Diana Fuss, for example, argues that essentialism may be unavoidable as a linguistic necessity even for feminists committed to fluid, multiple and socially-constructed identities (4). For Fuss, the critical determination is not *whether* feminist interventions rely on essentialisms; rather, it is *how* they deploy them and to what ends (4). Troubling the assumption of a fundamental opposition between essentialism and social construction might better account for the precarious positioning of birthmothers as biological and non-normative within dominant and critical feminist discourses on adoption.

Finally, another important dimension of this project, which has already been suggested by the important work of adoptee theorists, is that we need to take seriously the perspectives of those living on the margins of the adoption debates and incorporate them, not simply as objects of study, but as subjects and agenda-setters. Without explicit attention to those who occupy liminal and/or multiple spaces in these discussions, we risk (re) creating problematic exclusions in new theories of family. It is no secret that birthmothers, not to mention adopted persons and people of colour, have struggled to be recognized equally as epistemological authorities in this field. As feminist theorists of adoption, our theoretical interventions must be framed in ways that open up the field for birthmother participation. As is eloquently articulated throughout *Outsiders Within*, a more critical feminist engagement with adoption must actively work from the margins, interrogate its own assumptions and seek out the boundaries and exclusions articulated in new understandings of family life.

As birthmothers gain increasing visibility in our culture, the questions we ask as adoption scholars need to be guided by birthmothers' understandings of their experiences as much as anyone else's. The failure to include birthmothers in this way risks sustaining the normative boundaries that critical adoption studies purports to resist. If the implications of feminist interventions are that birthmothers remain "outside" the family, it is of little consolation to birthmothers that feminist theorists contribute significantly to unmasking birthmothers' marginalization in normative constructions of the family. For birthmothers, the message remains the same—the only thing that changes is the messenger.

[1]For the sake of continuity, "birthmother" refers to women who either

voluntarily elect, or are coerced, to terminate their parental rights through adoption. I recognize, however, that there is little consensus regarding the appropriate and accurate terminology in reference to these women. Many women who have experienced adoption in this way consider the term "birthmother" to be a deliberate and disrespectful attempt to undervalue their relationships with their children. I will use the words "birthmother," "birth family" and "birthparents" throughout this paper, although I recognize the descriptive limitations and controversies inherent in their use. I also assign no privileged value to these terms, although they are worthy of a separate analysis, but this is beyond the scope of this paper. [2]The term "Birthmother Dilemma" is inspired by the British political theorist, Carole Pateman, and her notion of "Wollstonecraft's Dilemma." In Pateman's famous critique of Mary Wollstonecraft's *A Vindication of the Rights of Women* (1792), she argues that Wollstonecraft employed two mutually exclusive justifications in defense of women's citizenship rights: "On the one hand, they have demanded that the ideal of citizenship be extended them, and the liberal-feminist agenda for a 'gender-neutral' social world is the logical conclusion of one form of this demand. On the other hand, women have also insisted simultaneously, as did Mary Wollstonecraft, that as women they have specific capacities, talents, needs and concerns so that the expression of their citizenship will be differentiated from that of men." The logic of the Birthmother Dilemma parallels Wollstonecraft's Dilemma in its exploration of the birthmother's problematic routes to inclusion in constructions of "family" that are rooted in liberal social/political sentiments (see Pateman, *The Disorder of Women* 196-197).

[3]There is by no means a consensus on the practical and theoretical implications of transracial and transnational adoption within feminist adoption scholarship. Many scholars, particularly transracial adoptees like Lisa Marie Rollins, John Raible and Deann Borshay Liem critique transracial adoption precisely because of adoptees' "hypervisibility."

[4]For example, the ability to pay for an adoption is a determinant of one's "choice" to adopt, as well as of one's ability to adopt the child of one's "choice," etc.

WORKS CITED

Allen, Anita L. "Open Adoption Is Not for Everyone." *Adoption Matters: Philosophical and Feminist Essays.* Eds. Haslanger, Sally and Charlotte Witt. Ithaca: Cornell University Press, 2005. 47-67. Print.

Bartholet, Elizabeth. *Family Bonds.* Boston: Beacon Press, 1993. Print.

Bartholet, Elizabeth. *Nobody's Children: Abuse and Neglect, Foster Drift and the Adoption Alternative*. Boston: Beacon Press, 1999. Print.

Brettschneider, Marla. *The Family Flamboyant*. Albany: State University of New York Press, 2006. Print.

Butler, Judith. *Gender Trouble*. New York: Routledge, 1990. Print.

Combahee River Collective. "A Black Feminist Statement" *Capitalist Patriarchy and the Case of Socialist Feminism*. Ed. Zillah R. Eisenstein. New York: Monthly Review Press, 1979. 362-72. Print.

Crenshaw, Kimberlé. "Demarginalizing the Intersection of Race and Sex: A Black Feminist Critique of Antidiscrimination Doctrine, Feminist Theory and Antiracist Politics." *The University of Chicago Legal Forum 1989* (1989): 139-167. Print.

Fogg-Davis, Hawley. *The Ethics of Transracial Adoption*. Ithaca: Cornell University Press, 2002. Print.

Fuss, Diana. *Essentially Speaking: Feminism, Nature and Difference*. New York: Routledge, 1989. Print.

Harris, Angela. "Race and Essentialism in Feminist Legal Theory." *Stanford Law Review* 42.3 (Feb 1990): 581-616. Print.

Haslanger, Sally. "You Mixed? Racial Identity without Racial Biology." *Adoption Matters: Philosophical and Feminist Essays*. Eds. Haslanger, Sally and Charlotte Witt. Ithaca: Cornell University Press, 2005. 265-289. Print.

Hirschmann, Nancy J. "Difference as an Occasion for Rights: A Feminist Rethinking of Rights, Liberalism, and Difference," *Feminism, Identity, and Difference*. Ed Susan J. Heckman. Great Britain: Rowe, 1999. 27-55. Print.

hooks, bell. *Yearning: Race, Gender, and Cultural Politics*. Boston: South End Press, 1990. Print.

Leighton, Kimberly. "Being Adopted and Being a Philosopher." *Adoption Matters: Philosophical and Feminist Essays*. Eds. Haslanger, Sally and Charlotte Witt. Ithaca: Cornell University Press, 2005. 146-170. Print.

Lind, Amy. *Development, Sexual Rights and Global Governance*. New York: Routledge, 2010. Print.

Levy, Traci M. "At the Intersection of Intimacy and Care: Redefining 'Family' Through the Lens of a Public Ethic of Care." *Politics and Gender* 1.1 (March 2005): 65-95. Print.

Lorde, Audre. "Age, Race, Class and Sex: Women Redefining Difference." *Sister Outsider: Essays and Speeches*. Freedom, CA: The Crossing Press, 1984. Print.

MacKinnon, Catharine. "From Practice to Theory, or What Is a White Woman Anyway?" *Radically Speaking: Feminism Reclaimed*. London:

Zed Books, 1996. Web.

Pateman, Carol. *The Disorder of Women: Democracy, Feminism and the Welfare State*. Cambridge: Polity Press, 1989. Print.

Pateman, Carole. *The Sexual Contract*. Stanford: Stanford University Press, 1988. Print.

Richardson, Diane. "Bordering Theory." *Intersections Between Feminist and Queer Theory*. Eds. Diane Richardson, Janice McLaughlin and Mark E. Casey. Hampshire: Palgrave Macmillan, 2006. 19-37. Print.

Shanley, Mary Lyndon. *Making Babies, Making Families*. Boston: Beacon Press, 2001. Print.

Smith, Janet Farrell. "A Child of One's Own: A Moral Assessment of Property Concepts in Adoption." *Adoption Matters: Philosophical and Feminist Essays*. Eds. Haslanger, Sally and Charlotte Witt. Ithaca: Cornell University Press, 2005. 112-131. Print.

Solinger, Rickie. *Wake Up Little Susie: Single Pregnancy and Race before Roe vs. Wade*. New York: Routledge, 1992. Print.

Solinger, Rickie. *Beggars and Choosers: How the Politics of Choice Shapes Adoption, Abortion and Welfare in the United States*. New York: Hill and Wang, 2001. Print.

Spivak, Gayatri Chakravorty. "Can The Subaltern Speak?" *The Norton Anthology of Theory and Criticism*. Ed. Vincent Leitch. New York: W. W. Norton, 2001. 2193-2208. Print.

Trenka, Jane Jeong, Julia Chinyere Oparah and Sun Yung Shin. *Outsiders Within: Writings on Transracial Adoption*. Cambridge: South End Press, 2006. Print.

Willke, Jack and Barbara Willke. *The Wonder of Sex: How to Teach Children*. Hiltz: Cincinnati, 1964. Print.

Winnubst, Shannon. *Queering Freedom*. Bloomington: Indiana University Press, 2006. Print.

Witt, Charlotte. "Family Resemblances: Adoption Personal Identity and Genetic Essentialism." *Adoption Matters: Philosophical and Feminist Essays*. Eds. Haslanger, Sally and Charlotte Witt. Ithaca: Cornell University Press, 2005. 135-145. Print.

Yngvesson, Barbara. "Negotiating Motherhood: Identity and Difference in 'Open' Adoptions." *Law and Society Review* 31.1 (1997): 31-70. Print.

5.
Reckless Abandon

The Politics of Victimization and Agency in Birthmother Narratives

FRANCES J. LATCHFORD

IN THE FILM *Then She Found Me* (2007), written and directed by Helen Hunt, a successful talk show host, Bernice Graves, is confronted by her birthdaughter as to the reason for her relinquishment. In the conversation that ensues, Bernice admits honestly, "you're right, I wanted a life more than I wanted you." What mother today could confess such feelings to her birth child and not raise the alarm and ire of anyone within earshot? Bernice, nevertheless, manages to avoid this censure. She does so, in part, because *Then She Found Me* is a comedy and as such, Bernice's confession, the cultural horror it would normally elicit, is contained by the absurd; unlike other genres, comedy facilitates the safe exploration of unthinkable ideas, events, or human acts that, in the real world, trouble us emotionally and psychically primarily because they threaten our socio-cultural norms. She also does so because Bette Midler, the actor who plays Bernice, is the consummate comedienne. Indeed, Midler, I suspect, is one of only a handful of women who could get away with, and really be forgiven for, not wanting to raise the child she bore. Her character on and off screen embodies an extraordinarily uncommon balance between traditional femininity and autonomy and, in so doing, she wins the sympathy of a heteronormative audience and enables it to understand and accept her as an "individual" who has a right to choose a life apart from motherhood. This is the genius of casting Midler as Bernice, because neither Midler nor her characters kid around when it comes to what they want, and this is why audiences admire her. Midler's persona renders bearable and intelligible the idea that a woman, genuinely and justifiably, could *choose* not to rear her birth child. She allows us to accept Bernice and not condemn her as "selfish," as I think Hunt intends, when she challenges her daughter with a real, but rarely articulated, truth: some women who relinquish their children are genuinely autonomous agents: they make independent decisions to place a child for adoption.

The discourse of naturalized motherhood that surrounds birthmothers enables us to look at how women's agency is effaced by bio-essentialist views of motherhood within and without adoption, search, and reunion discourse. In the simplest terms, it is a mode of knowledge that casts women as innately driven toward motherhood and bio-narcissistic nurturing. It understands women primarily in relation to their reproductive biology, and its success or failure, which is treated as the cause of women's natural inclination toward motherhood. It exiles from intelligibility critical questions asked by Judith Butler regarding the normative production of sex: "to what extent does a body get defined by its capacity for pregnancy? Why is it pregnancy by which that body gets defined?" (Butler 33). Naturalized motherhood is a discourse governed by bio-essentialist and heteronormative ideals of sex and reproduction, the family, gender, and sexuality, all of which continue to curtail women's freedoms. It holds that reproduction and bio-narcissistic nurturing are a kind of nuclei around which a woman's identity, as normal or pathologically abnormal, is centered. Thus, even as it is more acceptable for women today to pursue maternity and motherhood later in life, women *qua* women remain subject to the imperative of naturalized motherhood. Indeed, its contemporary impact on women's lives is clearly evident in the stigma to which childless women continue to be subject; these women are treated as suspect, social pariahs, and/or in-denial of the natural aims of their biological make-up as women. For instance, in a recent study on "voluntary childlessness," Sarah L. Pelton and Katherine M. Hertlein found that women who refuse childbirth and the role of motherhood outright are typically characterized as "selfish, deviant, immature, and unfeminine," because society still "equates motherhood with womanhood" or female adulthood (43). In effect, only women that utilize their reproductive organs and, further, assume bio-heteronormative maternal roles are read as normal. In adoption, search and reunion discourse, naturalized motherhood also informs the pathology that surrounds birthmothers. The pathology of these women stems from trauma that surrounds their inability, or perceived failure, as women and *ipso facto* as mothers to nurture the children they bear. Depicted almost exclusively as victims of coercion and trauma who must come to terms with the meaning of their biological motherhood, birthmothers are pathologized as incapable of either inner peace and/or a normal sense of self because they are denied a social role and recognition as mothers.

This paper interrogates the bio-essentialism of the dominant birthmother narrative: it examines its relationship to entrenched notions of feminine gender, and its re-inscription of a naturalized imperative of motherhood that forecloses women's possibilities and freedoms. It does *not* deny the real grief and loss experienced by so many birthmothers. Nor does it deny a history soaked with the tears of women who have been coerced into giving up their children for adoption. On the contrary, it assumes that too many surrenders have been compelled by systemic injustices due to class, family, peers, religion, racism, and/or the institution of adoption and social work, although this is not its central focus. Instead, it argues that birthmothers, like Bernice, who *are* agents in relinquishing their children, are the unacknowledged secret of the dominant birthmother narrative. It suggests that insofar as the stories of autonomous birthmothers are erased, so too is the political import of their decisions and experiences as sites of resistance against imperatives of naturalized motherhood and bio-essentialist notions of family. It contends not only the reality, but the validity of these choices is disavowed by the dominant discourse that positions birthmothers *as* fundamentally traumatized and bereaved women. It argues that a woman's complete social equality turns on a social and political understanding of herself as a free agent: she has a right to choose whether or not to mother her biological child, just as a pregnant woman has a right to choose whether or not she carries a child to term. It has implications for the subjectivity and rights of birthmothers as they are currently understood: it implies that to secure their rights as "mothers," birthmothers should not be forced to portray relinquishment as a phenomenon that is always and only intelligible when it is the result of some form of coercion. It concludes that in adoption, search and reunion discourse, birthmothers will be better served if and when maternal work replaces coercion and biological motherhood as the foundation that best sustains their identities and rights as mothers, their choices as women, and, ultimately, their access to their children.

In Western culture, the idea of a biological mother who chooses to relinquish a child conjures up images of an unnatural, aberrant, or monstrous woman—a Jocasta, who sacrifices her child for herself, her own interests and well-being. Indeed, there are no emblems, no positive archetypes, of the mother who voluntarily relinquishes the biological child. In spite of feminism's advances and hard-won right to abortion, the idea that a woman could or would abandon her child, autonomously and rationally, is still impossible. In our culture, it is generally the sign of a failed or depraved woman: her act is on a continuum with maternal infanticide. In adoption, search and reunion discourse, the dominant interpretation of the woman who "voluntarily" parts with her child is more nuanced. In reality, she is a woman who must lack agency. Positioned as a "birthmother," she is understood typically as compelled by circumstances beyond her control. As I have said, she is the victim of systemic injustice, class, racism, youth, abuse and/or circumstance; she is coerced, overtly or covertly, by social and familial pressures, religion, and social workers. These forces drive her toward her pathology and interminable grief over what is not solely the loss of a child, but also the lost realization of a maternal role that defines her identity as a woman. Birthmothers are practically never intelligible as women who can and do make free and reasoned choices to lead lives in the absence of their children. At best, it may be said that they "have limited choices" or "their choices are determined by others" and, at worst, "that women who surrender their children for adoption are enlisted in their own enslavement" (Weinreb and Konstam 316).

Ann Fessler's wrenching book, *The Girls Who Went Away* (2007), is a powerful illustration of the *real* lack of agency that many birthmothers experience in adoption. It is also an excellent example of the discourse of naturalized motherhood. Its stories recollect the experiences of American birthmothers prior to *Roe v. Wade* in 1973 and predate the advent of formalized open adoption. As is typical of such historical narratives, it focuses upon women who had no say in relinquishing their children (Fessler 103). One birthmother, Yvonne, describes giving up her child in the following way: "I actually had only one choice, which means there was no choice" (97). She goes on to say that "It's just ... my whole life has just been based on shame. I'm probably halfway through it. I can't go through life crying. I mean, it was so bad in the nineties I had scabs under my eyes from wiping them" (97). Her story, while only one among many that Fessler's book documents, is illustrative of the duress that is generalized to birthmothers by adoption, search and reunion literature overall. Admittedly, *The Girls Who Went Away* considers only the stories of birthmothers living in the particular historical context of the United States between 1945 to 1973. But, the dominance of the narrative of coercion, victimization and trauma prevails in the present—it has even proliferated, mainly because one of the "biggest change[s] in adoption psychology research has been the recognition of birthparent remorse and guilt over the relinquishment" (Baldassi 240).[1] What hasn't changed in the context of adoption, search and reunion discourse is the hush that continues to cloak the reality that some birthmothers are agents.[2]

Contrary to the idea of agency, birthmothers' experiences of relinquishment *as* coercion, or as surrender, are also linked to maternal grief, which is represented as pathological. This grief experience is depicted mainly as the natural consequence of the mother-child bond that is understood, uncritically, to form during pregnancy and childbirth; I say uncritically because crises of "maternal adjustment" and "post-partum depression," even as they, too, are pathologized, clearly trouble the idea that maternal bonds *are* either natural or biological—they are clear examples of women who, although they are biological mothers, do not take *naturally* to a social maternal role (Gameiro). While the birthmother's grief and pathology is said to vary in intensity, for instance, in relation to secret versus open forms of adoption, it is still presumed a virtually inevitable effect of relinquishment and its aftermath (See Henney et al). In their article, "Birthmothers: Silent Relationships," Maxine Weinreb and Varda Konstam state that the "meager research on the relinquishment of babies suggests that women experience profound feelings of loss, grief, and psychological pain" (315). Mary Jo Carr argues in "Birth Mothers and Subsequent Children" that the birthmother's "pathological grief" elicits "feelings of intense loss, enduring panic, and unresolved anger; episodes of searching for the lost child in waking life or in dreams; and a sense of incompleteness" (349). Susan Henney et al.'s study, "Evolution and Resolution: Birthmother's Experience of Grief and Loss at Different Levels of Openness," reiterates this pathology and typifies what has become the expert's common-sense belief in the connection between the separation of biological mother and child and grief that *naturally* disturbs the subjectivity of birthmothers as a group:

> It is clear to even the most casual observer that the process of relinquishing a child for adoption is an experience like no other. Imagine, if you will, what it is like to create a life, nurture that life in pregnancy—feeling the fetus grow and move—and then making the decision to relinquish. The magnitude of such a loss, even if the loss was "voluntary" in legal terms, produces the grief reaction experienced by so many birthmothers following the relinquishment of a child. (876)

To capture the momentousness of such a loss, Merry Bloch Jones has coined the term "Birthmother Syndrome" (272). Cast as a syndrome, it is a pattern of experience that is exclusive to birthmothers. As Henney et al. indicate, this syndrome is characterized by a variety of symptoms including: "unresolved grief," "Post Traumatic Stress Disorder," "diminished self-esteem," "arrested emotional development," "self punishment (often in the form of substance abuse and eating disorders)," and "unexplained secondary infertility" (876). Alternatively, J. A. Aloi refers to such phenomena as "disenfranchised grief" (29). Disenfranchised grief occurs when what are depicted as almost insurmountable obstacles block the birthmother from normal grief resolution. For example, an obstacle to the grief reaction arises "[w]hen the relationship between the griever and the lost person is not recognized" socially or institutionally (29). This lack of recognition condemns the birthmother to grieve inadequately, alone, and in silence (29). Aloi further contends that, because birthmothers are typically "denied expression of the emotional response to loss, [this] result[s] in feelings associated with grief that persist for a very long time, and, for some, a life time" (27).

When the discourse surrounding birthmothers is re-examined closely, however, there is another tale of relinquishment yet to be told and heard by adoption experts. It is the furtive narrative of women who did or do not understand their relinquishments to be coerced. It is the absent stories and investigations of women who did and do not pathologically grieve their choices. It is the invisible account of autonomy that can nevertheless cost a woman in guilt, and grief, precisely because she dares to resist a bio-heteronormative imperative of motherhood and bio-narcissistic nurturing, which precludes her unfettered existence apart from the norm. These tales of women's choice are rarely articulated because they continue to be taboo, a reality of which I am increasingly convinced based on stories birthmothers have shared with me in response to my research.

Given the elusiveness of the history of birthmother's agency, I offer two anecdotal stories about birthmothers who have told me directly about the reality of their experiences of agency. The first involves a conversation I recently had with my (adopted) aunt just before she died, one that began, "I have a story I bet you can use in your paper."[3] Having just asked me about my research, she then surprised me with a generous and daring gift: the untold truth of her relinquishment, which she urged me to recount here. She did so partly because her story corroborates this work and partly, I think, because she wanted the truth of her experience on record. "I had no second thoughts about it." "It was a relief." "What upset me most was the betrayal I felt over changes to the laws." She is referring here to Canadian adoption law, which has increased adoptee access to identifying information: it was a change that angered her because she "had been promised privacy."[4] When I asked if she had ever searched, she said, "no never, and I never wanted to." She also said she had "no regrets." Now, I recognize my aunt's story can be mis/read psychologically as one of denial. But she told it to me little more than a week before her death from cancer. In light of the nearness of her death, as well as what prompted our discussion, I surmise only that she wanted it known that relinquishing her child for adoption was what she wanted; she wanted it known that she experienced herself as an agent in the course of her child's relinquishment. The second story, while brief, is no less significant. It occurred in 2010, at the Alliance for the Study of Adoption and Culture conference. Following a presentation of an earlier version of this paper, a birthmother in the audience approached me and said, *sotto voce*, "That's my story." She had also *chosen* to give up her child. Her whispered admission, and my aunt's deathbed confession are evidence of the secret experience and knowledge of women's agency, a knowledge that contravenes the limits of women's identity within the ambit of naturalized motherhood.

Stories like these *are* just barely audible in the silences, gaps, and qualified exclusions of adoption, search and reunion discourse, which overtly aligns the birthmothers' subjectivity with grief. Untold tales of women's choices *are* implicit in carefully articulated sentences like this one: "*Most* of the women I interviewed did not refer to the surrender of their child as a choice at all" (Fessler 103).[5] Or this one: "*Many* of those who did make contact communicated their deep feelings of pain, guilt, anger, and regret regarding the relinquishment" (De Simone 67).[6] Women who are agents—and who as such may or may not experience grief and pain over their choices—appear as the "few" and "less" or through the reverse signification that is implied by the "many" and "more."[7] The vague palimpsest of women's choices also appears in discussions intended to contextualize research, which devolves all too soon into strong resolutions that birthmothers *en masse* are victims of trauma and duress:

> Although a number of studies have compared factors that influence a woman's decision to surrender, abort, or keep her baby ... *few* studies have specifically investigated the decision to relinquish a baby in relation to the voice that the women thought they had in the decision, the manner in which they made their decision, and how their decision affected subsequent choices in their lives. The studies that have explored this decision ... have found that *many* women who surrender babies believe that external pressure from family members, agency staff, and societal attitudes influenced their decision and that they had little say in it. (Weinreb and Konstam 316)[8]

If a deep and nuanced understanding of women's agency, or lack thereof, is to be developed when it comes to mothering, the hidden choices of women that are veiled by "many" and "more" women who "surrender" must be explored. If some women, even a few, understand themselves to choose relinquishment, there is a need to consider seriously how their stories bespeak experiences of autonomy and empowerment, and to undertake their study as real and worthy alongside, not in spite of, birthmothers who are coerced. These women's stories, rare as they may seem, prompt us to ask how adoption, search and reunion discourse, as well as our culture, prevents women from freely telling their stories and feeling at liberty to make their choices, openly, without the threat of becoming social pariahs. These women's whispers should be understood to texture, not undercut, birthmother research.

This behooves us to ask why there is so little interest in committing the experience of relinquishment as a choice to knowledge, especially when there *is* so much interest in relinquishment as trauma and loss. It bespeaks the need for inquiry into modes of knowledge and relations of power that are served by what is only a partial investigation of women's relinquishment experience. It points to responsibilities, more broadly, on the part of feminists, to direct more critical analysis toward research that effectively excludes the voices of some women in favour of the many. It also has implications for better understanding the production of birth-mothers' subjectivity wherein women are granted only one narrative with which to make sense of either their relinquishment desire or experience.

The birthmother's depiction as a grieving subject who lacks agency is often the result of studies that simply treat trauma and coercion as an organizing principle or focus, even when their findings suggest other foci could lead to a more multifaceted account of birthmother subjectivities. Michael De Simone's study, "Birth Mother Loss: Contributing Factors to Unresolved Grief," is a fascinating example of this phenomenon. His work shows that birthmothers often are agents in relinquishment, albeit to varying degrees, and that choice should be, if not *the*, then at least, *a* key pivot on which his findings turn. De Simone's statistics show that:

> In response to the question which measured the degree to which the adoption was based on the birth mother's decision, 46.1% responded that it was 'not at all as I wanted.' The remainder reported "a little" (17.4%), "moderately" (12.8%), considerably" (9.7%), and "completely as I wanted it" (14.0%). Fifty Seven percent reported that they considered changing their minds after the relinquishment. (68)

The number of autonomous birthmothers documented in De Simone's study is not inconsequential (14.0 percent). His work further complicates the overarching conflation of birthmother subjectivity with coercion, grief, loss and trauma, because he identifies choice as a *variable* that contributes to a sense of well being amongst birthmothers who exercise it in relinquishment. Despite tangible evidence to the contrary, however, the "grief process" remains the *invariable* cynosure of his study's title, discussion, and analysis. De Simone contends that, amongst birthmothers, "the greater the perception of coercion by others, the higher the levels of unresolved grief" (69). Ironically, he has the statistical data to re-skew the issue in the direction of choice, rather than grief, which would model women's agency. Indeed, his study is fascinating because of the ways in which it contradicts the dominant depiction of birthmother subjectivity in adoption search and reunion discourse. De Simone's statistics show that different birthmothers really do have different experiences with respect to the question of agency. But, he neither argues, nor observes that where birthmother experience is depicted as unified in grief, the multiplicity of their subjectivities is collapsed. His study also implies it is autonomy, as much or more than reunion, that may actually diminish grief in relinquishment; yet he does not make this inference. He also fails to examine (mis)characterizations of birthmother grief as the outcome of naturalized views of motherhood and separation in light of his findings. In my view, they suggest the origin of grief might be more accurately characterized as the result of a woman's lack of freedom. De Simone admits that his "self-selected" sample "*decrease*[s] the ability to generalize the findings … to the population of birthmothers," because "the overall population of birth mothers is both un-known and unaccessible" (74).[9] But this is an admission that seems somewhat disingenuous in that the absences in his discussion belie an intention to do just this. Taken together, these facts essentially disclose De Simone's and, really, any study's fundamental inability to properly generalize about birthmothers at all, primarily because "a random sampling for this population is not possible" (74).

What De Simone's study fails to pursue but, nonetheless, elicits through his study is the critical question that needs to be asked of birthmothers and studies that address their subjectivity: what social forces and/or attitudes are at work in the determination of the coercion or agency of birthmothers that are un/willing to give an account of their experience and how can adoption experts locate better samples in light of the recognition of these forces?

A return to Henney et al.'s two-wave grief study illustrates how birthmother subjectivity is produced as a lack of agency by means of what is said and left unsaid in adoption discourse. Here, the lack is realized by virtue of the study's highly determined focus on the idea that "[b]irthmother grief is a complicated and complex process that evolves over the life span" (886). Like De Simone, Henney et al. acknowledge that some "birthmothers felt that, even though relinquishing a child had been a difficult choice, a positive result of that choice had been an increased sense of self-efficacy and personal power" (886). Their focus on female agency, however, is even more fleeting than De Simone's—a passing addendum really—the goal of which appears to be the proof of their professional ethics. Although their statistics indicate certain women experienced "[n] o feelings of grief" over relinquishment—4.9% of respondents in the first wave of interviews, and 24.6% in the second—the authors revert too quickly back to the dominant discourse of grief (885). They do not entertain the possibility that these birthmother accounts reflect a "normal" grief process, one that involves little or no grief because it is built upon a foundation of agency. Nor do they seriously consider, for future birthmothers, the positive implications of stories in which women do not grieve. They fail to investigate these stories *as* models of empowered relinquishment. They ignore the possibility that these mothers could be role models for women coerced to surrender, not a child, but their choice, because of the effects of naturalized motherhood. Their study and elucidation of these mothers' experiences could protect autonomous birthmothers from being treated as monstrous anomalies and from the fear and anxiety this elicits, as well as the pressure to keep their choices secret, but it does not.

What does the profound commitment to grief and victimization as the central object of study in the literature on birthmother experience say about the operations of naturalized motherhood as a normative meaning in adoption? What is the effect of the rhetorical reiteration of qualifiers in adoption literature that obfuscate the agency of these women? What purpose is served, for instance, when J. A. Aloi writes, "[t]he decision to place a child for adoption is *almost always* a heart-wrenching one; and, with it, some of the most significant losses that one can face" (27)?[10] And what of the birthmothers who neither experience themselves as victims, nor grieve the choice to relinquish, so much as they grieve the pain of an obligatory secret that is necessitated by a real choice, one that nevertheless must remain a secret to avoid being cast as monsters and retain their identities as "women" and/or "mothers"?

Within the discourse of adoption, search and reunion, the logic of naturalized motherhood, which informs the birthmother's pathology due to coerced separation, also functions as the naturalized basis for a right—the right of access to her birthchild. The political strategy that adoption experts and search activists have derived from this logic is umbilically bound to a broader bio-genealogical imperative that already naturalizes Western ideals about "family" and familial rights *as* biological in origin.[11] This strategy helps to establish the birthmother's access to her child insofar as her biological tie already operates as the material foundation for other rights in our culture. In addition to this, it institutionalizes the birthmother's right *as* the cure for her pathology. Still, it traps the birthmother in the horns of a dilemma: her right is only deemed valid where she identifies as a birthmother who is also a victim of pathology and coercion. This identification, within naturalized motherhood, is what proves that the materiality of her biological tie and/or her motherhood is real, which is the foundation upon which her right depends. It does so because naturalized motherhood undercuts the possibility that a "mother" is ever free to relinquish a child; where autonomy is claimed, the bio-logic of naturalized motherhood necessarily denies a birthmother's access to the identity of "mother." Nevertheless, to identify as the "birthmother coerced" renders a woman's motherhood and rights suspect too because *as* any kind of birthmother she still has relinquished a child, which remains contrary to the rule of bio-narcissistic nurturing entailed by naturalized motherhood. There is then a great price to be paid by the birthmother whose relinquishment *within* the discourse of naturalized motherhood is openly coerced *or* secretly chosen.

To solve this dilemma, the naturalized basis upon which the birthmother lays claim to her rights to child access and knowledge must change: to prevent her victimization and coercion, to minimize her grief, to ensure her access, and to instate her autonomy. To resist naturalized motherhood entails the rejection of the biological tie, in and of itself, as proof that the right to the child is real. But if we refuse the edict of naturalized motherhood, how does this alter the meaning and dimensions of the birthmother's right? Does it mean she will lose this right? And if not, how is the right to be retained? What, in effect, would a new right that insures access to the child while resisting naturalized motherhood look like?

An alternative basis upon which to establish the birthmother's right is her work; her care and activity in pregnancy, her labour, birth, and the physical, perhaps even the psychic aftermath of reproduction. All of these can operate as the ground for a newly conceived right to child access. Indeed, some birthmothers already argue the process of reproduction is a kind of nurture and parenting, precisely, to respond to arguments that claim "parenting" *is* solely the work of *extra utero* nurture as a means to exclude birthmothers from the right to access.[12] And let's face it, pregnant women today are under more pressure than ever to nurture children *in utero*: through diet, exercise, avoiding certain activities, foods, drugs, and alcohol, prenatal training, talking to their tummies, altering their social and sex life, and reduced employment and income. They may also have to manage depression before and after birth, caesarean sections, the risk of death—their own and the child's—and, further, negotiate the adoption system. So why not acknowledge this real, material work with a right, one that balances not only the best interests of the child, but the interests of the people involved in any aspect of the fundamental work of the child, including the birthmother and adoptive parents? Of course, you may ask: "What of birthfathers? How are their rights to be determined?" The answer, again, is work. Insofar as it is balanced against the best interests of the birthmother and child, the birthfather should have a right that turns on whether he is involved, seriously, in the work and support of the pregnancy: financially, physically, and psychically, as well as in the process of adoption. Now you might find this idea of a right to remuneration for pregnancy work to be cold, measured, calculating, self-interested, or even unromantic. But perhaps it can be rethought or wrapped up in some other romantic ideal, such as, "it takes a village." Indeed, this ideal promises greater equity than the false romanticism of naturalized motherhood which still subjects women to most, often all, of the hard work related to child bearing and rearing with little or no compensation. Moreover, when pregnancy and birth are recast as work, women potentially achieve more freedom and agency to give up the "job" if and when they choose and, at the same time, maintain a surety that they can collect on their original investment through access that is balanced against the rights of others involved.

Obviously, the idea that pregnancy be cast as work that grants a right to access creates a concern that children might come to be treated as products, objects or as private property, particularly in a capitalist context. Yet, it is precisely the refusal of capitalist patriarchy to fairly recognize and value all manner of mothering as labour that continues to diminish women socially and economically as a class. The best response to this concern is that it is unwarranted, not only in a context that already recognizes the rights of children as "persons" whose "best interests" are and should be protected under the law as such, but in the context of my own argument which has stipulated that the rights of birthmothers, birthfathers and, I would add, adoptive parents, must be balanced against the rights of children and/or their best interests.

Finally, I want to imagine how to diminish secrecy that surrounds the agency of some birthmothers, without denying the victimization, coercion, and grief of others. In relation to a norm, Judith Butler says, "crafting a sexual position, or reciting one, always involves becoming haunted by what's excluded. And the more rigid the position, the greater the ghost, and the more threatening..." (Butler 34). The birthmother's position in adoption discourse, the rigidity with which her victimhood is almost universally acclaimed, implies her ghost—her threat—*is* agency; it is the desire to reject motherhood as a natural consequence of childbirth. Of course, the reverse could be true too, as Butler contends, because "one is defined as much by what one is not as by the position one explicitly inhabits" (35). Were birthmothers normatively intelligible *solely* as agents, therefore, they would be haunted by the coercion and victimization in relinquishment that is excluded by the substitution of the imperative of agency. My goal, however, is not to merely expose the ghost, so much as it is to expose the norm of naturalized motherhood and its relations of power. I want to envision new relations that better represent and enable a broader range of birthmother's experiences and stories to be told. Without neglecting the grief and coercion of so many birthmothers, I suggest that those who choose relinquishment need to be liberated from the cultural shame that at present erases their autonomy.

[1] It is worth noting that the vast majority of "birthparent" research focuses on data and interviews gathered from birthmothers, rather than fathers; this has implications for grief and loss over relinquishment as facets of the construction of sex and gender identities, something that remains largely unexplored in light of sex and gender studies in the context of adoption studies.

[2] The question of agency, whether it is real, is often paired with questions of race, class, sex, and ability. In effect, it raises the question of who enjoys the historical, social and legal privileges that are necessary to underpin agency. While these are undeniably important questions, they are not my focus herein. This paper addresses the question of women who have and do experience themselves as agents with respect to relinquishment—it assumes they exist in all races and classes and that the trace and implications of their existence lies in the interstices of adoption, search and reunion discourse.

[3] My aunt was not an adoptee; she was adopted as an aunt by my family.

[4] What made my aunt's account profound is that she divulged it to me so close to her death; she left me with the impression that she finally had nothing to lose—no stigma to face—if the truth be known that she was a woman who experienced herself as a willing agent in the context of her relinquishment.

[5] Italics mine.

[6] Italics mine.

[7] I say "may or may not experience grief and pain over their choices" because not all choices are pain free or even free of regret, even as they

really are choices, for example, that a woman makes between competing interests and desires. Choosing between competing interests is not identical with coercion, which is why women who choose to relinquish their children can also be understood to want to make or maintain contact. In other words, when a woman chooses between interests, it does not necessarily mean that she retains no interest in the child at all, nor should it mean that she has no right to retain an interest in the child.

[8]Italics mine.

[9]Italics mine.

[10]Italics mine.

[11]This imperative (which I investigate in my forthcoming monograph, *Steeped in Blood: Crimes Against the Family Under the Tyranny of a Bio-genealogical Imperative*) plays a role in over-determining family bonds *as* biological bonds and has various implications for the subjectivity of birthmothers, adoptees, and adoptive parents alike, although I do not discuss them here. Where biological bonds are set-up as ontologically superior in (modern Western) discourse and knowledge, the self that is a birthmother, is adopted, or adopts is prone to measure "family" experience against the presence or absence of biological ties. The effects of this discourse on one's subjectivity can manifest, therefore, as grief and loss on the part of all members of what is commonly referred to as the adoption triad: the birthmother and adoptee because their biological tie is severed and the adoptive parent because her tie is not biological. This raises the question of whether or not these experiences are actually rooted in either the absence or severing of biological ties *per se* (i.e., the *Cri du Sang*) or in a totalizing and socially constructed meaning of family that is attached to biological ties.

[12]This argument has been made to me in conversations I have had with different birthmothers.

WORKS CITED

Aloi, J. A. "Nursing the Disenfranchised: Women Who Have Relinquished an Infant for Adoption." *Journal of Psychiatric and Mental Health Nursing* 16 (2009): 29. Print.

Baldassi, Cindy L. "The Quest to Access Closed Adoption Files in Canada: Understanding Social Context and Legal Resistance to Change." *Canadian Journal of Family Law* 21 (2005): 211-65. Print.

Butler, Judith. "Gender as Performance: An Interview with Judith Butler." *Radical Philosophy* 67 (1994): 32-9. Print.

Carr, Mary Jo. "Birth Mothers and Subsequent Children: The Role of

Personality and Attachment Theory." *The Handbook of Adoption: Implications for Researchers, Practitioners and Families.* Eds. Rafael Havier, Amanda L. Baden, Frank A. Biafora, and Alina Camancho-Gingerich, Eds. London: Sage Publications, 2007. 348-358. Print.

De Simone, Michael. "Birth Mother Loss: Contributing Factors to Unresolved Grief." *Clinical Social Work Journal* 24.1 (1996): 65-76. Print.

Fessler, Ann. *The Girls Who Went Away: The Hidden History of Women Who Surrendered Children for Adoption in the Decades Before Roe v. Wade.* New York: Penguin Books 2007. Print.

Gameiro, Sofia, Mariana Moura-Ramos and Maria Cristina Canavarro. "Maternal Adjustment to the Birth of a Child: Primiparity Versus Multiparity." *Journal of Reproductive and Infant Psychology* 27. 3 (2009): 269-286. Print.

Henney, Susan M., Susan Ayers-Lopez, Ruth G. McRoy and Harold D. Grotevant. "Evolution and Resolution: Birthmother's Experience of Grief and Loss at Different Levels of Openness." *Journal of Social and Personal Relationships.* 24.6 (2007): 875-889. Print.

Jones, Merry Bloch, *Birthmothers: Women Who Have Relinquished Babies for Adoption Tell Their Stories.* Chicago: Chicago Review Press, 1993. Print.

Pelton, Sarah L. and Katherine M. Hertlein. "A Proposed Life Cycle for Voluntary Childfree Couples." *Journal of Feminist Family Therapy* 23 (2011): 39-53. Print.

Then She Found Me. Dir. Helen Hunt. Perf. Helen Hunt, Bette Midler, Colin Firth, Matthew Broderick. Killer Films, John Wells Productions, Blue Rider Pictures, 2007.

Weinreb, Maxine and Varda Konstam. "Birthmothers: Silent Relationships." *Affilia* 10.3 (1995): 315-27. Print.

6.
Re-Thinking Motherhood and Kinship in International Adoption

SARAH WALL

THE STORY OF INTERNATIONAL ADOPTION is a dramatic one. Although most people are familiar with international adoption as a way of creating a family, it prompts continued questioning, theorizing, and research about the creation and meaning of non-biological motherhood and kinship. Adoption is a highly stigmatized mode of family formation largely because of the ways in which Western society privileges biological kinship (Fisher 352). Adoptive kinship and motherhood are often judged according to familiar and "natural" models of biological reproduction (Brakman and Scholz 56). The heightened social and cultural value of biological motherhood seeps into discussions about adoption, which results in a pervasive understanding of adoptive motherhood and kinship as second-rate and over-determines the experience of adoptive motherhood (Brakman and Scholz 55, 56, 62). Given the emphasis placed on biological relatedness, the story of international adoption too easily becomes one about otherness, disruption, and risk. In this chapter, I use my experience as the mother of an internationally adopted child to challenge idealistic and stereotypical notions of motherhood and adoption and to re-think the meaning and nature of non-biological kinship.

For fifteen years, I have mothered my son, now 17 years old, who is adopted from Romania (my family also includes my husband of 24 years, who has parented alongside me, and my two biological daughters). While academic analyses of adoption, as presented in the literature, do not always inform ordinary life, I have, as an academic and an adoptive mother, ventured into the literature in order to analyze my experiences sociologically. The value of personal experience in the development of social knowledge has received increasing attention. Elliott Eisner emphasizes that knowledge is rooted in experience and argues that personal experience requires a method for its representation (15). Thus, my approach to using my personal experience as a source of knowledge about adoption and mothering is autoethnography. Autoethnographies are "personalized accounts that draw upon the experience of the author/ researcher for the purposes of extending sociological understanding" (Sparkes 21). Barbara Laslett claims that stories of personal experience "can address key theoretical debates in contemporary sociology: macro and micro linkages; structure, agency and their intersection; [and] social reproduction and social change" (392), offering a new vantage point from which to contribute to social science. By combining my personal experience with extant adoption literature from a range of disciplines, I will arrive at a unique understanding of the processes, meanings, and issues in international adoption and adoptive motherhood. In this chapter, I speak for myself, as a mother, about the motherhood experience. I avoid sharing details about my son's experiences and perceptions; his story is not my story to tell (Wall 49-50).

DECIDING TO ADOPT

According to research cited by Allen Fisher (353), only one in 50 women in the U.S. have ever applied to an adoption agency and only one-third of women who say they have taken steps to adopt actually do adopt. Generally, adoptive mothering is seen as inferior to biological mothering, often undertaken as a last resort as a consequence of infertility (Brakman and Scholz 56; Gailey 13, 54; Park 206). Adoptive mothers are often understood to be compensating for failed womanhood unless they are otherwise able to prove their fertility (Gailey 19). Under the assumption that women wish to fulfill their biological destiny through motherhood, fathers are also thought to require persuasion to adopt as a way of supporting their wives (Gailey 19).

Certainly, I am protected from the judgments of others regarding my status as a woman because I had biological children before becoming an adoptive mother. My desire to parent, however, did not originate out of a stereotypical or essentialist desire to be a mother; nor did my husband have any particular desire to perpetuate his genetic lineage. We had children simply because we wanted children in our lives and family relationships beyond ourselves as a couple. Driven by this desire generally, and not idealized notions of biological motherhood and fatherhood, we made a mutual and egalitarian decision to add another child to our family through adoption. In this light, adoptive motherhood is really "a story of social agency," one "that rejects the idea that a woman's anatomy is her destiny" (Park 214). It is a story that enables us to rethink and recreate notions of family that resist the "biologic paradigm" (Brakman and

Scholz 56), a paradigm that "pressure[s] adults to produce new children at all costs, using their own ... genetic material" and neglects "children already born who [are] in need of homes" (Bartholet ix).

THE ADOPTION PROCESS IN RELATION TO PREGNANCY

Because I have experienced both pregnancy and adoption, I can say that there are clear parallels between the process of adoption and pregnancy and birth; I experienced the same excitement, anxiety, and anticipation in both cases. Yet, my adoption experience highlighted for me that it is possible to "demystify pregnancy, to take away the patriarchal lens that presents it solely as gratifying, joyous, fulfilling, and the completion of a woman's being" (Brakman and Scholz 66) and strengthened my inclination to resist romanticized versions of the gestating maternal body (Park 215). I actually did not enjoy the physical experience of pregnancy; I tolerated it as a means to a desired end. My adoption experience also re-emphasized the paradoxical nature of pregnancy, in the sense that it was an "injury" combined with the more expected feelings of enrichment (de Beauvoir 495). In fact, my desire *not* to experience pregnancy for a third time was a motivator in my choice to adopt. It meant that, like other adoptive mothers, I did not have to experience the rapid, exhausting, and traumatizing physical changes associated with pregnancy and childbirth (Park 214). As well, by resisting motherhood through further procreation, I was able to maintain my identity and interests (i.e., those unrelated to motherhood), and combine my desire for another child with the strong value I place on sharing resources with a child in need.

While the adoption process can be seen as analogous to pregnancy, with prospective parents moving through some similar psychological stages (Ouellette and Belleau 22; Howell 470-471; Smith, Surrey, and Watkins 146), I am not attempting to demonstrate that adopting is "just as good as" being pregnant. Rather, I support Signe Howell's claim that the "kinning" process, through which a fetus, newborn, or previously unconnected child is brought into significant and permanent relationship with a group of people, follows a similar trajectory, regardless of biology (465). Howell describes the pregnancy-like adoption process as a time when adoptive parents "create the mental and emotional space for a non-biological child" (471). Thus, as with a biological child, the adopted child is "incorporated into its adopters' sense of their own identity as expecting parents" and "the kinning of the distant and unseen child is actively pursued" (471).

It is often assumed that only adoptive mothers work to make this initial connection with their future child, and yet both biological and adoptive routes to motherhood culminate in the arrival of a stranger. In the moments that my biological children were handed to me in the delivery room, I felt relief and happiness, but I also felt a sense of disconnectedness. I looked at each of them with awe but also with the realization that I did not yet know them. Likewise, when I first saw my adopted son walking toward me in the orphanage, I felt the deep significance of the moment and knew that the waiting was over, but I also looked at him with amazement and a sense of wonder as to who this little boy was and would become. In my experience, I know that whether the child is biological or adopted, prospective mothers and fathers are required to make physical and emotional space for their new child, evaluate the quality of their anticipated child's biological heritage, and consider how this child will become part of a newly-defined family, while they also worry, wonder, and hope for a healthy, happy child.

THE FAMILY CIRCLE

Prospective adoptive parents can be apprehensive about pursuing an adoption that requires contact with the birth mother/family because of the fear of interference from the birth family and the possibility that they will always feel that they are not fully the child's parents (Siegel 181).[1] While it is claimed that "concerns about birth parents intruding into adoptive families have not been corroborated" (Siegel 182), "it must be admitted that, despite their recognized virtues, open adoption practices, at least for potential adoptive parents, can discourage and complicate adoption" (Allen 60). I found it uncomfortable to consider sharing the role of mother with another, especially for the purpose of perpetuating the dominant discourse of the primacy of biological connectedness.

International adoption makes it possible to pursue a relatively closed adoption, an option that is still more comfortable for many prospective adoptive families. Often, parents adopting internationally receive their children from orphanages, with little or no interaction with the birth-mother or family (Dorow 142-143; Goldberg 88). Once the adoptive parents return home with their child, it is practically difficult to maintain any meaningful contact with the biological family. Indeed, this type of arrangement was appealing to me. I did not, like other internationally adoptive parents, suffer from an "illusion of kinlessness" (Gailey 50). I was aware that my son's biological mother was alive and regretted that the circumstances of my son's adoption did not allow me to assure her that he was well. Still, it was strange to me to think of sharing the role of mother with her, and for some time after the adoption, I felt moments of brief panic when I considered that there was someone out there who had a claim on my son.

As well, I was reluctant to accept uncritically the totalizing conceptualization of birthmothers in international adoption as powerless and exploited. In fact, there are many different ways that women facing the same circumstances can respond. While women make choices that are informed by the context of their lives at a given time, that does not negate the fact that they can and do make conscious and individual decisions. Given that women in Romania were forced to have five children each, for the good of the nation (Hubing 658), it is conceivable that some of these children were actually unwanted, especially given the fact that under circumstances of extreme economic deprivation, such as those in Romania at the time, traditional notions of motherhood and maternal attachment can be challenged (Scheper-Hughes qtd. in Stryker 4). An emphasis on the plight of birthmothers in the international adoption literature glorifies biological motherhood without giving real consideration to the idea that some biological mothers do not want to keep a child. It also obscures the fact that some mothers are abusive, negligent and fail to display behaviours associated with positive family relationships (Weston 34; Smith et al. 154). I have limited knowledge about my son's birthmother and the circumstances of her decision to relinquish him for adoption. While I did not want to diminish her experience, neither did I wish to make assumptions about her interests based solely on her biological connection to my son.

Feminist writers argue that kinship need not be associated with ownership or possession, increasingly emphasizing nurturing and an ever-expanding circle of kin (rather than a separation from one set to another) (Gailey 20; Brakman and Scholz 67). However, I prefer, as Anita Allen (52-53) describes, the comfort of a nuclear family configuration rather than one that is fused or extended to include the adopted child's biological parents. I see my comfort with a closed adoption as signifying connection and belonging, not possessiveness and proprietary exclusion (Smith 130). It has been important to me to maintain our family privacy and intimacy (Allen 63) and to have the parental rights required for responsible parenting (Smith 130). My choices challenge the assumption that "knowledge of one's biological origins is a necessary component of normal identity development" (Wegar 546) and that something (or someone) is missing in a family formed by adoption.

RACE AND CULTURE:
DEALING WITH EXPRESSIONS OF BIOLOGICAL DIFFERENCE

After WWII, due to an increased awareness of the child victims of war and famine, both European and Asian children began to be adopted to homes abroad. Asian countries have been the key sending countries for the last several decades (Hubing 662; Strong-Boag 200). During the 1990s, Romanian children became available for adoption (Goldberg 81; Strong-Boag 201, 205), and this represented one of the first opportunities for (white) North Americans and Europeans to adopt white children transnationally.

According to Mary Watkins, "most adoptive parents do not set off on the path of adoption in order to transgress societal norms regarding family, kinship, race, and ethnicity" (269). Because I am white, my own desire for social conformity led me to seek a white child. Family resemblances have an important social nature because they attribute relational properties to individual family members, bond family members together, and serve to explain the behaviour of individuals within the family context (Witt 141). Because "race doubles as an expression of biological difference between parent and child" (Dorow 21), I sought racial similarity to avoid stigmatized reactions to my adopted child and family. In retrospect, my focus on family resemblances was excessive. During the adoption process, I was fixated on adopting a blue-eyed child since my husband and I are both blue-eyed. I imagined that observers would know immediately of the adoption in our family were I to adopt a brown-eyed child. As it happens, my son is brown-eyed, which has been of no consequence in others' perceptions about the strength of our kinship.

My sensitivity to family resemblance was based on prevailing discourses that privilege a genetic relationship between mother and child, leading me to want a family that would appear "as if begotten" (Modell 5). I have since learned that adoptive mothers can resist a range of normative and traditional ideas about family and embrace diversity, multiplicity, and complexity (Park 215). Nevertheless, while an individual family might effectively create its own forms of relationality, racism is still alive and well (Watkins 262), as is the influence of the biologic paradigm, and resistance to these takes energy. I am happy that I do not have to comfort my child who has been insulted with racial slurs and I am relieved that I do not to have to field questions about whether my child is "really mine" (Smith et al. 146; Dorow 21; Homans 267). At the same time, I am also inspired by the many successful families that challenge and oppose the genetic essentialism of family resemblances (Witt 143) with and through racial hybridity (Dorow 21).

Minimizing racial difference has not eliminated questions about ethnicity and culture in my family. Adoptive parents are compelled to account for their child's cultural and geographical origins in order to create a sense of belonging and integrate them into the ongoing narrative of the adoptive family (Howell 468). International adoption has been seen to involve a child being separated from one nation and transferred to another, forcing the child to leave behind one past and identity in order to be assimilated into a new family and nation (Yngvesson 7). Today, contemporary adoption discourses pressure adoptive parents to embrace difference (rather than assimilation) and recognize the loss inherent in such transitions, acknowledge the differences between parent and child along national, ethnic, and cultural lines, and respect and embrace the child's culture of origin (Volkman 8, 10-11). The adopted child is no longer freestanding but rooted (Yngvesson 8). Furthermore, the question of the maintenance of the child's culture and ethnicity has become a moral concern insofar as children adopted internationally are thought to be deprived of their *right* to identification with their ethnic, cultural, or national origins (Hollingsworth 212-213).

Adoptive parents can be torn between wanting to be a "normal family" and feeling compelled to meet the expectations of adoption experts with regard to nurturing their child's "original culture" (Homans 264; Howell 476). Practically speaking, however, parents are unable to access, cultivate, and reinforce elements of their child's culture in any depth in everyday life (Homans 265; Scroggs and Heitfield 6). Further, the extent to which reinforcing the child's original culture is important to adoptive parents can vary according to whether the child is a member of a majority or minority ethnic group in society (Scroggs and Heitfield 9).

The expectations that adoptive families should strive for the continuance of an adopted child's culture are linked to dominant discourses about biological motherhood, resulting in the confounding of biology and culture and an over-determination of the adoption experience. Very commonly, although seldom made explicit, an adopted child's national culture is perceived as an essence that he/she carries with him/her from the moment of birth; the child is presumed to be born with "culture in [his/]her blood" (Homans 262). In the case of adoption, disrupted links between biological mothers and children require adoptive mothers to manage and heal a fracture (Gailey 20), including the cultural damage that has been done. Generally, mothers bear the responsibility for teaching cultural values in the family (Park 207). Thus, white adoptive mothers who adopt internationally undertake emotional, mental, and physical work to respond to the challenges of conveying culture in the context of non-biological kinship (Jacobson viii). Mothers' approaches to maintaining the child's culture of origin can involve a range of approaches including attempting to erase the pre-adoption phase, striving for complete assimilation, balancing two (or more) cultural identities in the child's life, and/or narrating elaborate origin stories (Yngvesson 7; Scroggs and Heitfield 6; Honig 217, 219; Watkins 262; Dorow 216; Gailey 50; Jacobson 114).

My initial response to the question of culture was to attempt assimilation. Although I recognized that my son was not a blank slate with no past, I also knew that his cultural past was inaccessible to me and that I could not reasonably or practically incorporate it into our family life. My early desire to assimilate him was replaced by a desire to pursue a balanced perspective. I would point out whenever Romania was mentioned in the media or featured in cultural events. However, that had little effect because it was sporadic and superficial and, moreover, my son was never interested. His disinterest also kept me from having to derive a story about his cultural origins. Additionally, our shared racial heritage has undercut the impact of this demand to some degree. Fundamentally, however, I do not see my son's life as fractured or defined by the moment of his adoption. I do not believe that his origins are his identity, as if culture is genetic or fixed at birth.

Moreover, I do not support the uncritical notion that the reinforcement of culture, as embodied, is necessarily good for adopted children (Homans 262). Culture should not be treated as though it is something that means the same thing to all (former) citizens of a given nation. For instance, my son's initial experiences of "culture" are not universally representative of the cultural experiences of all other Romanians, nor vice versa. Indeed, the conditions in his orphanage were sub-optimal: the food was inadequate, the building was in disrepair, each day followed the same routine as the one before, and there was no life outside of the orphanage walls. For him, then, the experience of Romanian culture was simply not that which was experienced by families living in homes, nor that which was displayed at the cultural centre we visited while in Romania. Certainly, he shared language with those outside of the orphanage, but I am not convinced that his experience of "original culture" is enough to create, for him or me, a demand that it continue.

My own life (I am not adopted) has involved international migration, a decision made for me by my parents. Like my son, I might ask whether there are ways in which I have been denied my heritage. My experience provides evidence that all of "our life stories are filled with contingency and circumstance" (Witt 140). Furthermore, as we live in societies that are increasingly characterized by cultural hybridity, it is suspect that adopted children alone are assumed to possess such a fixed social identity that it must be continuously reinscribed (Allen 64). Such an approach to identity clearly derives from "myths" that biological "roots" are and must always be privileged by and for adopted children (Homans 266). Yet, given life's contingencies, it is not unreasonable to think that, adopted or not, "no child has a right to a certain identity" (Allen 66). My son brings with him a past, but the circumstances of his life, like mine, have brought him to *this* place, in which his real existence is situated. There is no parallel universe in which an alternate life might be lived, raising the question as to whether it is necessary or appropriate to attempt to connect him with something that does not and, perhaps, never did, exist.

FAMILY LIFE AFTER ADOPTION

A significant and unfortunate lack of research within the social sciences about the positive aspects of non-biological kinship and the social factors that influence adoption experiences has left room for considerable fascination among the practice disciplines (psychiatry, psychology, social work and education) with the negative outcomes of international adoption (Fisher 336; Howell 465; Wegar 542; Engel, Phillips, and Dellacava 257). Research conducted since adoption from Romania began has "consistently reported a number of consequences of early institutionalization that could be problematic for adoptive parents" (Mainemer, Gilman, and Ames 165). The severe effects of institutionalization upon the adopted child are observed to include illness, physical, intellectual and psychological delays, and decreased motor, living, and social skills (Johnson and Edwards 495). They are said to have difficulty in school (Dalen 40) and are noted to be overrepresented among people seeking psychological or psychiatric treatment (Pertman 85; Dalen 42; Smith et al. 148). Impoverished children without families are portrayed as "unsocialized or antisocial dangers to the established order and as primary causes of escalating social problems" (Stephens 12). They are transformed from "children at risk" to "children as a risk" (Stephens 13). Adoption, therefore, is perceived as a very risky venture that frustrates idealistic parents who are likely to have troubled children (Fisher 344).

The discovery of "truth" in studies of adoption outcomes is always constrained by methodological limitations and philosophical orientations.

Some researchers have raised serious concerns about the results and methodological limitations of many adoption studies (Groza, Ryan, and Cash 7; Wegar 541). There is merit, then, in questioning the data collection and testing tools that are used in both adoption research and practice. For example, the accuracy of testing non-English-speaking children who lived in deprived environments with tools that are standardized against a normal North American population has been questioned (Miller 230). It is also acknowledged that the variation in the academic achievements of adopted children can reflect variations or bias in teachers' evaluation criteria when they are aware of the adoptive status of the child (Dalen 53). It has also been suggested that the overrepresentation of adoptees in clinical settings is due less to the fact that adoptees are more troubled and more to societal beliefs that expect them to be so (Smith et al. 148; Pertman 86).

The powerful assumption that "genetics plays a determining role in the social potential of an individual, focused variously on criminality, intelligence, or personality, depending on the context," underpins (and constructs) social and psychological analyses of the effects of adoption on the adopted child (Gailey 18). Psychological models of adoption outcomes rely on prevailing Western assumptions about biologically-based human development (Smith et al. 148-149). Adoptive kinship, not regarded as "natural," is considered to be "fragile" because it lacks "genetic infrastructure" (Gailey 22). "The absence of blood relations has generally been thought to render adoption pathogenic" (Wegar 540) and the focus on genetic explanations has overshadowed any consideration of the role of structural forces and cultural norms in family life (Wegar 545).

Adoption practitioner literature still recommends assessment and intervention based on findings of pathology and promotes a paternalistic approach to working with adopted children and their families. The "pervasive sense of adoption as risky, even 'dangerous', stigmatize[s] the adoptive child as different, potentially damaged in ways that require heightened vigilance and expert intervention" (Melosh 39). Yet, many adoptive parents resist information about the risks inherent in adopting an institutionalized child (Mainemer et al. 178), refusing to accept "the range of ignorant and prejudicial attitudes by educators, counsellors, and community members regarding adoption" (Gailey 24) because even in the absence of a biological tie, they know their child intimately and are able to assess their potential. My son has not escaped the consequences of early institutionalization, although he is resilient, healthy and intelligent. Like many adoptive parents described in the adoption research literature, I have resisted negative predictions and professional interventions because I prefer to draw on my own strengths and abilities as an intelligent, resourceful mother. Nevertheless, I have faced considerable pressure from educators and health practitioners to monitor and label my son's abilities and character traits. Some educators with whom I have interacted have put considerable faith in the results of the testing and referred to me as "a parent in denial" when I questioned them about the validity of standardized testing for him and the incongruence between their findings and my knowledge of him. For reasons such as these, it is a constant struggle to navigate our social context effectively.

The daily work of this navigation falls mainly to me as my son's mother. While my husband and I have an egalitarian relationship and reject stereotypical gender roles, I have a greater aptitude for family management and my daily work life is more flexible than his. As well, motherhood is mediated by cultural expectations and norms, to which my family has yielded to some degree, so our recognition that parenting work need not be associated with either sex does not negate the reality that many of its responsibilities are typically assigned to women (Ruddick qtd. in Park 207). Thus, mothers tend to be held accountable for their children's negative outcomes (Gailey 23). To manage the ordinary expectations and responsibilities of mothering is hard enough, but as an adoptive mother, I must do so within a context that expects me to engage with professionals, comply with their assessments and expectations, and express gratitude for their assistance, all the while perceiving that their preconceptions about our circumstances and my mothering are disruptive, unsettling, and even traumatic.

My attempts to navigate a paternalistic professional environment have been supported by my theoretical and practical knowledge of adoptive motherhood, which has provided me with a standpoint from which to resist pathologizing discourses surrounding the adoptive family. For instance, clinical research shows that while some children can "be deemed 'high risk' in terms of the number of problems that they showed, many of their families were very positive about the adoption and expressed no negative feelings at all" (Groothues, Beckett, and O'Connor 19). Knowing this empowers me to question the values of an adoption system that is biased in favour of the biological family. Knowing also that these researchers conclude that "it is not easily predictable why this should be the case" and that they wonder whether "perhaps it may only be explained by personal qualities and feelings that are hard to tap" (19) suggests to me that what these researchers have discovered is that successful kinship transcends what is understood usually and narrowly as biological.

EXTENDING THEORY ON ADOPTIVE KINSHIP

Adoption is commonplace, and yet it receives remarkably little attention from social scientists who critically examine the negative and biologically biased social assumptions that surround it (Fisher 356). Several adoptive mothers who are academics have started to question more deeply these pervasive discourses of adoption. As I add my voice to theirs, I too challenge the "bias toward biological reproduction and [the way] this bias infiltrates the language and experience of adoptive mothers" (Brakman and Scholz 55). In effect, my goal has been to critique this bias, not only in society, but in myself; it impacted the kind of adoption I pursued, my approach to negotiating issues of race and culture in my family, as well as my experiences of the adoption process and my ongoing family life.

I love my son. My connection to him is not genetic but it is fully embodied. As with my biological children, I have experienced fatigue in caring for him, a visceral sense of worry during hard times, a swelling of my heart when I am proud of him, and a feeling that part of me is missing when I am away from him. That my connection to him should be seen as anything but natural distresses me, yet I am edified by Howell's description of kinship that is constituted apart from biogenetic procreation: by eating the same food over time, sharing emotional states, being in close physical proximity to people and objects, and being part of the shared creation of a family's destiny, a child becomes one's own, not just legally but *physically* (467). Not only is this a new and productive way for our society to think about kinship, it genuinely describes kinship as I have experienced it; my experience opens up questioning and provides a portal to the pursuit of new theories about motherhood and kinship in international adoption.

[1]In much of the adoption literature, apart from that specifically related to pregnancy and infertility, the perspectives, roles and responsibilities of "parents" are seldom distinguished from those of "mothers." However, the use of the word "parent" is often used as a code word for "mother," which subtly places obligations upon mothers to cope with or manage the issues surrounding adoption (Gailey 20).

WORKS CITED

Allen, Anita L. "Open Adoption is not for Everyone." *Adoption Matters: Philosophical and Feminist Essays.* Ed. Sally Haslanger and Charlotte

Witt. Ithaca, NY: Cornell University Press, 2005. 47-67. Print.

Bartholet, Elizabeth. *Family Bonds: Adoption, Infertility, and the New World of Child Production*. Boston: Beacon Press, 1999. Print.

Brakman, Sarah-Vaughan and Sally J. Scholz. "Adoption, ART, and a Re-conception of the Maternal Body: Toward Embodied Maternity." *Hypatia* 21.1 (2006): 54-73. Print.

Dalen, Monica. "School Performances Among Internationally Adopted Children in Norway." *Adoption Quarterly* 5.2 (2001): 39-58.

de Beauvoir, Simone. *The Second Sex*. London: Vintage Books, 1952. Print.

Dorow, Sara K. *Transnational Adoption: A Cultural Economy of Race, Gender and Kinship*. New York: New York University Press, 2006. Print.

Eisner, Elliot W. "The Primacy of Experience and the Politics of Method." *Educational Researcher* 17.5 (1988): 15-20. Print.

Ellis, Carolyn and Arthur Bochner. "Autoethnography, Personal Narrative, Reflexivity." *Handbook of Qualitative Research*. Ed. Norman K. Denzin and Yvonna S. Lincoln. Thousand Oaks, CA: Sage, 2000. 733-768. Print.

Engel, Madeline, Norma K. Phillips and Frances A. Dellacava. "International Adoption: A Sociological Account of the US Experience." *International Journal of Sociology and Social Policy* 27.5,6 (2007): 257-270. Print.

Fisher, Allen P. "Still 'Not Quite as Good as Having Your Own'? Toward a Sociology of Adoption." *Annual Review of Sociology* 29 (2003): 335-361. Print.

Gailey, Christine W. "Ideologies of motherhood and kinship in U.S. adoption." *Ideologies and Technologies of Motherhood*. Ed. Heléna Ragoné and France Winddance Twine. New York: Routledge, 2000. 11-55. Print.

Goldberg, Roberta. "Adopting Romanian Children: Making Choices, Taking Risks." *Marriage & Family Review* 25.1/2 (1997): 79-98. Print.

Groothues, Christine, Celia Beckett and Thomas O'Connor. "Successful Outcomes: A Follow-up Study of Children Adopted from Romania into the UK." *Adoption Quarterly* 5.1 (2001): 5-22. Print.

Groza, Victor, Scott Ryan and Scottye Cash. "Institutionalization, Behavior and International Adoption: Predictors of Behavior Problems." *Journal of Immigrant Health* 5.1 (2003): 5-17. Print.

Hollingsworth, Leslie. "International Adoption Among Families in the United States: Considerations of Social Justice." *Social Work* 48.2 (2003): 209-217. Print.

Homans, Margaret. "Adoption and Essentialism." *Tulsa Studies in Women's Literature* 21.2 (2002): 257-274. Print.

Honig, Elizabeth A. "Phantom Lives, Narratives of Possibility." *Cultures of Transnational Adoption*. Ed. Toby A. Volkman. Durham: Duke University Press, 2005. 213-222. Print.

Howell, Signe. "Kinning: The Creation of Life Trajectories in Transnational Adoptive Families." *Journal of the Royal Anthropological Institute* 9 (2003): 465-484. Print.

Hubing, Bridget M. "International Child Adoptions: Who Should Decide What is in the Best Interests of the Family?" *Notre Dame Journal of Law, Ethics & Public Policy* 15 (2001): 655-698. Print.

Jacobson, Heather. *Culture Keeping: White Mothers, International Adoption, and the Social Construction of Race and Ethnicity*. Diss. Brandeis University, 2006. Print.

Johnson, Alice K. and Richard L. Edwards. "Foster Care and Adoption Policy in Romania: Suggestions for International Intervention." *Child Welfare* 72.5 (1993): 489-506. Print.

Laslett, Barbara. "Personal Narratives as Sociology." *Contemporary Sociology* 28.4 (1999): 391-401. Print.

Mainemer, Henry, Lorraine Gilman and Elinor Ames. "Parenting Stress in Families Adopting Children from Romanian Orphanages." *Journal of Family Issues* 19.2 (1998): 164-180. Print.

Melosh, Barbara. *Strangers and Kin: The American Way of Adoption*. Cambridge: Harvard University Press, 2002. Print.

Miller, Laurie C. "Initial Assessment of Growth, Development, and the Effects of Institutionalization in Internationally Adopted Children." *Pediatric Annals* 29.4 (2000): 224-232. Print.

Modell, Judith S. *A Sealed and Secret Kinship: The Culture of Policies and Practices in American Adoption*. New York: Berghahn Books, 2002. Print.

Ouellette, Françoise-Romaine and Hélène Belleau. *Family and Social Integration of Children Adopted Internationally: A Review of the Literature*. Montreal: INRS-Urbanisation, Culture et Société, 2001. Print.

Park, Shelley, M. "Adoptive Maternal Bodies: A Queer Paradigm for Rethinking Mothering?" *Hypatia* 21.1 (2006): 201-226. Print.

Pertman, Adam. *Adoption Nation*. New York: Basic Books, 2000. Print.

Scroggs, Patricia Hanigan and Heather Heitfield. "International Adopters and their Children: Birth Culture Ties." *Gender Issues* 19.4 (2001): 3-30. Print.

Siegel, Deborah H. "Open Adoption and Family Boundaries." *Adoptive Families in a Diverse Society*. Ed. Katarina Weger. New Jersey: Rutgers University Press, 2006. 177-189. Print.

Smith, Janet F. "A Child of One's Own: A Moral Assessment of Property

Concepts in Adoption." *Adoption Matters: Philosophical and Feminist Essays*. Ed. Sally Haslanger and Charlotte Witt. Ithaca, NY: Cornell University Press, 2005. 112-131. Print.

Smith, Betsy, Janet L. Surrey and Mary Watkins. "'Real' Mothers: Adoptive Mothers Resisting Marginalization and Recreating Motherhood." *Adoptive Families in a Diverse Society*. Ed. Katarina Wegar. New Jersey: Rutgers University Press, 2006. 146-161. Print.

Sparkes, Andrew C. "Autoethnography and Narratives ofSelf: Reflections on Criteria in Action." *Sociology of Sport Journal* 17 (2000): 21-43. Print.

Stephens, Sharon. "Introduction: Children and the Politics of Culture in 'Late Capitalism.'" *Children and the Politics of Culture*. Ed. Sharon Stephens. Princeton, NJ: Princeton University Press, 1995. 3-48. Print.

Strong-Boag, Veronica. *Finding Families, Finding Ourselves: English Canada Encounters Adoption from the Nineteenth Century to the 1990s*. Don Mills, ON: Oxford University Press, 2006. Print.

Stryker, Rachael. "'Trading Children for Childhood': Deciphering Modes of Exchange in Russia's State-Run Orphanages." *Center for Slavic and East European Studies Newsletter* 18.1 (2001): 4-5, 23-25.

Volkman, Toby A. "Introduction: New Geographies of Kinship." *Cultures of Transnational Adoption*. Ed. Toby A. Volkman. Durham: Duke University Press, 2005. 1-22. Print.

Wall, Sarah. "Easier Said than Done: Writing an Autoethnography." *International Journal of Qualitative Methods* 7.1 (2008): 38-53. Print.

Watkins, Mary. "Adoption and Identity: Nomadic Possibilities for Reconceiving the Self." *Adoptive Families in a Diverse Society*. Ed. Katarina Wegar. New Jersey: Rutgers University Press, 2006. 259-274. Print.

Wegar, Katarina. "Adoption and Mental Health: A Theoretical Critique of the Psychopathological Model." *American Journal of Orthopsychiatry* 65.4 (1995): 540-548. Print.

Weston, Kath. *Families We Choose: Lesbians, Gays, Kinship*. New York: Columbia University Press, 1991. Print.

Witt, Charlotte. "Family Resemblances: Adoption, Personal Identity, and Genetic Essentialism." *Adoption Matters: Philosophical and Feminist Essays*. Ed. Sally Haslanger and Charlotte Witt. Ithaca, NY: Cornell University Press, 2005. 135-145. Print.

Yngvesson, Barbara. "Going 'Home': Adoption, Loss of Bearings, and the Mythology of Roots." *Social Text* 21.1 (2003): 7-27. Print.

7.
Mothering Chineseness

Celebrating Ethnicity with White American Mothers of Children Adopted from China

AMY E. TRAVER

A T THIS WRITING, American citizens have adopted more than 65,000 children from China.[1] Significantly, the vast majority of these adoptions pair White Americans with Chinese girls. Recent studies indicate that, among international adopters in the United States, White parents who adopt from China are unique in the extent to which they celebrate their children's ethno-cultural heritage (i.e. Jacobson; Scroggs and Heitfield; Pertman). Drawing on original data gleaned from semi-structured in-depth interviews with ninety-one Americans interested or involved in an adoption from China, this chapter examines the central role *adoptive mothers* play in the cultural celebrations of these new "Chinese-American" families.[2] In doing so, it interweaves literature on ethnicity and mothering to reveal how these *ethnic* efforts might best be understood as White, middle-class adoptive *mothering* strategies.

This chapter begins with a brief introduction to literature on gender and ethnicity, as well as a discussion of the methods employed in the research for this study. It then segues into an exploration of two celebratory practices that are popular among White American mothers of children adopted from China: consuming Chinese cultural objects for display in the home and connecting with Americans of Chinese heritage.[3] The chapter concludes with a summary of mothers' motivations with respect to these efforts.

GENDER AND ETHNICITY

The family is widely recognized as an institution that is central to *maintaining* ethnic cultures and ethno-racial collectives. For example, Richard Alba describes how the "family provides the original nurture for ethnicity" (164). He explains that ancestral heritage tends to orient ethno-cultural/ethno-racial identifications and that families almost always serve as the primary agents of ethno-cultural/ethno-racial socialization (see also Portes and Zhou; Knight et al.; Rumbaut; Rumbaut and Portes; Suárez-Orozco; Jiménez).

Women and girls are considered vital to identification *maintenance*, as they are most often responsible for intra-family ethno-cultural/ ethno-racial socialization (Kurien; Spitzer et al.) and positioned as familial markers of ethno-cultural/ethno-racial purity and tradition-alism (Gold; Anthias and Yuval-Davis; Ferber). Given their gendered position, women and girls are reportedly more interested in matters of ethno-cultural heritage (Bolling; Ting-Toomy) and more likely to enact an ethno-cultural identity than their male counterparts (Dion and Dion). In fact, given the interchange between the maintenance of ethno-cultural/ethno-racial groups and gender(ed) roles, scholars tend to characterize race/ethnicity and gender as mutually constitutive social forces (i.e., Kimmel and Ferber).

Interestingly, the family is also an institution of ethno-cultural/ethno-racial *change*, or a place/space where ethnic and racial groups/identities are adapted and amended via intimate social interaction (Nagel; Cornell and Hartmann). This flux is particularly evident in the intra-familial socialization and categorization of multiethnic or multiracial children. For example, parents in interethnic or interracial marriages often differ on the ethno-cultural/ethno-racial designations of their children (Waters; Roth) and individual parents frequently fluctuate about the ethnic designations they attribute to the same multiethnic/multiracial child (Lieberson and Waters). In fact, given the fluidity of such categories within their interethnic or interracial families, many parents assign non-ancestrally-inherited ethnic labels to a child that exhibits "appropriate" traits and behaviours (Lieberson and Waters).

Women and girls are considered central to this flux and fluidity as well. For instance, studies indicate that many women convert ethnicities (i.e., learn to speak new languages, take the lead in new cultural traditions, and consume/prepare new types of cuisine) when they marry or partner across ethno-cultural/ethno-racial boundaries (i.e., di Leonardo, *The Varieties*; Johnson; Leonard; Luke), especially when those relationships render offspring who can be categorized and stigmatized as minorities (i.e., Twine; Reich). Likewise, given their anticipated role in the socialization of future generations of ethno-cultural and ethno-racial actors, it is the identities of multiethnic/multiracial *female* offspring that most frequently are of concern to researchers (i.e., Storrs; Rockquemore).[4]

METHODS

The data for this chapter was collected as part of a larger research project. Beginning in January 2005, I spent one calendar year conducting semi-structured in-depth interviews with ninety-one Americans interested or involved in an adoption from China. These individuals were located via a "snow-ball sampling" technique initiated from a variety of starting points. These points included friends and their acquaintances, adoption research websites and newsletters, and adoption blogs, chat-groups, and listservs. In selecting these starting points, I made a concerted effort to capture a wide range of individuals within the population. I also divided the sample into three groups of interviewees, each of which represented a particular stage of the adoption process: pre-adoption, waiting, or post-adoption.[5] As in the broader study, this spectrum continues to give my current project a sense of longitudinal time, capturing the *process* by which parents' Chinese cultural enactments begin, develop, fade, and/or solidify.[6] In the original study, I was careful to ensure that each group reflected the diversity of American parents who adopt from China; the groups contained interviewees from different races, ages, genders, and socioeconomic status, as well as interviewees from various geographic locales and family forms. In the context of this discussion, however, I focus on only a sub-set of the interviewees. I focus on parents who, in light of the data, were the most likely to engage in Chinese cultural practices: White, middle-class American mothers.

Additionally, throughout the course of 2005 I read a number of first-person texts about adoption from China, including family narratives like Karin Evans's *The Lost Daughters of China: Abandoned Girls, Their Journey to America, and the Search for a Missing Past* and edited collections of parent narratives like Amy Klatzkin's *A Passage to the Heart: Writings from Families with Children from China*. As autobiographical accounts of an array of China-related adoption issues, these texts provide further insight into adoptive mothers' Chinese cultural practices, and they do so in their own words.

I organized all interview transcripts and first-person texts through a process of open-coding. The same conceptual categories or codes were applied to all data (Emerson, Fretz, and Shaw).

MOTHERING CHINESENESS

Consistent with the literature on gender and ethnicity, White American mothers of children adopted from China are the principal organizers of their family's Chinese cultural practices; however, as data on two such practices popular among White American families with children from China reveal, this is more reflective of the intricacies of (middle-class, adoptive) mothering in the United States than it is of traditional inter-sections of gender and ethnicity.

Consuming Chinese Cultural Objects for Display in the Home

Given the structural order and emphasis of our global post-Fordist economy, consumption is a primary mechanism for ethno-cultural/ethno-racial identification in the contemporary era (Giroux; Halter). Thus, White Americans who adopt from China view the consumption and display of Chinese cultural décor (i.e., art reflecting a traditional Chinese aesthetic, standard household décor of Chinese cultural themes, and Chinese holiday decorations) as central to their family's connection to China (Tessler, Gamache, and Liu; Rojewski and Rojewski).

Also consistent with contemporary ethno-cultural/ethno-racial con-sumption patterns, the consumption and display of Chinese cultural objects by White Americans who adopt is largely a feminized practice (Etzioni; Zelizer; Spitzer et al.; Zukin and Maguire). Unlike biological mothers who consume similar objects to identify with their ethno-cul-tural/ethno-racial communities (see, for example, Kurien), however, White American women who adopt Chinese children consume Chinese cultural objects to affirm their membership in the *symbolic* community of American mothers.[7] This is particularly evident among women who have yet to complete their adoption from China. In the absence of a positive pregnancy test and a protruding belly, many pre-adoptive mothers draw on Chinese cultural objects to signal to themselves and to others that they are indeed becoming mothers.[8]

Vivian, a waiting parent, describes using Chinese cultural objects to announce her emergent status:

> I decided, whoever was left to tell, I would make a big an-nouncement at Christmas. So I bought China related gifts. I bought a bunch of Chinese tea and a China children's calendar and things like that. Then I wrapped everything in red and gold and I bought these pretty chopsticks and used them to tie the ribbon and all. I think word had gotten around the family and I'm pretty sure they pretended not to know. So I said, "This is a guessing game," but they still swear that they were surprised.

Similarly, waiting women use Chinese cultural objects to represent their potential child (see also Anagnost). In an essay titled "The Labor of Waiting," one mother explains how, during a particularly long and complicated adoption journey, an object came to symbolize her future child:

> There was something else that got me through, and only today do I realize how important it was. A friend at work cut out a photo from a tourist guide that showed a group of Chinese children standing together, giggling at the photographer. I taped it to my computer and speculated daily which my future daughter might look like. ... No longer how painful the wai—and how heartless the international conditions that prolonged it—that picture promised that if I somehow maintained hope, somewhere out there a child would come to me. (Kukka 20)

These women remain invested in the display of Chinese cultural objects even after a child joins their family. Once the child arrives in the United States, however, the meaning of this investment shifts. Where originally the objects, themselves, were significant, it is now the *act of displaying* these objects that is central and symbolic. This act of display is intimately bound to middle-class American conceptions of good mothering; Vivian, again:

> *I keep thinking of those sorts of stereotypes of mothers in the '50's who were always worried that everything had to be clean and had to be, you know, "Oh my God, what if you get in an accident and your underwear isn't right?" And I'm sort of thinking, I betcha some Chinese comic girl is going to become a comedian and make fun of, you know, "My mother was so, she was always hanging up these Chinese calendars."*

While the desire to mother well is not unique to White American mothers who adopt from China, the use of de-contextualized Chinese cultural objects to express and address this desire *is* specific to these mothers (Anagnost). In fact, they use these objects to signal that they are not only *good* mothers, but that they are *better* mothers than an earlier cohort of similar women: the White American mothers who ignored issues of ethno-cultural/ethno-racial difference in their adoption of children from Korea during the 1960s and 1970s. Kim, a waiting parent, mentions this negative reference group as she explains her plans to display Chinese cultural objects in her home:

> *And in our agency meeting there was a woman who had been*

adopted from Korea and it was really wonderful to hear first-hand how, she loves her family dearly, but they didn't make her culture a part of their life. I think they had a Korean flag in her bedroom, she described that, and there were a couple of other Korean things in her room, but there was nothing up in the rest of the apartment.

Additionally, as many adult Korean adoptees in the United States now relay angry stories of "growing up thinking they were White like their parents," the contemporary use and display of Chinese cultural objects can also be read as a form of intensive mothering (Trenka 35). According to Sharon Hays, intensive mothering is "a gendered model that advises mothers to expend a tremendous amount of time, energy, and money raising their children" and that expects, as payment for this expenditure, "the promise of ... long-term intimate ties" (x, 127; see also Douglas and Michaels). Diane, a mother of a five-year-old girl, defends her identification with Chinese culture by appealing to her daughter's eventual gratitude:

I think that when your heart's in the right place, that makes up for a lot of stuff and I think what will happen is that twenty years from now Nina (her daughter) will probably say, "You know, that whole you trying to be Chinese thing was so lame, but I really appreciate you trying."

Finally, something that is implied by the interview excerpts in this section is that mothers are thought to be most responsible for the cohesion of the adoptive family (Gailey). Such is evident not just in the actions and emotions conveyed in each interview excerpt, but also in the words—particularly the singular, first-person pronoun—used to convey them. According to Pierre Bourdieu, this is true of mothers in *all* families because, largely, they perform the labor central to the transformation of family "from a nominal fiction into a real group whose members are united by intense affective bonds" (68; see also DeVault). Barbara Katz Rothman describes the function of mothers' consumption in this transformation. She notes that shopping is one way mothers create "households as families" and "make, display, (and) distinguish" family units (39, 37; see also Zaretsky). Katie, a mother of a seven-year-old girl, exemplifies this as she describes her search for Chinese cultural objects to display as family artifacts: "Because I have a lot of antiques from my family, I wanted to make sure I had something for Sydney (her daughter) that was an antique from her country, from her culture." In fact, as Laura, a mother of two girls under the age of three, explains, it is often a mother's decontextualized display of these objects that best captures her construction of what Bourdieu refers to as "family feelings" (68):

> *It's a funny story. I decorate my house. I collected all of these cool things to put up for Chinese New Year. For a while we had a Chinese teacher coming in from the city to teach piano to my girls. Anyway, for Chinese New Year he came and my house is all decorated up. I put the Chinese flag out in front and he came in and he just shakes his head. He goes, "You know, people don't do this in China." I'm like, "What? Of course they don't do that in China! It's a minimalist society! They don't carry on and decorate all over the whole house." And he's like, "We don't do this in China." So I thought about it and said, "Do I want to change that?" And I thought, "No, because it's how we celebrate."*

CONNECTING WITH AMERICANS OF CHINESE HERITAGE

In his classic analysis of social stigma, Erving Goffman designated any deviation from the ethno-racial norm of a community a "tribal stigma," or an interactional contaminant "transmitted through lineages" (4). In doing so, he both rooted race/ethnicity in perceptions of genetic relatedness and recognized the social impacts of these perceptions. Yet, equally social is the gendered work required of this purportedly natural or descent-based "tribalism." For example, employing the construct of "mother-work," Patricia Hill Collins describes how women of color toil to foster kin sentiments and connections within their ethno-racial collectives. Similarly, coining the phrase "kin work," di Leonardo details the "mental (and) administrative labor" necessary to bond the bedrock of the Italian-American community, which is the Italian-American family (*The Varieties* 194). Like Collins, Micaela di Leonardo specifies that this labor is largely performed by women, who tend to experience more "felt responsibility" for the work of family and ethno-cultural/ethno-racial preservation ("The Female" 445).[9]

The "fictive kin work" of White American adopters, or their efforts to connect their multiethnic/multiracial families to a "tribe" of Chinese-American kin, is equally feminized. For example, mothers most frequently accompany their children to the places or spaces thought to best facilitate interaction with Americans of Chinese heritage (i.e., Chinatown neighborhoods and Chinese restaurants). Mothers also tend to initiate the activities (i.e., Chinese dance/language lessons and foreign-exchange partnerships) that promise similar relationships. Brenda, a mother of two girls under the age of seven, attributes this gender-based discrepancy to her role as a stay-at-home-mom in a single-earner two-parent family:

> Honestly, I don't see any man, I'm not a man basher or anything, I just don't see any man doing that because even when they get home from work, they just, they play with the kids but not the cultural things and stuff. I think it's more on whoever is the primary caretaker.

Interestingly, the two stay-at-home-dads in my sample confirm Brenda's hypothesis. In each of these unique families, the child's father assumes primary responsibility for the family's interplay with Chinese culture. Jackie, a mother of a two-year-old girl, relays how her husband's role as the primary caregiver encourages him to take the lead in the family's fictive kin work:[10] "He is full time with her (their daughter), so when he's going about his day with her and they run into Asian people, you know, he has no qualms talking to them or saying, 'Are you Chinese?' and 'Oh, my daughter is Chinese.'"

As Arlie Russell Hochschild and Anne Machung demonstrate, however, the meaning and value of household and family labor is best revealed in the context of *dual-earner* two-parent families. Significantly, the overwhelming majority of the married couples in my sample are dual-earner and, in each and every one of these families, *mothers* assume primary responsibility for their family's fictive kin work. It is important to note, however, that while this finding is consistent with the work of women in ethno-racial minority communities (i.e., Kibria; Collins), White American mothers of children adopted from China don't interpret fictive kin work as an act of community or cultural responsibility. Instead, they see it as an extension of their *mothering* role. For example, while describing her intended culture work, Sienna, a waiting parent, states: "While we have race to be concerned about, what we are describing is a fear that I'm pretty sure every mother has: how do I do this right?" In this way, White mothers' fictive kin work in international adoption from China more closely resembles the time-intensive "motherwork" required by the production of an "adjusted and achieving" middle-class child than it does the work on the part of minority women who "mother the race" (Epstein 197; Rothman 231).

This analysis is verified by the fact that White mothers tend to liken their fictive kin work to their facilitation of extra-curricular activities for their children. Drawing on the cultural ideal of the devoted White, middle-class "soccer mom," Willa, a mother of two girls under the age of ten, explains how she drives her two children across state lines every Saturday to attend Chinese school: "It's (Chinese school) an hour and fifteen minutes away, but I think soccer moms do that. My husband thinks I'm nuts, all my friends think I'm nuts, but if I was doing soccer I would be doing it."

Notably, White mothers frequently make inroads into Chinese and Chinese-American communities through their mothering practices. Jill, a mother of two girls under the age of 13, explains her family's participation in Chinese dance:

> Jill: *In Liz's (her youngest daughter's) age group, ten kids were adopted and ten were Chinese children. In Mary's (her oldest daughter's) class there were two adopted and the rest were from Chinese families.*
>
> Amy: *Were they able to make connections with the Chinese-American community through that?*
>
> Jill: *Yes, oh yes, particularly for me because it's the moms that do all the work. They are the volunteers. So I got to be a part of the Chinese community as much as anybody does in Stamford, Connecticut.*

Yet, while driven by the desire to help Chinese adoptees manage stigma and find community, these labors are equally informed by the fact that they provide White mothers with a distinctly *public* arena in which to demonstrate their successful negotiation of classed "regimes of child nurture" *and* racialized ethnic differences (Anagnost 155; see also Allen and Daly).

CONCLUSION

To conclude, White American mothers of children adopted from China assume the central role in their family's Chinese cultural celebrations. While consistent with the gendered nature of more traditional constructions of ethnicity/race in American families, the meaning of their role is best ascertained through an analysis of the felt and functional dimensions of mothers' ethnic identifications.[11] For example, these mothers often identify with their children's ethno-cultural heritage to make visible and maintain their maternal relationships, which are largely characterized in the culture in which they mother as "unnatural" and "in need of continual support" (Eng 22; see also Rapp; Ragoné and Twine; Luker). Mothers also attach or identify themselves with their children, as well as with the social position of "mother," through ethnic performance. In other words, through Chinese cultural practice White American mothers enact the culturally-specific, middle-class "role identities" of their position (Howard 371), often becoming "good mothers" of "well-developed" children through their efforts to manage intra-family difference (Nelson 448).

[1]See the U.S. Department of the State for more statistics on Americans' adoptions from China ("China").

[2]Despite vast ethnic, gender, class, and historical differences in the experience and definition of Chinese culture, American parents of children adopted from China regularly characterize it as a singular entity. As Hein indicates, this characterization is more reflective of a nation-centered cultural orientation than an ethnicity-centered cultural orientation. Even then, however, it neglects the salient provincial divisions that exist within China's national borders (Honig).

[3]A version of my analysis of mothers' consumption of Chinese cultural objects for display was previously published in "Home(land) Décor: China Adoptive Parents' Consumption of Chinese Cultural Objects for Display in their Homes" (see *Qualitative Sociology* 30.3:201-220). A version of my analysis of mothers' efforts to connect with Americans of Chinese heritage was previously published in "Towards a Theory of Fictive Kin Work: China Adoptive Parents' Efforts to Connect their Children to Americans of Chinese Heritage" (see *International Journal of Sociology of the Family* 35.1:45-67).

[4]As 95 percent of American adoptees from China are girls, the gendered nature of ethno-cultural/ethno-racial maintenance is likely to influence adoptive parents' concerns with matters of Chinese heritage.

[5]Pre-adoptive parents are people who are committed to adopting from China but have yet to initiate their adoption paperwork. Waiting parents are people who have initiated their adoption paperwork but have yet to adopt a child from China. Post-adoptive parents are people who have successfully completed at least one adoption from China. I categorized any parent who was in the process of initiating a second or third adoption from China at the time of our interview as a post-adoptive parent.

[6]See Katz on temporal structure in research design.

[7]Anderson uses the phrase "imagined communities" to describe when a

community (or "image of communion") is comprised of individuals who will "never know most of their fellow members" (6).

[8]Similarly, in her study of pregnancy loss, Layne shows how women use angel figurines, sonogram images, and baby toys to "assert their claim that a 'real baby' existed" and to "claim for themselves the social credit to which they feel entitled as real mothers" (113).

[9]Gilroy explores the negative effects of kin conceptions on ethno-racial group members, noting, in particular, how such conceptions can essentialize gender roles.

[10]Studies indicate that the ethno-racial identity of a child's primary caregiver has a significant associative impact on the felt identity of that child (i.e., Rockquemore and Arend; Roth).

[11]For a similar example of how women can and do "draw upon ethnicity as a resource," see Otis (377).

WORKS CITED

Alba, Richard D. *Ethnic Identity: The Transformation of White America.* New Haven, CT: Yale University Press, 1990. Print.

Allen, Sarah M. and Kerry Daly. "Fathers and the Navigation of Family Space and Time." *Situated Fathering: A Focus on Physical and Social Spaces.* Eds. William Marsiglio, Kevin Roy, and Greer Litton Fox. Lanham, MD: Rowman & Littlefield Publishers, Inc., 2005. 49-70. Print.

Anagnost, Ann. "Maternal Labor in a Transnational Circuit." *Consuming Motherhood.* Eds. Janelle S. Taylor, Linda L. Layne, and Danielle F. Wozniak. New Brunswick: Rutgers University Press, 2004. 139-167. Print.

Anderson, Benedict. *Imagined Communities: Reflections on the Origin and Spread of Nationalism*, 2nd ed. London: Verso, 1991. Print.

Anthias, Flora and Nira Yuval-Davis. *Racialized Boundaries: Race, Nation, Gender, Colour and Class and the Anti-Racist Struggle.* New York: Routledge, 1992. Print.

Bolling, John L. "The Changing Self-Concept of Black Children." *The Journal of the National Medical Association* 66 (1974): 28-31. Print.

Bourdieu, Pierre. *Outline of a Theory of Practice.* Cambridge, UK: Cambridge University Press, 1977. Print.

"China." *Bureau of Consular Affairs, U.S. Department of the State.* U.S. Department of the State, n.d. Web. 10 February 2012.

Collins, Patricia Hill. "Black Women and Motherhood." *Justice and Care: Essential Readings in Feminist Ethics.* Ed. Virginia Held. Boulder, CO: Westview Press, 1995. 117-138. Print.

Cornell, Stephen and Douglas Hartmann. *Ethnicity and Race: Making Identities in a Changing World*. Thousand Oaks, CA: Pine Forge Press, 1998. Print.

DeVault, Marjorie L. *Feeding the Family: The Social Organization of Caring as Gendered Work*. Chicago: The University of Chicago Press, 1991. Print.

di Leonardo, Micaela. "The Female World of Cards and Holidays: Women, Families, and the Work of Kinship." *Signs* 12.3 (1987): 440-453. Print.

di Leonardo, Micaela. *The Varieties of Ethnic Experience: Kinship, Class, and Gender among California Italian-Americans*. Ithaca, NY: Cornell University Press, 1984. Print.

Dion, Karen K. and Kenneth L. Dion. "Gender, Immigrant Generation, and Ethnocultural Identity." *Sex Roles* 50.5/6 (2004): 347-355. Print.

Douglas, Susan J. and Meredith W. Michaels. *The Mommy Myth: The Idealization of Motherhood and How it has Undermined Women*. New York: The Free Press, 2004. Print.

Emerson, Robert M., Rachel I. Fretz, and Linda L. Shaw. *Writing Ethnographic Fieldnotes*. Chicago: University of Chicago Press, 1995. Print.

Eng, David L. "Transnational Adoption and Queer Diasporas." *Social Text* 21 (2003): 1-37. Print.

Epstein, Cynthia Fuchs. *Deceptive Distinctions*. New York: Russell Sage Foundation and Yale University Press, 1988. Print.

Etzioni, Amitai. "Holidays and Rituals: Neglected Seedbeds of Virtue." *We Are What We Celebrate: Understanding Holidays and Rituals*. Eds. Amitai Etzioni and Jared Bloom. New York: New York University Press, 2004. 1-42. Print.

Evans, Karin. *The Lost Daughters of China: Abandoned Girls, Their Journey to America, and the Search for a Missing Past*. New York: Jeremy T. Archer/Penguin, 2000. Print.

Ferber, Abby. "Whiteness Studies and the Erasure of Gender." *Sociology Compass* 1.1 (2007): 265-282. Print.

Gailey, Christine Ward. "Ideologies of Motherhood and Kinship in U.S. Adoption." *Ideologies and Technologies of Motherhood*. Ed. Heléna Ragoné and France Winddance Twine. New York: Routledge, 2000. 11-55. Print.

Gilroy, Paul. *Small Acts: Thoughts on the Politics of Black Cultures*. London: Serpent's Tail, 1993. Print.

Giroux, Henry A. *Disturbing Pleasures: Learning Popular Culture*. New York: Routledge, 1994. Print.

Goffman, Erving. *Stigma: Notes on the Management of Spoiled Identity*. Englewood: Prentice-Hall, Inc., 1963. Print.

Gold, Steven J. "Ethnic Boundaries and Ethnic Entrepreneurship: A Photo-Elicitation Study." *Visual Sociology* 6.2 (1991): 9-22. Print.

Halter, Marilyn. *Shopping for Identity: The Marketing of Ethnicity.* New York: Schocken Books, 2000. Print.

Hays, Sharon. *The Cultural Contradictions of Motherhood.* New Haven, CT: Yale University Press, 1996. Print.

Hein, Jeremy. *Ethnic Origins: The Adaptation of Cambodian and Hmong Refugees in Four American Cities.* New York: Russell Sage Foundation, 2006. Print.

Hochschild, Arlie Russell and Anne Machung. *The Second Shift.* New York: Penguin Books, 2003. Print.

Honig, Emily. *Creating Chinese Ethnicity: Subei People in Shanghai, 1850-1980.* New Haven, CT: Yale University Press, 1992. Print.

Howard, Judith A. "Social Psychology of Identities." *Annual Review of Sociology* 26 (2000): 367-393. Print.

Jacobson, Heather. *Culture Keeping: White Mothers, International Adoption, and the Negotiation of Family Difference.* Nashville, TN: Vanderbilt University Press, 2008. Print.

Jiménez, Tomás R. "Negotiating Ethnic Boundaries: Multiethnic Mexican Americans and Ethnic Identity in the United States." *Ethnicities* 4.1 (2004): 75-97. Print.

Johnson, Colleen Leahy. *Growing Up and Growing Old in Italian-American Families.* New Brunswick, NJ: Rutgers University Press, 1985. Print.

Katz, Jack. "From How to Why: On Luminous Description and Causal Inference in Ethnography (Part I)." *Ethnography* 2.4 (2001): 443-473. Print.

Kibria, Nazli. "Migration and Vietnamese American Women: Remaking Ethnicity." *Women of Color in U.S. Society.* Eds. Maxine Baca Zinn and Barrie Thornton Dill. Philadelphia: Temple University, 1994. 247-261. Print.

Kimmel, Michael and Abby Ferber, eds. *Privilege: A Reader.* Oxford, UK: Westview Press, 2003. Print.

Klatzkin, Amy, ed. *A Passage to the Heart: Writings from Families with Children from China.* St. Paul, MN: Yeong and Yeong Books, 1999. Print.

Knight, George P., Martha E. Bernal, Camille A. Garza, Marya K. Cota, Katheryn A. Ocampo. "Family Socialization and the Ethnic Identity of Mexican-American Children." *Journal of Cross-Cultural Psychology* 24 (1993): 99-114. Print.

Kukka, Christine. "The Labor of Waiting." *A Passage to the Heart: Writings from Families with Children from China.* Ed. Amy Klatzkin. St. Paul, MN: Yeong and Yeong Books, 1999. 19-20. Print.

Kurien, Prema. "Gendered Ethnicity: Creating a Hindu Indian Identity in the United States." *American Behavioral Scientist* 42.4 (1999): 648-670. Print.

Layne, Linda L. "Baby Things as Fetishes? Memorial Goods, Simulacra, and the 'Realness' Problem of Pregnancy Loss." *Ideologies and Technologies of Motherhood: Race, Class, Sexuality, Nationalism*. Eds. Heléna Ragoné and France Windance Twine. London: Routledge, 2000. 111-138. Print.

Leonard, Karen. *Making Ethnic Choices: California's Punjabi-Mexican-Americans*. Philadelphia: Temple University Press, 1992. Print.

Lieberson, Stanley and Mary C. Waters. "The Ethnic Responses of Whites: What Causes Their Instability, Simplification, and Inconsistency?" *Social Forces* 72.2 (1993): 421-451. Print.

Luke, Carmen. "White Women in Interracial Families: Reflections on Hybridization, Feminine Identities, and Racialized Othering." *Feminist Issues* 94.14 (1994): 49-73. Print.

Luker, Kristin. "Afterward." *Ideologies and Technologies of Motherhood: Race, Class, Sexuality, Nationalism*. Eds. Heléna Ragoné and France Winddance Twine. New York: Routledge, 2000. 295-297. Print.

Nagel, Joane. "Constructing Ethnicity: Creating and Recreating Ethnic Identity and Culture." *Social Problems* 41.1 (1994): 152-176. Print.

Nelson, E. D. (Adie). "The Things That Dreams Are Made Of: Dreamwork and the Socialization of 'Stage Mothers.'" *Qualitative Sociology* 24.4 (2001): 439-458. Print.

Otis, Eileen M. "The Reach and Limits of Asian Panethnic Identity: The Dynamics of Gender, Race, and Class in a Community-Based Organization." *Qualitative Sociology* 24.3 (2001): 349-379. Print.

Pertman, Adam. *Adoption Nation: How the Adoption Revolution is Changing America*. New York: Basic Books, 2000. Print.

Portes, Alejandro and Min Zhou. "The New Second Generation: Segmented Assimilation and its Variants." *Anals of the American Academy of Political and Social Science* 530.1 (1993): 74-96. Print.

Ragoné, Heléna and France Winddance Twine. "Introduction: Motherhood on the Fault Lines." *Ideologies and Technologies of Motherhood: Race, Class, Sexuality, Nationalism*. Eds. Heléna Ragoné and France Winddance Twine. New York: Routledge, 2000. 1-8. Print.

Rapp, Rayna. "Foreword." *Ideologies and Technologies of Motherhood: Race, Class, Sexuality, Nationalism*. Eds. Heléna Ragoné and France Winddance Twine. New York: Routledge, 2000. xiii-xvi. Print.

Reich, Jennifer A. "Building a Home on a Border: How Single White Women Raising Multiracial Children Construct Racial Meaning."

Working Through Whiteness: International Perspectives. Ed. Cynthia Levine-Rasky. New York: State University of New York Press, 2002. 179-208. Print.

Rockquemore, Kerry Ann and Patricia Arend. "Opting for White: Choice, Fluidity and Racial Identity Construction in Post Civil-Rights America." *Race & Society* 5 (2002): 49-64. Print.

Rockquemore, Kerry Ann. "Negotiating the Color Line: The Gendered Process of Racial Identity Construction among Black/White Women." *Gender and Society* 16.4 (2002): 485-503. Print.

Rojewski, Jay W. and Jacy L. Rojewski. *Intercountry Adoption from China: Examining Cultural Heritage and Other Post-Adoption Issues.* Westport, CT: Bergin and Garcey, 2001. Print.

Roth, Wendy D. "The End of the One-Drop Rule? Labeling of Multiracial Children in Black Intermarriages." *Sociological Forum* 20.1 (2005): 35-68. Print.

Rothman, Barbara Katz. *Weaving a Family: Untangling Race and Adoption.* Boston: Beacon Press, 2005. Print.

Rumbaut, Rubén G. "The Crucible Within: Ethnic Identity, Self-Esteem, and Segmented Assimilation Among Children of Immigrants." *International Migration Review* 28.4 (1994): 748-794. Print.

Rumbaut, Rubén G. and Alejandro Portes, eds. *Ethnicities: Children of Immigrants in America.* Berkeley: University of California Press, 2001. Print.

Scroggs, Patricia Hanigan and Heather Heitfield. "International Adopters and their Children: Birth Culture Ties." *Gender Issues* 19.4 (2001): 3-30. Print.

Spitzer, Denise, Anne Neufeld, Margaret Harrison, Karen Hughes, and Miriam Stewart. "Caregiving in Transnational Context: 'My Wings Have Been Cut; Where Can I Fly'?" *Gender & Society* 17.2 (2003): 267-286. Print.

Storrs, Debbie. "Whiteness as Stigma: Essentialist Identity Work by Mixed-Race Women." *Symbolic Interaction* 22.3 (1999): 187-212. Print.

Suárez-Orozco, Carola. "Formulating Identity in a Globalized World." *Globalization: Culture and Education in a New Millennium.* Eds. Marcelo M. Suárez-Orozco and Desirée Baolian Qin-Hilliard. Berkeley: University of California Press, 2004. 173-202. Print.

Tessler, Richard, Gail Gamache, and Liming Liu. *West Meets East: Americans Adopt Chinese Children.* Westport, CT: Bergin and Garvey, 1999. Print.

Ting-Toomy, Stella. "Ethnic Identity and Close Friendship in Chinese-American College Students." *International Journal of Intercultural*

Relations 5 (1981): 383-406. Print.

Trenka, Jane Jeong. *The Language of Blood: A Memoir.* Minneapolis, MN: Borealis Books, 2003. Print.

Twine, France Windance. "Bearing Blackness in Britain: The Meaning of Racial Difference for White Birth Mothers of African-Descent Children." *Ideologies and Technologies of Motherhood.* Eds. Heléna Ragoné and France Winddance Twine. New York: Routledge, 2000. 76-108. Print.

Waters, Mary. "Multiple Ethnic Identities and Identity Choices: Implications for American Pluralism." *Beyond Pluralism: The Conception of Groups and Group Identities in America.* Eds. Wendy Katkin, Ned Landsman, and Andrea Tyree. Champaign, IL: University of Illinois Press, 1998. 28-46. Print.

Zaretsky, Eli. *Capitalism, the Family, and Personal Life.* New York: Harper and Row Publishers, 1973. Print.

Zelizer, Viviana A. *The Social Meaning of Money.* New York: Basic Books, 1994. Print.

Zukin, Sharon and Jennifer Smith Maguire. "Consumers and Consumption." *Annual Review of Sociology* 30 (2004): 173-97. Print.

8.
Narrating Multiculturalism in Asian Adoption Fiction

JENNY HEIJUN WILLS

T HE ADOPTIVE MOTHERS of transnationally and transracially adopted Asian children have felt the burden of explaining their choices for years. They are asked to put into words the reasons they have turned to adoption, transnational adoption, and transracial adoption by scholars like Sara Dorow, who straightforwardly asks of some of her interviewees, "Why China?" (*Transnational Adoption* 35). They are also asked to explain the choices they make when raising their adopted children, as scholars like Kristen Johnson et al. seek to better understand their "efforts to socialize their children in the culture of the child's birth country and to teach their children about racial bias" in their adoptive lands ("Mothers' Racial, Ethnic, and Cultural Socialization of Transracially Adopted Asian Children"). These interests, and often judgments, of adoptive motherhood have been intriguingly represented in contemporary Asian adoption fiction insofar as an archetypal adoptive mother figure has begun to emerge. Here, I address the ways that mothers of transnationally, transracially adopted Asian characters in contemporary fiction are satirically represented as both progressive liberals and Orientalists, which posits them as foils to their adopted children's development of identity. This, in turn, causes a degree of estrangement between adoptive mother characters and their children that inverts the traditional positions held by these characters and reframes adoptive mothers as a kind of marginalized Other.

The field of adoption studies has recently seen a rapid increase in literature and scholarship that represents and discusses the particularly unique experiences involved in transnational, transracial adoption from Asia. Anthologies like Tonya Bishoff and Jo Rankin's *Seeds from a Silent Tree* and Sara Dorow's *I Wish for You A Beautiful Life* feature the voices of people affected by Asian adoption, ranging from adoptees to biological mothers. These collections demonstrate the turbulent emotional circumstances of transnational, transracial Asian adoption and address ideas of kinship, race, ethnicity, and nation from multiple perspectives. Adult adoptees like Jane Jeong Trenka, Kim Sunée and Mei-Ling Hopgood have gained acclaim and recognition for life narratives. These narratives undermine many of the expectations and assumptions held by their respective societies with regard to transnational, transracial Asian adoption in the past (i.e. the idea that overseas adoption is an entirely altruistic and selfless practice performed by adoptive parents for the benefit of orphaned children). Often these texts are critical examinations of the systems of adoption that have transformed and influenced the lives of their book's subjects. Trenka and Dorow have also contributed scholarly analyses to discourses of Asian adoption to bridge the distance between anecdotal representations of personal adoption stories and analytic research in *Outsiders Within* (Trenka, Oparah and Shin) and *Transnational Adoption: A Cultural Economy of Race, Gender and Kinship* (Dorow). Along with these works, anthologies like *International Korean Adoption* (Bergquist et al.), *Cultures of Transnational Adoption* (Volkman), and *The Adoption Reader* (Wadia-Ell) comment on issues like kinship formation, class and power imbalances, and social adjustment as they pertain to transnational, transracial Asian adoption. Literary critics, such as Marianne Novy, Mark Jerng, Margaret Homans and David Eng have also begun to explore transnational, transracial Asian adoption in light of the complex and unique narratives that involve its development, subsistence, and representation. In short, transnational, transracial Asian adoption is a highly contentious and fruitful field of study for scholars and individuals from a variety of personal and professional backgrounds.

While these texts initiate many important conversations about Asian adoption, especially as they identify questionable practices related to transnational and/or transracial adoption in general, I am drawn, in this essay, to fictional representations of transnational, transracial Asian adoption as a way of thinking about narratives and representations of adoptive mothers and their children. The texts I am most interested in are written by contemporary, acclaimed and accomplished writers who approach transnational, transracial Asian adoption from a perspective that is unburdened by the emotional weight of life writing, as well as the goal of critical, political theory that drives scholarly work on adoption. As such, I analyze literary representations of transnational, transracial Asian adoption through what I think is a common theme or issue that has begun to form in new fiction: it is the use of the adoptive mother as a character through which the paradoxical merging of fetishistic multiculturalism and liberal colour-blindness is explored in relation to her children who are transnational, transracial Asian adoptee characters. Specifically, this article draws on Gish Jen's, *The Love Wife*, Larissa Lai's *When Fox is a Thousand* and Anne Tyler's *Digging to America* in order to highlight a pattern in transnational, transracial Asian adoption fiction that represents adoptive mothers as simultaneously celebratory of their daughters' cultural heritage and colour-blind to their racial differences because their behaviours as characters are shaped by Orientalist beliefs. The result is adoptive mothers become complex and contradictory characters through their selective colour-blindness, wherein they discredit the importance of biology, origins and race at the same time that they uphold the cultural symbols of their adopted children's difference through practices of fetishistic Orientalism. These depictions of adoptive mothers in fiction also create a notable distance between themselves and adopted people, in that they come to signify and embody the force that causes the awkward precariousness of transnational, transracial Asian adoptees' racial, ethnic and national identities.

Despite the differences in genre and tone in *When Fox is a Thousand*, *The Love Wife*, and *Digging to America*, each novel's approach to the topic of Asian adoption is strikingly similar. *When Fox is a Thousand* was published in 1995 by Canadian novelist and scholar Larissa Lai. It subtly slides into the realm of speculative fiction, or fantasy literature that consists in science-fiction and magic realism, because it shifts between centuries, sexualities and scenarios. Lai's narrative follows several characters, one of whom is a young adult called Artemis Wong. Artemis is determined to establish an identity for herself despite being a Chinese adoptee who lacks important information about her past. *The Love Wife*, published in 2004 by the American novelist Gish Jen, is more traditional in literary style. It explores conventional Asian-American literary themes, such as generational conflict between parents and children and the culture shock of immigration. Here, Lizzy (age fifteen) and Wendy (age nine) are Chinese adoptees living in a family that consists of a Chinese American father and Caucasian-American mother. The girls feel as though their mother fails to listen to them and is more interested in the image she projects to the rest of the world, especially as this image relates to her Asian daughters. Finally, *Digging to America*, published in 2006 by Anne Tyler, reveals the intricacies of race and ethnicity as the characters' different immigrant identities are layered one on top of another. In this novel, two families, one American and one Iranian American, adopt Korean infants at the same time and compare notes as to the best ways to raise their children. These three novels elicit the same sorts of questions about Asian adoption, especially in relation to the role of adoptive mothers and their choices with respect to how they raise their children.

In a self-reflexive and semi-autobiographical essay, "Embodying Chinese Culture," author and adoptive mother Toby Alice Volkman identifies what she calls "parents' fascination with the imagined 'birth culture' of their adopted children" (29). Volkman charts some of the phenomena that have caused adoptive parents' recent interest in the preservation of their adopted children's cultures of origin, especially in contrast to the experience of a larger and earlier cohort of Korean-born adoptees who were "widely dispersed over time and space" and for whom "adoption was not freely discussed, and racial assimilation was the goal" (31). Volkman points to the historical significance of time, because adoption regulations, as well as attitudes toward immigration and multicultural-ism, in "receiving nations" have been significantly transformed relative to the early years of Korean adoption in the 1950s. Early adoptee-authored memoirs, such as those by some of the authors I mention above, as well as other anachronistic fictional representations of transnational, transracial Asian adoption (i.e. Chang-Rae Lee's *A Gesture Life* that is set in the 1960s), reflect Volkman's historical observation that adoptive parenting practice in the 1950s was predicated on values of assimilation and incorporation. For instance, in *The Language of Blood*, Trenka recalls that in her childhood home "the a-word, adoption" was not mentioned and "[n]either was the k-word, Korea" (35). As attitudes toward ethnic difference and alternative kinship formations have shifted, however, so too have approaches to rearing transnationally and/or transracially adopted children, a phenomenon that that is evident in Lai, Tyler and Jen's novels as well. In *The Love Wife*, *Digging to America* and *When Fox is a Thousand*, both of which are set in the 1990s or early 2000s, adoptive mothers are also depicted as Volkman describes: they are "fascinated" with their adopted children's cultures or origin.

In *When Fox is a Thousand*, the reader is led to believe a fascination with China is a motivating factor in Artemis' parents' decision to adopt her as an Asian child. Artemis is a young woman in Vancouver who attempts to explore her racial and ethnic identity despite missing information that relegates her past to a mystery. In effect, Lai's novel presents adoption as the cause of Artemis' confusion. Like characters featured in many transnational, transracial Asian adoption narratives, Artemis exhibits a struggle faced by many adopted people who feel ethnically connected to their adoptive societies and communities, but are racially marginalized as visible minorities in the context of their adoptive families and communities. When outsiders begin to question why Artemis' race and ethnicity do not match up, she is conflicted as to how and to whom she is supposed to belong. Artemis' adoptive mother is not a main focus in the novel; she appears somewhat estranged from Artemis and is presented as an obstacle in Artemis' effort to understand her identity. The way in which the reader does experience Artemis's mother is through Artemis' conversations with other characters in which she reminisces about her childhood, growing up Chinese Canadian in a Caucasian family. Early in the narrative, Artemis discusses adoption with her friend Diane, another Chinese Canadian woman that others believe Artemis resembles so much they could be sisters. Artemis and Diane discuss how being an adopted person has influenced Artemis' understanding of selfhood, and more specifically, how Artemis fits into her adoptive parents' lives and interests. Learning that Artemis' parents are specialists in East Asian art and antiques, Diane calls them "Asian-philes" and claims that Artemis is one of their "artefacts;" she is comparable to the "Chinese poetry, silk hangings, and scrolls of calligraphy" that make up "part of the collection" (50). Although Artemis denies Diane's interpretation of her family, and defends her parents as she nonchalantly explains, "My mother wants to make sure that I am aware of my history" (50), she admits the Asian food, customs and objects that her adoptive mother imposes upon her make her feel alienated from the rest of the family. She also recounts a story in which her mother, whenever her father was away on business, would take her and sneak away to the Asian dry goods store. Although she always felt uncomfortable around what to her were unrecognizable items in the shop, Artemis always remained silent, because she did not want to disappoint her mother who believes exposure to these items is important to Artemis' understanding of herself. Artemis is also made to feel an outsider in her own family, because her mother, who decides she should keep her biological name, denies her the name of her family ("Artemis Spinner"). She is also bound by her mother to the mysterious foods and objects with which her mother is keen for her to identify. Although Lai is careful not to label the Spinners as Orientalists directly, characters in *When Fox is a Thousand* that critique other characters who express what is considered to be unusual fascination with the East, serve this function in the novel by proxy. For instance, the father of one of Artemis' friends collects traditional Chinese gowns and Diane becomes the house sitter for some young women who hang Chinese scrolls and art pieces on the walls of their apartment. All of these characters are scoffed at by others as unusual and eccentric and they are presented to the reader as comparisons to Artemis' mother and father. In this manner, Lai prompts us to make connections between parents who are involved in transnational, transracial Asian adoption with other fetishizing, Orientalist characters in the book that further encourage the reader to wonder about the Spinners' motives.

This representation of Artemis' parents is reminiscent of some of the adoptive parents interviewed by Sara Dorow in *Transnational Adoption* who admit that adopting from China makes sense because they already "like Chinese people and food and things and culture" (43). In another interview from Dorow's book, a mother pauses in the midst of conversation to declare: "You know, I was just thinking as we're sitting here, looking at our house, ... we have a lot of Asian influence, and most of this was before we adopted her. This was just our taste" (43). Lai presents Artemis' adoptive mother in the same light as this second mother. Her adoption of an Asian child did not motivate her to learn more about a foreign culture—her fascination with this culture precedes Artemis' adoption, which renders Artemis a cultural object of sorts.

Lai's representation of an adoptive mother who already has a curiosity with Asian customs and objects is repeated in Gish Jen's *The Love Wife* as well, wherein, Lizzy and Wendy Wong's mother, Blondie, fondly describes how her fascination with Chinese culture and language led to her to major in East Asian studies in college; she is fluent in Mandarin and a collector of Asian household objects. Blondie unintentionally, but admittedly, envisions Lizzy and Wendy as part of her collection of Oriental objects. She is happy that her children "match" and thrilled when strangers stop her on the street to inquire about her daughters: "Is she yours?" (132). Alarmingly, when Blondie imposes her interest in Asia onto her adopted children, her Orientalist version of the East is also transmitted to her daughters, which simultaneously (re)produces Lizzy and Wendy as fetishized objects and Orientalists, the latter of which makes them complicit in their own racialized objectification. So before Wendy and Lizzy meet their immigrant nanny, Lan, their perspectives of Asia are already shaped by Western notions of the Orient on which they have been fed by their mother. Their father Carnegie's deadpan comments summarizes Blondie's good intentions, but also points to the shortcomings of her decisions in a critically comedic way; "Concentrating the chinoiserie in the adopted children's bedrooms: a classic mistake," he says. "How mightily we had strived to build [their] self-esteem, to give [them] 'tools for [their] tool kit[s].' Did we not balance our chequebook on the abacus? Find the girls Asian dolls? Provide them with multiracial crayons?" (206) Reducing Chinese culture to antiquated objects, racialized figures and notions of colour, or worse, easily consumable objects like stuffed pandas and Chinese lantern wallpaper, Blondie and Carnegie transform their daughters into imperialist, cultural consumers, wherein the Chinese objects their children now consume stand-in also as the signifiers of their Asianness.

Like Artemis in *When Fox is a Thousand*, Lizzy and Wendy grow resentful of their mother's Orientalist leanings and begin to search for answers about their cultural heritage in other places. For Artemis, this is with other Chinese Canadian women of various generations and histories in Vancouver. Whereas Wendy and Lizzy turn to their Chinese nanny who, in her own unassuming way, introduces the girls to a version of Chinese subjectivity that is rooted in Chinese mythology and philosophy (for instance, she teaches them that "Every day Chinese people eat better"); even the Chinese food they normally receive from Blondie "tastes better when Lanlan gives it to [them]" (140) This leaves Blondie feeling left out, marginalized and excluded from their secret forms of communication, which ironically prompts her to ask, "How did I end up an outsider in my own family?" (132).

In Anne Tyler's *Digging to America*, performances of Asian culture are even more superficial with respect to Bitsy Donaldson's mothering as she raises her adopted daughter, Jin Ho. Bitsy also decides to keep Jin Ho's Korean name, as well as the "squared-off hairstyle she had arrived with" (28) and presents her at parties in "full Korean costume – a brilliant Kimono-like affair and a pointed hat with a chin strap and little embroidered cloth shoes" (39). In this novel, the Orientalist performances of Asian culture on the part of the adoptee character Jin Ho are not merely private experiences; they are not concentrated in children's bedrooms, as in *The Love Wife*, or acted out in secret as they are for Artemis, whose mother steals away with her to the Asian market in *When Fox is a Thousand*. In *Digging to America*, Bitsy's insistence that Jin Ho enact her mother's Orientalist beliefs is transformed into a public spectacle. While Bitsy regards these Korean garments as a means that ensures American Jin-Ho will connect with her Korean past, these items actually perpetuate what Eleana Kim has elsewhere referred to as "auto-Orientalizing" (80). In effect, the spectacle Bitsy creates around Jin Ho is like that created around some transnationally, Asian adopted people by well-meaning parents. In effect, they are made to wear so-called traditional Korean dress that is now uncommon in contemporary Korean contexts and, thereby, become symbols of inauthenticity. For this reason, Bitsy's character operates as a warning, much like Vincent Cheng's theoretical book, *Inauthentic: The Anxiety Over Culture and Identity*; Cheng warns adoptive parents against the exaggerated display of Asian adoptees' cultural foreignness in that "a little knowledge is a dangerous thing, resulting most frequently (and unconsciously) in Orientalisms and fetishizations of an exoticized otherness, evocations of an exoticized but dead past" (79). Whether it is through the Orientalist objects in *The Love Wife*, the mysterious food in *When Fox is a Thousand* or the exotic costumes in *Digging to America*, these novels characterize adoptive mothers as conduits for Orientalism and fetishization that profoundly influence and undermine transnational, transracial Asian adoptees who are raised in North American families.

In each of these novels, adoptive mothers impose what they believe to be authentic Asian culture onto reluctant adoptees that also long to feel as though they belong in their predominantly white communities. The items, or "chinoiserie" as it is referred to by Carnegie Wong (206), with which the mothers in these stories surround their children—Asian-themed trinkets, food, costumes, and traditions—marginalize these adoptees within their families, despite their mothers' desires to create cultural awareness and pride. Through the personal opinions of the adopted characters in these texts, the figure of the transnational, transracial adoptive mother is lampooned in terms of any fascination with Asian cultural symbols and practices she may exhibit. Indeed, these mothers are depicted in a kind of comic relief when adoptee characters become exasperated over their mothers' insistence that they learn to cook Chinese food, instead of lasagne and chicken pot pie (Lai 114), or wear some annoying traditional costume with the "stiff, sharp seams inside" (220). In *The Love Wife*, for example, Blondie's efforts are depicted ironically to the reader who recognizes that she often conflates all Asian cultures, because she gives her China-born children Japanese trinkets and treats. Her ignorance of her children's culture of origins is also evident in the fortune cookies she reverently bestows upon them, because they are really an American invention and, thus, a metaphor for her Orientalist naivety. While these representations of adoptive mothers are fictional, hyperbolic, and presented mainly from the perspective of their distant and self-focused adoptee characters, what we can glean from them is that the idea that (any) culture is authentic or recoverable is problematic; race, ethnicity and culture within the contexts of transnational, transracial Asian adoption are ambiguous concepts which bring to light the complexities of identity as the world becomes increasingly intercultural and interracial.

Multiculturalism and what often seems to be its counterpart, colour-blindness, are also common themes in each of these novels. On the one hand, the adoptive mothers in these novels are emphatic about the need to participate in multiculturalist practices. They embrace what David Theo Goldberg refers to as "commitments to cultural diversity," which "emerged out of [a] conflictual history of resistance, accommodation, integration, and transformation" (7). In other words, the adoptive mothers in these stories hold multiculturalist beliefs that entail cultural diversity should be celebrated and individual cultural differences should be preserved within our heterogeneous societies. In the three novels I address, each of the adoptive mothers exhibit multiculturalist leanings. Through spectacle, they display values of cultural preservation and difference that are domesticated and incorporated into their practices of child rearing. In *The Love Wife*, Blondie constantly assures her family that she is a progressive, open-minded person who "believe[s ...] in openness. In the importance of cultural exchange, especially what with globalization and whatnot" because, as she adds, "My family had always hosted exchange students" (6). Bitsy also makes repeated efforts to declare her multiculturalism, for example, when she objects to the idea of Jin Ho having a friend over for the afternoon, at least, until she realizes the girl in question is Athena, a black girl in her daughter's kindergarten class, whose diversity makes her a desired guest. As is pointed out in the novel, "Athena was African American, which Jin Ho's mother approved of" (219); clearly, Bitsy wants to be seen to encourage interactions between people of different ethnic backgrounds.

On the surface, multiculturalism appears to be in opposition with liberal notions of colour-blindness, since the former celebrates diversity and the latter, in the words of Jim Sleeper, intends to "eliminate racial differences," which has implications for cultural and moral differences as well (7). Multiculturalism, as we are most likely to encounter it (i.e., at multicultural festivals, ethnic restaurants, etc.), makes a spectacle out of difference—its aim is to open our minds to experiences of difference. Conversely, colour-blindness is about *not* seeing or overlooking difference and undermining the significance of race in terms of an individual's identity. In reality, however, these two perspectives actually play into the same liberal mandate and can be used, albeit in different ways, to support the same claims. Colour-blindness, in a sense, is a way of rationalizing the multiculturalist belief in unwavering equality, since it is premised on the idea that there is no substantial meaning behind difference. Being different makes no difference. Put another way, multiculturalism is not about highlighting peoples' differences; it is about eradicating the need to talk about difference. In the same way, colour-blindness is not so much about not seeing people's differences, it is about overlooking them as important aspects of a person's identity. In this way, a proponent of multiculturalism might argue that one should be able to celebrate another person's cultural differences but not see how those differences might shape their social experiences. Both notions are born from the liberal idealism that all members of society are equal and discount the significance of the many social boundaries that create imbalanced access to power. Put simply, although multiculturalism exalts the role of difference and co-lour-blindness undermines the importance of difference in our society, their project is one and the same: both proclaim a liberal notion of equality. Of course, there are also flaws with both perspectives. Multiculturalism is often relegated to fetishistic performances and feel-good celebrations of Others' differences, whereas colour-blindness (or post-raciality as it is sometimes labelled) supposes an inherent undesirability in certain racial groups to which we should blind ourselves while accepting the hegemony of the racial group that represents the norm.

In many transnational, transracial Asian adoption narratives, we can see that adoptive mothers are commonly depicted as both champions of either multiculturalism (celebrating difference) and/or colour-blind-ness (undermining difference). While the paradoxical experiences of transnationally, transracially adopted people (such as disconnections between space, race and ethnicity or biology and environment) are often examined sympathetically in Asian adoption literature, the complex-ity of adoptive mothers' paradoxical relationships to difference tends to escape examination in any such light. For instance, in *Digging to America*, Bitsy is devastated when other characters mention the pos-sibility that one person might have a different skin tone than another. She insists that she really could never notice such a thing and tries to present herself as immune to seeing racial difference. On the other hand, she obviously recognizes Jin Ho's racial and ethnic background is different than the other members of the family, because she goes to extreme lengths to address and highlight these differences. She dresses her daughter in different costumes and introduces her alone to certain customs and foods. Put another way, Bitsy engages in what I call "selective color-blindness;" she is a person whose approach to race and ethnicity, multiculturalism and difference, is paradoxically complicated because of her status as an adoptive parent. Transnational, transracial Asian adoption, after all, is dependent on a level of liberal colour-blindness as much as best practices in adoption demand the preservation of culture and intercultural connection.

Let us think about this issue of selective colour-blindness and adop-tion as it pertains to an already fraught notion of essentialism. Adoptive mothers seek to undermine the validity of essentialism because they must challenge the possibility that there is an impermeable link between biology and identity. They must do so because their own ties to their children are non-biological. Since they wish to challenge traditional ideals about biology, namely that kinship is predicated on genetics and blood connections, adoptive mothers like Bitsy, Blondie and Artemis' mother (who, it is noteworthy, remains unnamed and nearly voiceless in *When Fox is a Thousand*) must therefore position themselves as anti-essentializers. On the other hand, the Orientalist spectacle that they impose on their adopted children, because they believe their children must retain a connection to Chinese or Korean culture and heritage, directly contradicts their anti-essentialist posture. This is the paradox in which these mothers are caught in these novels: at the same time that they believe, or are expected to believe, that Artemis, Jin Ho, Lizzy and Wendy must have access to their cultural history and origins (a history to which their children are tied by virtue of their biological origins), they also believe, or are expected to believe, that kinship is not biological in origin.

My goal in this discussion is not to condemn the adoptive mothers' practices or behaviours that are set out in these novels; there is no easy solution to the unique and complicated experience of raising a transnational, transracial Asian adoptee. What I want to highlight, instead, are the implications of a new literary genre, one which surrounds transnational, transracial adoption, that tends to represent adoptive mothers in a one-dimensional way. In the past, scholars like Mark Jerng have challenged what he sees as the archetypification of transracial Asian adoptee subjects through the production of textual narratives that depict them as melancholic, angry and fragmented people. In a similar vein, I wish to alert us to the fact that a new archetype has begun to develop in fictional texts about transnational, transracial adoption, wherein adoptive mothers are shaped by a textual pattern that depicts them satirically, but fundamentally, as contradictory and self-serving liberals who perpetuate Orientalist stereotypes that undermine and traumatize their adopted children.

In stories that focus on how adopted people become marginalized outsiders in their respective communities, particularly as a result of their mothers' contradictory and Orientalist approaches to maintain their ethnic identities, it is important to observe that adoptive mothers in these novels are also outsiders within the context of their own families. In *The Love Wife*, Blondie admits that she begins to feel like "a kind of guest" in her own family (132). In *When Fox is a Thousand*, Artemis' adoptive mother is completely absent, while Gish Jen's adoptive mother Blondie eventually leaves the family and finds a home for herself with her biological son. Aside from this literal outsider-ness, the adoptive mothers in these texts are never made privy to the anxieties and challenges the adoptee protagonists explore; because of their Orientalist tendencies, the reader is left to assume these mothers could not possibly understand the complexities of their adopted children's experience. Thus, the adoptive mothers who strive to protect adoptees from alienation in relation to their cultures of origin are now alienated in and by these new adoption narratives.

While the biological mother is a metonym for an adoptee's lost Asian culture, in these novels, the adoptive mother is a metonym for Western colonization and the consumption of transracial and transnational adoptees. In contemporary adoption narratives, the adoptive mother appears doomed to be a symbol of naivety and insufficiency. She is a foil or obstacle to be overcome in the adoptee's quest for self-fulfilment. In contemporary fiction about Asian adoption, she is a lampooned and satirized figure through which adopted characters challenge restrictive categories and strictures of race. The adoptive mother's common depiction as a one-dimensional Orientalist, on the part of Jen, Lai and Tyler, enables these novels to critique conditions of Otherness that are placed upon Asian adoptees as immigrants and racialized subjects. She also allows these authors to explore the indefinable status of the Asian adoptee, a reality to which David Eng alludes when he asks, "[i]s the transnational adoptee an immigrant [or is she] Asian American?" (2) For my purposes, however, these characters of adoptive mothers are also a reminder that adoption is a complicated, ambiguous and paradoxical experience for all people involved, not just the adoptee, as the narratives I have explored seem to suggest. In effect, while each of these novels can be read to remind us that many adoptive mothers of transnational, transracial Asian adoptees are challenged in terms of race and ethnicity, they also suggest adoptive mothers face important challenges with respect to these issues, challenges that make their perspectives and motivations as important and intriguing as their children's.

WORKS CITED

Bergquist, Kathleen Ja Sook et al., eds. International Korean Adoption: A Fifty-Year History of Policy and Practice. New York: Haworth Press, 2007.

Bishoff, Tonya and Jo Rankin, eds. Seeds from a Silent Tree: An Anthology by Korean Adoptees. 3rd ed. San Diego: Pandal Press, 1997. Print.

Cheng, Vincent. Inauthentic: The Anxiety Over Culture and Identity. New Brunswick: Rutgers University Press, 2004. Print.

Dorow, Sara K., ed. I Wish for You a Beautiful Life. St. Paul: Yeong and Yeong Book Company, 1999. Print.

Dorow, Sara. *Transnational Adoption: A Cultural Economy of Race, Gender and Kinship*. New York: New York University Press, 2006. Print.

Eng, David. "Transnational Adoption and Queer Diasporas." *Social Text* 21.3 (2003): 1-37. Print.

Goldberg, David Theo, Ed. *Multiculturalism: A Critical Reader*. Boston: Blackwell, 1994. Print.

Hopgood, Mei-Ling. *Lucky Girl*. Chapel Hill, NC: Algonquin Books, 2010. Print.

Jen, Gish. *The Love Wife*. New York: Random House, 2004. Print.

Jerng, Mark Chia-Yon. *Claiming Others: Imagining Transracial Adoption in American Literature*. Doctoral dissertation. Harvard University. English and American Literature and Language. 2006. Print.

Johnson, Kristen E., Janet K. Swim, Brian M. Satsman, Kirby Deater-Deckard and Stephen A. Petrill. "Mothers' Racial, Ethnic, and Cultural Socialization of Transracially Adopted Asian Children." Web. 6 Sep. 2007.

Kim, Eleana. "Consuming Korean Bodies: Overseas Adoptees and the South Korean Media." *Proceedings of the First International Korean Adoption Studies Research Symposium*. Eds. Kim Park Nelson, Eleana Kim and Lene Myong Peterson. Seoul: International Korean Adoptee Associations, 2007. 77-90. Print.

Lai, Larissa. *When Fox is A Thousand*. 2nd ed. Vancouver: Arsenal Pulp Press, 2004. Print.

Lee, Chang-Rae. *A Gesture Life*. New York: Riverhead Trade, 1999. Print. Sleeper, Jim. *Liberal Racism*. New York: Penguin, 1997. Print.

Sunée, Kim. *Trail of Crumbs: Hunger, Love, and the Search for Home*. New York: Grand Central Publishing, 2008. Print.

Trenka, Jane Jeong. *The Language of Blood*. Saint Paul: Graywolf Press, 2003. Print.

Trenka, Jane Jeong, Julia Chinyere Oparah and Sun Yung Shin, eds. *Outsiders Within: Writing on Transracial Adoption*. Cambridge: South End Press, 2006. Print.

Tyler, Anne. *Digging to America: A Novel*. New York: Random, 2007. Print.

U.S. Department of State. *Immigrant Visas Issued to Orphans Coming to the United States*. Web. Date Accessed: 30 March 2008

Volkman, Toby Alice, ed. *Cultures of Transnational Adoption*. Durham: Duke University Press, 2005. Print.

Volkman, Toby Alice. "Embodying Chinese Culture: Transnational Adoption in North America." *Social Text* 74 (21.1) 2003: 29-55. Print.

Wadia-Ells, Susan, ed. *The Adoption Reader: Birth Mothers, Adoptive Mothers, and Adopted Daughters Tell Their Stories*. Emeryville, CA: Seal Press, 1995.

9.
Adoptive Mothering

A Transracial Adoptee's Viewpoint

JUDITH MARTIN AND GAIL TRIMBERGER

TRANSRACIAL ADOPTION IS A COMPLEX, multifaceted, and often contested phenomenon because it amplifies some of the major differences in society, such as class, race, and gender. Bringing children from different racial or ethnic backgrounds into white homes, for example, changes the racial makeup of the family and forces parents to examine the place of white entitlement in their communities and in their personal lives (Gailey). Furthermore, transracial placements are often viewed as an effective alternative to leaving children in impermanent and endangering situations. Some argue, however, that removing children from their cultures and communities is detrimental (Trenka, Oparah and Shin 4). This chapter examines the relationship between a transracially adopted son and his adoptive mother in order to illuminate how the changing racial makeup of the family intersects with the mothering experience.

Most research on adoptive mothering tends to focus on caretaking responsibilities and measures success by assessing how well the emotional and physical needs of children have been met (see, for example, Welsh et al.). In contrast, the present study applies an empowering model to explore the adoptive mothering experience. Using Andrea O'Reilly's mothering paradigm, this study examines the role of authority, agency, autonomy, and authenticity in adoptive mothering.

One approach to examining transracial adoption is to analyze the autobiographical materials of adoptive mothers (Grice). While there is much to learn about transracial adoption from mothers, their personal accounts may reflect the limited, lived experience of racial entitlement. The present study explores this phenomenon from a different standpoint; that of an adult African-American male who was adopted as an infant, in the 1960s, by a white family. Jaiya John's autobiography, *Black Baby White Hands: A View from the Crib*, provides rich detail that allows for a race-based analysis of the adoptive mothering role through the eyes of an adopted child. Furthermore, the depth of his writing allows for the role of maternal authenticity, autonomy, control, and authority to be explored. The situation of this adoptee and his white mother represent a singular example of a multi-dimensional phenomenon that is still largely unarticulated.

The diverse and controversial nature of transracial adoption, particularly with regard to racial concerns, is initially discussed in order to provide a context for this study. Secondly, the positioning of mothers in the transracial adoption experience is explored and, finally, a paradigm for analyzing a transracial adoptee's relationship with his adoptive mother is presented from the unique perspective of the adoptee.

THE DIVERSE NATURE OF TRANSRACIAL ADOPTIVE MOTHERING

Transracial adoption is a wide-spread occurrence, applying to more than 380,000 individuals; 18 percent of the 2.1 million adopted children whose caretakers participated in the 2000 U.S. Census (U.S. Census Bureau). The concept of transracial adoption basically "…refers to circumstances where children have been adopted across racial groups" (Patel 328). In adoption literature, the term most often refers to the adoption of Black children by white parents (Patel 328). However, the range of transracial adoptive experiences is enormously broad and not limited to a particular race, ethnicity, or situation.

Transracial adoptions occur in homes that have been approved and selected by private or public adoption agencies, in homes where adoptive and birthparents select the placement with the assistance of attorneys, or through informal adoptive placements where an adoptee's birthparents choose an adoptive family without involving the courts. Transracial adoptees may live with relatives (kinship care), former foster parents, or with parents who were strangers to them prior to their adoption. Some transracial adoptees may live with neighbors in the communities in which they grew up, while others are transported across the globe from other countries. Some transracial adoptees are in placements made and accepted by their birthmothers, while others are in placements bitterly opposed by their birthmothers, who want their children returned to their own homes.

Each of these circumstances describes a different position from which adoptive mothers come to the adoption experience, impacting the family's construction of its racial identity, and the parents' and children's management of their experiences of oppression. While each of these unique experiences deserves attention in its own right, the present study focuses on the lived experience of only family and one of these circumstances.

CONTROVERSIES

The impact of adoption on mothers is complex and highly controversial in our society. There is still a sense that adoptive mothers bypass an essential aspect of mothering because they adopt rather than give birth. By not giving birth, adoptive mothers are inevitably faced with questions regarding their ability to be "real" mothers. Birthmothers and adoptive mothers alike are subjected to a societal stigma of insufficiency; for example, inferiority rooted in a "disputed" ideology of biological motherhood (Gailey). For adoptive mothers, the underlying cause of social stigma is their failure to protect bloodlines by giving birth to the child. Adoptive mothers, particularly those who have children who do not look like them, are commonly asked by strangers and friends, "But what about the real mother?" Although adoptive mothers are often applauded for offering to raise "unwanted" children, this admiration amounts to "faint praise" because it diminishes the meaning of their act to one of charity, or a kind of selfishness, rather than a voluntary act of love. Conversely, the underlying cause of social stigma faced by birthmothers is their alleged inability or unwillingness to carry out an essential function of womanhood—successful child rearing. Labeled "bad mothers" by society, birthmothers' decisions to relinquish their children are seen as "...an indication of irresponsible sexuality and abnormal motherhood" (Gailey 25).

Women seeking to adopt transracially face additional challenges. Transracial adoption remains a widely contested approach to resolving the need for permanent, stable homes for children. While some adoption experts view transracial placements to be an effective way to "save" children by moving them out of impermanent and endangering situations, others argue that it is a homogenizing and destructive force that is tantamount to cultural genocide, "stealing" children away from their cultures and communities (Trenka, Oparah and Shin 4). In fact, some published literature, which asks "Should Whites Adopt African American Children?" (Satz), challenges the right of prospective adoptive mothers to contemplate taking this step at all.

The main argument centres around the question of identity and cultural formation, especially in a society abound with racial discrimination (Gailey 13). This concern is echoed in the literature discussing white women who give birth to children of color, suggesting that the mental health of these children is dependent on their white birthmother's ability to teach them the realities of racism (Verbian 216). With respect to transracial adoptive mothering, therefore, the issue is "... whether White parents, whose unmarked racial identity is continually reinforced as the social norm, are capable of teaching their Black children how to resist and undercut potentially devastating and ubiquitous racial stereotypes and racist ideology" (Patton 13). The literature surrounding transracial mothering sometimes suggests that white mothers can never perform competently in this regard, no matter how much they try (Verbian 216).

Thus, women with transracially adopted children are often thought to be "transgressive" in that they are considered to have violated racial divisions. As a result, they are further "subjected to forms of surveillance, discipline, and moral censure usually restricted to women of color" (Twine 130). As white women, their mothering may be further stigmatized by suggesting that they lack the tools to effectively analyze and counteract the impact of this censure on themselves and their families because of their racial privilege (Robinson).

Two pieces of federal legislation in the United States reflect the ambivalence with which transracial adoption is perceived. While the 1978 Indian Child Welfare Act directs child welfare agencies to give "preference to extended family or tribe in placement of Native children" (Park and Green 7), the 1996 Multi-Ethnic Placement Act made "consideration of race in adoptive placement impermissible, unless such considerations could be documented as relevant to an individual child's particular needs" (Park and Green 9; See also Quiroz). Adoption workers are required to meet both of these contradictory directives in their placement practices.

The multi-faceted and ongoing debate about transracial adoption provides the impetus for this study which examines the experiences of one transracial family in an attempt to articulate the interconnections between questions of "capability" and adoptive mothering. Furthermore, it explores the means by which adoptive mothers and children can negotiate and resolve these questions over time.

DIMENSIONS OF MOTHERING

Andrea O'Reilly has offered a paradigm for a feminist analysis of motherhood. It challenges the "patriarchal profile and script of 'good' mothers and 'good' mothering" (802), which prescribes responsibility without power, giving without receiving, and nurturing without being nurtured in return. O'Reilly describes four dimensions that empower motherhood: authority, agency, autonomy and authenticity. Authority reflects the mother's insistence that her role include the power to make decisions. Agency, or the capacity to make personal decisions, provides the means to carry out mothering in an authoritative manner. Autonomy invokes the right to make decisions without obtaining a male's permission to do so. Although a woman may have a partner in parenting, her own ability to act independently should not be impaired. The fourth dimension, authenticity, involves the mother's responsibility to position her mothering in the context of her life goals as a whole. Ultimately, a feminist analysis of mothering is designed to "reclaim that power for mother" (O'Reilly 802).

O'Reilly's paradigm is useful for exploring the ways that mothering is articulated in transracial adoptive families because it allows for the integration of responsibility towards self with responsibility towards others. While the enactment of the four mothering abilities suggests women should be empowered and satisfied in their parenting, the impact of transracial adoption on mothering is not clear. Amy Middleton points out that, "When framed in terms of feminist mothering . . . the four conditions of empowered mothering are difficult to achieve for women mothering under duress" (76). France Twine sought to answer the question, "How do racism and sexism intersect in the lives of white women who were seen as racial transgressors?" (134). The present study explores the concept of racism through the eyes of a transracial adoptee and asks the question: Are adoptive mothers in transracial families able to carry out their parenting roles effectively, or do racialized and oppressive factors create barriers to empowered mothering because of the duress of racism?

REFLECTING ON BIRTHMOTHERS:
THE TRANSRACIAL ADOPTEE'S STANDPOINT

This study is based on the writing of Jaiya John (2005) who was transracially adopted as a young child. John's *Black Baby White Hands: A View from the Crib* was chosen because it is a widely known and well-respected autobiographical work; it was not selected because it somehow "represents" the viewpoint of transracial adoptees, nor was it chosen because of the particular views the author expressed regarding his adoptive mother. A different autobiographical selection might provide very different answers to the questions posed in this research. We chose an autobiographical approach, in part, to gain distance from one of the author's situation as an adult woman who has adopted transracially, and to create a more balanced perspective by beginning with the voice of a child in this type of family situation.

To carry out the study, a qualitative approach was utilized; all references to John's adoptive mother were noted during an initial reading of the text and were subsequently systematically re-examined with regard to each of the key questions of the study. For the most part, Jaiya John distinguishes between his adoptive mother and father, although occasionally he talks about his adoptive parents as a couple. Following O'Reilly's paradigm for empowered mothering, and to understand the impact of racism on adoptive mothers, the key questions explored in this study include:

•Does this adult adoptee describe adoptive parenting as an authentic aspect of his mother's life?
•Does this adult adoptee describe his adoptive mother as having the autonomy to make effective parenting decisions?
•Does this adult adoptee describe his adoptive mother as having control (agency) over her parenting choices and changes?
•Does this adult adoptee describe his adoptive mother as having authority over him as a parent?

Background

Born in the summer of 1967, Jaiya John was placed with his adoptive family when he was nine months old. His adoptive parents, the Potters, had a birthdaughter who was three months older than he, adopted another Black infant one year later, and brought two more birth children into the family when Jaiya was seven and ten. His adoptive mother worked in the home while his adoptive father ultimately obtained his Ph.D. and worked as a scientist at Los Alamos National Laboratory. Jaiya's birthmother had come to New Mexico to work and had briefly known his birthfather, who was in the military. Seriously ill at the time of his birth and struggling to care for two older children, Jaiya's birthmother decided to place him for adoption. He was reunited with his birthmother and father when he was in his twenties. Jaiya's birthparents are Black and Native American, and his adoptive parents are white.

Authenticity

Like many women in the 1960s, Jaiya portrays his adoptive mother as embracing a more traditional, patriarchal view of her role. Nurturance, protection and sacrifice were hallmarks of her mothering stance:

> Mom's whole world was her children and family. She put everything she had into us. It was her identity, her reason for being, although I am sure she had other life desires that she subdued over time. (63)

Jaiya describes his adoptive mother as highly creative and emotionally expressive, enjoying parenting and finding pleasure in life. She is a woman who likes to express her feelings, but then let go, one who thinks a person should "take it on the chin and then get on with things" (64).

Her flamboyant, expressive approach to life was incongruent with Jaiya's who metaphorically describes himself as a shy, private child who would retreat, like a turtle, into his shell. "I walked slowly, begrudgingly away from my emotions, especially the solemn, sullen ones.... I held onto my emotions like a bag lady hordes her stash" (64).

Jaiya traces some of his mother's frustrations with parenting to this incompatibility in their approaches to self-expression and problem-resolution. He also believes his adoptive mother harbored some feelings of insecurity and resentment aimed at people who had gone to college when she had not. In general, however, Jaiya perceives his mother's caretaking as an authentic and personally meaningful dimension of her life.

Autonomy

Jaiya places his adoptive mother at the "center" of his parenting experiences. His father, while important, appears to play a quieter, more peripheral role:

> She was the center of my life, and as my life evolved into a processing of constant racial messages and interactions, I needed her to play the role of conductor, explainer, and the one who made the bad things go away. (65)

Although both parents loved him, it was his adoptive mother to whom Jaiya turned for affirmation and guidance. Jaiya does not describe a single instance in which his father overrode his mother's directives or decisions. In his eyes, his adoptive mother had the ability to make critical decisions about mothering without needing his father's permission to do so.

Agency

Although he sees his mother as having an authentic and autonomous experience with mothering, Jaiya raises questions about her ability to carry out caretaking in an authoritative way. It is in this arena that he raises questions concerning her attempts to deal with the racial dimensions of family life. Jaiya believes his parents attempted to deal with race by trying to disconnect it from parenting. Like other transracial adopters of their generation, Jaiya's parents appeared to believe that loving nurturance would give their children all the support they needed to survive and thrive in the world (Simon and Roorda 2007):

We were spoiled with a diet of love, support, opportunities, and education. But love is more complex than the concept we dress it up as. My parents' only source of security in their decision to adopt us was that they would simply love and treat the Black children just like their own biological children. They had to believe that this loving environment would be all that we would need, because it was all they could conceive of offering us. (152)

However, this strategy to engage in "colorblind" parenting was actually "white parenting":

Mom and Dad inherently were engaged in cultural parenting. They were constantly attending to their White children's ethnicity simply by relating to them through the White cultural styles that had shaped them. (147)

Furthermore, their "colorblind parenting" was ineffective in buffering the family from racial oppression. Jaiya's mother became acutely aware, through the stares of hatred from others, that she and her husband were considered traitors by virtue of their transracial adoption and, in turn, became targets for discrimination (33):

It was not that I felt my parents hated or disliked African Americans. They were openhearted to everyone they came across. They taught that lesson as a matter of priority to their children. But accumulated moments led me to sense in them a distinct yet slight discomfort with the *idea* of African Americans. It was a hard-to-grasp but tangible combination of barely perceptible discomfort with spending time in Black environments, and interacting with Black persons. More importantly it had to do with what was not said. (209)

Afraid that, in acknowledging his racial pain, she would have to recognize the deep-seated racism surrounding her, Jaiya's mother was silent about her own racial attitudes and silenced his attempts to explore them. Jaiya interpreted his mother's "love is all we need" approach as a major barrier to his efforts to explore his own sense of identity, and he describes this as a major source of growing conflict in his relationship with her:

I could not discern between her emotions that came from the pressures of maintaining a household, raising children, and the discomfort she seemed to have specific to my growing racial unrest. It did not help Mom that I could not articulate exactly what was troubling me. All I expressed were banners of distress in the form of gloom, mope, and increasingly angry tones. (64)

One particular incident in Jaiya's childhood highlights his mother's insufficiency in helping him sort through his identity. As he struggled watching Alex Haley's *Roots* for the first time, his mother responded, "You've been acting weird. I'm not gonna let you watch that show anymore if you don't straighten up" (158). Jaiya was devastated by this reaction: "*You're acting weird.* The words made me feel as if I was the discontent field slave planning an uprising against the big house, and she was the Master's wife, discovering the treachery of Nat Turner in my eyes" (160). Jaiya describes his reaction to this scenario as one of betrayal, and he perceived this overt silencing as his mother's "inability, even *unwillingness,* to 'see'" him (115). Eventually, Jaiya interpreted his mother's silence to mean that she did not really like him. In Jaiya's eyes, this sense of disconnection and increasing conflict were powerful indicators of his mother's diminishing opportunities for authoritative parenting.

Authority

Jaiya's perspectives on his adoptive mother's parental authority changed dramatically over time. "There was a time, up until I was about 10 years of age, when I enjoyed an open and unbound ability to love Mom with nothing held back" (166). However, in his adolescence and increasingly in his young adult years, Jaiya's rejection of his adoptive family was filled with strong personal emotion. Eventually, he stopped speaking to his family, especially his mother (288-289). His adoptive mother's inability to address Jaiya's racial experiences resulted in her loss of authority in their relationship.

After a long period of disconnection during his adult years, Jaiya came to recognize the strengths of his relationship with his family. By his thirties, he says, "I gained more appreciation for what my family had been to me all along. I saw that they had been steady in their support, their forgiveness, and their embrace" (302). As a child, Jaiya's interpretation of certain events led to his feeling of disconnection. He remembered his mother's reaction to his moody adolescence, "'Quit hanging your lip!' she would snap at me, fatigued by the Scorpio mood I dragged around the house" (64). In childhood he felt misunderstood and alienated by this reaction. In his later years, Jaiya reinterprets this experience, recognizing that, through her enactment of parenting, "she gave me her grit, tough-ness, determination. *We stand by for the long haul.* Mom's life enabled me. I had precedence" (333).

CONCLUSION

Jaiya John's articulation of his path toward an integrated sense of self illuminates the centrality of race, racism, and white privilege on that process. For Jaiya, trying to realize "who I am" without embracing his racial background is tantamount to offering "unclean" love:

> It was clean love that made the world of difference for me. The vibes weren't polluted with a discomfort with my race, and avoidance of the idea of my race, or a strained tolerance or for-giveness for my race. Crisp and clean, that's how I needed it. (53)

Jaiya perceived, early in his life, that their racial differences created bar-riers between his mother and himself. While he identified his mother's parenting as authentic and autonomous, he described her control and authority diminishing as their racial conflicts increased.

This analysis supports the utility of O'Reilly's mothering paradigm and the significance of assessing each of the four dimensions of parenting, since life events in the family can reflect differences in outcomes along each of these dimensions. In addition, this study reflects the importance of examining "the ongoing, lifelong impact of the adoption experience itself on adoptees and their families" (Raible 181). Jaiya's changing perspectives on the meaning of his interactions with his mother indicate the importance of following the unfolding dialogue between mother and child regarding the nature of parenting and the intersection of racial and mothering concerns.

Jaiya's struggle to develop a holistic, integrated sense of his own iden-tity is reflected in the words of Sandra Patton: "We live our lives at the margins of difference—ative and foreigners" (7). Jaiya's work compels us to continue examining the nature of the relationship between adoptive mothers and their children in transracial families. Clearly, any further study of transracial adoption requires that this issue be placed at the centre of the analysis.

This analysis reflects the importance of analyzing mothering experi-ences, not only from a non-patriarchal perspective, but also from the viewpoint of the transracial adoptee. Jane Trenka recognizes that adoptees have been effectively silenced. As an adoptee, she argues adoptees are frequently "viewed as perpetual children, with views easily dismissed as 'angry,' 'ungrateful,' or 'bitter,' especially if our views are politicized, raced, or consider the women who gave birth to us" (2). Tina Patel argues for "the need for the adoptees to speak for themselves about their own lives" and the efficacy of using qualitative methods to give them voice (331). The responsibility to recognize the authority, and reflect the standpoint, of those whom a researcher is studying is articulated in Afrocentric research methodology. As stated by Ruth Reviere, "...the experiences of community members are the ultimate authority in determining what is true and, therefore, are the final arbiter of the validity of research about their lives" (713). This is verified in the present study whereby Jaiya's account of his mother's parenting on his development and self-identity illustrates a critical view in understanding the implications of transracial adoption.

This analysis could be enriched by addressing one additional element: the voice of Jaiya's adoptive mother, Mrs. Potter, has not been heard. Perhaps her views would be congruent with his, but this can only be discovered if she were asked to articulate her mothering experiences. Future research in this area could benefit from including the mother in such analyses and, where feasible, her perspectives could be compared with those of her adopted children.

WORKS CITED

Gailey, Christine Ward. "Ideologies of Motherhood and Kinship in U.S. Adoption." *Ideologies and Technologies of Motherhood: Race, Class, Sexuality, Nationalism.* Eds. Heléna Ragoné and France Winddance Twine. New York: Routledge, 2000. 11-55. Print.

Grice, Helena. "Transracial Adoption Narratives: Prospects and Perspectives." *Meridians* 5.2 (2005): 124-148. Web. 19 December 2000.

John, Jaiya. *Black Baby White Hands: A View from the Crib.* Silver Spring, MD: Soul Water Rising, 2005. Print.

Martin, Judith. "A Social Work Perspective on Birth Parents' Grief and the Adoption Experience." Association for Death Education and Counseling. *The Forum* 33.4 (2007): 8. Print.

Middleton, Amy. "Mothering Under Duress: Examining the Inclusiveness of Feminist Mothering Theory." *Mothering and Feminism* 8 (2006): 72-82. Print.

O'Reilly, Andrea. "Feminist Mothering." *Maternal Theory: Essential Readings.* Ed. Andrea O'Reilly. Toronto, Canada: Demeter Press,

2007. 792-821. Print.

Park, Shelley and Cheryl Evans Green. "Is Transracial Adoption in the Best Interests of Ethnic Minority Children?: Questions Concerning Legal and Scientific Interpretations of a Child's Best Interests." *Adoption Quarterly* 3.4 (2000): 5-34. Print.

Patel, Tina. "The Usefulness of Oral Life (Hi)story to Understand and Empower: The Case of Trans-Racial Adoption." *Qualitative Social Work* 4.3 (2005): 327-345. Print.

Patton, Sandra. *Birth Marks: Transracial Adoption in Contemporary America*. New York: New York University Press, 2000. Print.

Quiroz, Pamela Anne. "Color-blind Individualism, Intercountry Adoption and Public Policy." *Journal of Sociology and Social Welfare* 34.2 (2007): 57-68. Print.

Raible, John. "Lifelong Impact, Enduring Need." *Outsiders Within: Writing on Transracial Adoption*. Eds. Jane Jeong Trenka, Julia Chinyere Oparah, and Sun Yung Shin. Cambridge, MA: Southend Press, 2006. 179-188. Print.

Reviere, Ruth. "Toward an Afrocentric Research Methodology." *Journal of Black Studies* 31 (2001): 709-728. Print.

Robinson, Tracy. "White Mothers of Non-White Children." *Journal of Humanistic Counseling, Education and Development* 40 (2001): 171-184. Print.

Satz, Martha. "Should Whites Adopt African American Children? One Family's Phenomenological Response." *Imagining Adoption: Essays on Literature and Culture*. Ed. Marianne Novy. Ann Arbor: University of Michigan Press, 2004. 267-276. Print.

Simon, Rita and Ronda Roorda. *In Their Parents' Voices: Reflections on Raising Transracial Adoptees*. New York: Columbia University Press, 2007. Print.

Trenka, Jane Jeong. "Whywrite." 19 September 2008. Web.

Trenka, Jane Jeong, Julia Chinyere Oparah, and Sun Yung Shin, Eds. *Outsiders Within: Writing On Transracial Adoption*. Cambridge, MA: Southend Press, 2006. Print.

Twine, France Winddance. "Transgressive Women and Transracial Mothers: White Women and Critical Race Theory." *Meridians* 1.2 (2001): 130-153. Print.

U.S. Census Bureau. "Adopted Children and Stepchildren: 2000." *Census 2000 Special Reports*. October, 2003. Print.

Verbian, Channa. "White Birth Mothers of Black/White Biracial Children: Addressing Racialized Discourses in Feminist and Multicultural Literature." *Mothering and Feminism* 8 (2006): 213-222. Print.

Welsh, Janet, Andres Viana, Stephen Petrill and Matthew Mathias. "Interventions for Internationally Adopted Children and Families: A Review of the Literature." *Child and Adolescent Social Work Journal* 24.3 (2007): 285-311. Print.

10.

Are You My Mother?

How Transracial Adoption Provides Insight into Who Can Be a Mother and Who Can Be Mothered

ELISHA MARR

T
RANSRACIAL ADOPTION OFFERS a unique opportunity to better understand how the structural forces of race and class shape mothering in contemporary society. It is characterized by two major trends: from a domestic standpoint, it involves White women who adopt children of colour and, from an international standpoint, it involves White American women who adopt children from predominantly non-White countries (Solinger 22-24). Since many women who desire to be mothers are not (Roberts 246-248) and many children are still available for adoption (Bartholet, *Where Do* 1166), we are compelled to seek an understanding of why certain mothers have the opportunity to adopt as well as why certain children are more likely to be adopted.

This chapter employs a conflict theorist perspective to illustrate how broad forces interact with individual decisions to create and maintain inequality in adoption and mothering. It reveals that at the macro-level, politics (e.g. China's one-child policy, Romania's mandate to procreate), economics (i.e. poverty), and culture (i.e., a racial hierarchy that favours White culture) produce a disproportionately large number of children of colour available for adoption. At the micro-level, these racial and cultural preferences are evident in the decisions of women privileged enough (primarily middle- and upper-class White Americans) to choose to be a mother through adoption; this is because they show an initial preference for White children, followed by Asian and Hispanic children, over and above Black children.[1] However, rather than critiquing the decisions of adoptive women or the policies of adoption agencies, this chapter asks the reader to consider how the act of transracial adoption perpetuates the structural race and class inequality responsible for creating the environment within which transracial placements are necessary. It adds to the scholarship on adoption and mothering by creating awareness about the fact that a race/class hierarchy plays an integral role in determining who can be a mother and who can be mothered.

LITERATURE REVIEW

Why Study Transracial Adoption to Learn About Mothering?

Adoption offers a more visible opportunity than biological reproduction to examine how mothering choices are made in a raced and classed society. Prior to 1960, adoptive parents were matched with children of the same race and religion. As access to birth control and abortion increased in the United States, fewer White infants became available for adoption (Solinger 22-24). In the 1970s and 80s, White women were more willing to consider adopting a child of colour as a shortage of White children converged with growing racial tolerance and an increasing number of interracial relationships (Simon and Altstein 3). Despite controversy and great opposition by many in the United States, transracial placements increased. These changes in adoption practice created an environment within which race and social class significantly influenced mothering choices and opportunities. Twentieth-century scholars began to learn about how access to resources, as well as domestic and global race relations, affected a woman's ability to become a mother through adoption as well as a child's opportunity to be mothered.

Toward the turn of the twenty-first century, the controversy associated with transracial adoption was much less concerned with *whether* it should occur, and more concerned with *how* it should occur. A number of adoption scholars note that the practice of allowing adoptive mothers to select children based on the child's racial categorization creates inequality amongst the children available for adoption because certain racial groups, particularly Black and African American children, languish much longer in foster care and orphanages than children from other racial groups. White children are the first children selected for adoption (with the exception of children with physical and mental health issues) since many mothers who adopt are White and prefer children who are similar in appearance. When White children are not available, these mothers often prefer to adopt Asian and Hispanic children over Black or African American children (Bartholet, *Where Do*; Banks; Maldonado). The implications of these trends are three-fold; first, it demonstrates that White, Asian, and Hispanic children have a greater opportunity to be mothered than Black children. Second, recognizing the disproportionate number of children of colour available for adoption, these trends reveal that White American women enjoy the greatest autonomy, opportunity, and choice about if and who to mother, whereas many women of colour are constrained from mothering the children they bear. Third, these trends in transracial adoption illustrate how the structural forces of race and class shape mothering in the twenty-first century.

This chapter explores how race and class affect contemporary experiences of adoption and mothering. Empirical data on transracial adoption is complemented by ethnographic voice to provide a more thorough picture of the phenomenon. The macro-level data on transracial adoption trends consists of academic research on adoption, publications from private adoption organizations, and reports from government agencies. The micro-level data, primarily interview excerpts, is original research I conducted between 2002 and 2004 on six transracially adoptive mothers and three transracially adoptive fathers, all of whom self-identified as White or Caucasian.[2] In this analysis of transracial adoption (TRA), I illustrate how race and class hierarchies factor into women's choices and opportunities to mother (effectively favouring White women) as well as children's opportunities to be mothered (favouring children who are not Black).

Why Conflict Theory?

Conflict theory helps us to better understand that the struggle over the resource of children is central to the issue of adoption and women's interests as mothers. Conflict theorists posit that social life is best understood by acknowledging that there are different and unequal groups in society and they struggle over resources (i.e., money, assets). Because resources are limited, the only way for a person and/or group to profit and have excess money and assets is for another person or group to go without. Additionally, as a person and/or group excels financially, their accumulated resources place them in a position of power and advantage that increases their ability to obtain additional resources (Schaefer 16; Farrington and Chertok 360-361). In regard to transracial adoption, the resource at stake is children; the only way for one woman to adopt is for another woman to voluntarily or involuntarily (i.e. removal by the child welfare system) relinquish the child she bore. Most adoption studies focus on the family created by adoption yet this obscures the fact that in order for adoption to occur another family must be disbanded.

Conflict theory can also be used to understand the ways in which race and social class shape adoption and mothering through the favouritism of middle- and upper-class White women as mothers and children who are not Black as the most likely to be adopted. For instance, social class is an economics-based categorization determined by income, assets, education and other wealth-related attributes. As a result, people at the top of social class hierarchies, the middle and upper classes, are also more able to easily acquire resources (Schaefer 17-18; Farrington and Chertok 370-371). In the context of transracial adoption, this ultimately means that women with higher levels of income, wealth, and education are more likely to be granted children because they are deemed more able to afford the expenses associated with the adoption, care, and education of a child. Conversely, poor women who lack an education and financial resources are not even considered as viable adoptive mothers.

Conflict theory provides insight not only into how social class factors into which women are selected as adoptive parents, but also into the decisions and experiences of the women who gave birth to the children available for adoption: birthmothers. The population of women who are considered birthmothers is diverse and their reasons for voluntary or involuntary relinquishment are numerous and varied, yet all indicate disenfranchisement. Domestically, being unmarried, lack of financial resources, and undocumented immigration status are cited as reasons for surrender.[3] Internationally, women surrender due to poverty, political pressure (i.e. China's one-child policy), and cultural preferences for boys.[4] From this perspective, conflict theory helps us to understand how disadvantage works to create a population of children available for middle- and upper-class White women to adopt.

Although conflict theory is grounded in social class inequality, it is also applicable to race. Race is a social construct based on cultural meanings that are attached to bloodlines, appearance, and phenotypes (Omi and Winant). Although I may believe that as human beings all races are intrinsically equal, it has been repeatedly shown that people are treated differently based on their perceived race (Schaefer 269-273). Consequently, social scientists indicate that, domestically and globally, a generalized racial hierarchy exists in which White people enjoy the most financial, social and cultural advantage followed by Asians, Hispanics, and Blacks in that order (Wynter 280; Gans).[5] This is evidence of not only a pattern of racial inequality, but of the interconnectedness of race and social class. Understanding this race and social class dynamic provides insight into why middle- and upper-class White women have more opportunities and choices in mothering, why poor and/or women of colour are the most restrained in their mothering choices, and why Black children are the least likely to be selected for adoption.

Why Focus on Mothers?

Adoption literature often refers to the activities of adoptive parents, however, adoptive mothers are the driving force behind adoptive choices and parenting. "Parenting" and "parents" are relatively new terms. More common are the concepts of mothering and fathering. Mothering is widely recognized as caring for, feeding, loving, and nurturing children. Traditionally, fathering is more simply defined as impregnating, although it may also include protecting and providing, which means that historically fathers have had much less and even minimal interaction with children (Strong 329-332; Gailey 120-121). American culture and definitions of fathering have changed and now include some of the responsibilities originally associated with mothering. However, research on the actual conduct of contemporary mothers and fathers reveals that mothers do more of the hands-on, labor-intensive work; in effect, mothers still perform a vast majority of the parenting (Strong 329-332; Coltrane 53-106). Consequently, as this discussion progresses, I assume that it is mothers who play the central parenting role in adoptive families today.

Adoptive mothers' domination over parenting and parenting decisions was evident in the interviews I conducted with transracially adoptive families. It was the adoptive mothers who typically initiated the decision to adopt, researched options, dominated adoption choices, and acted as the primary caregivers of their adoptive children. Although fathers agreed to adoption, expressed broad preferences (i.e. gender, age), and took an interest in parenting their adoptive children, they were less concerned with the details (i.e. skin tone, potential height). Adoptive mothers were the driving force behind the adoption process. In light of this gendered difference, it is clear that a focus on adoptive mothers ensures a more nuanced understanding of how race- and class-based trends in transracial adoption emerge.

DATA

Who Can Be a Mother?

> In fact the way the "adoption market" took form after Roe v. Wade is a case study of how some women's choices depend on exploiting the relative choicelessness of other women.
> —Rickie Solinger (22)

White, middle- and upper-class women have greater opportunities and choices with regard to becoming mothers in the "adoption market" compared to poorer women and women of colour. Prior to the 1900s, pregnancy was largely unmanageable with respect to choice and a mandatory expectation imposed on married women. The advent of birth control and safe, legalized abortion gave some women control over their fertility and made childbearing and rearing more of a choice. From many perspectives, adoption offers an additional choice for women by providing another option to become a mother. However, the conflict theorist perspective shows that the choice to mother a child is not equally available to all women since poor women and women of colour are more likely to be forced to surrender a child for adoption while White, middle- and upper-class women often have the "choice" to adopt.

Socioeconomic status is a determining factor not only in creating the opportunity to mother, but the societal support to do so. Currently, financial security, which is enjoyed by middle- and upper-class women, is a more important litmus test for becoming a parent than parenting skills. Previously, societal acceptance of women who became mothers was based on marital status, but now income and assets are the primary factors considered (Solinger; Patton 117-146). Financial stability and disposable income are even more important considerations in the context of adoption, especially if a White woman is in pursuit of a White infant; depending on the type of adoption (i.e. domestic/international, open/closed) expenses can range from $8,000 to over $100,000 dollars (Waldman and Caplan 64-65).

The role of class in providing White women with more mothering choices than any other group of women in the American context was evident in my research. Of the six adoptive families I interviewed, only one had an annual income of less than $75,000. Interviewees indicated spending between $4,500 to $30,000 on adoption expenses. Although most took advantage of the U.S. federal tax credit, it seemed inconsequential to their adoption decision.

> Interviewer: *How much did the adoption cost?*
> TRA Mother: *[International] adoption was $30,000 dollars. Domestic was free.*

> Interviewer: *I've heard from other parents that they received [financial] help from their work and tax credits from the government. [Did you?]*
> TRA Father: *Not really. There's a federal tax break [shakes head dismissively].*

Comparatively, poor and working-class women struggle more to become mothers due to circumstances beyond their control, such as lack of housing, child care, and employment (Solinger 182-224; Patton 117-146). The use of social services (i.e. food stamps, cash assistance, Medicaid) to provide for a family is discouraged formally through welfare reform and informally through social discrimination (Brush; Patton 130-167; Solinger 139-224). Poor women's lack of resources makes them particularly vulnerable to having their children removed by child welfare agencies and decreases the likelihood of reunification with removed children (Arons 10). In a similar vein, poor and working-class women are not deemed appropriate adoptive parents by adoption agencies which require a demonstration of financial security and the ability to pay adoption expenses (Roberts 272-275). Poor and working class women are greatly discouraged from mothering as either birthparents or adoptive parents.

One of the reasons poor and working-class women have fewer choices in mothering is because it is more difficult for them to utilize the family planning and medical services that are essential to be able to make choices about motherhood. For instance, the cost of prescription birth control (i.e. contraceptive hormones) may exceed the budgets of poor women. Long-term birth control options (i.e. tubal litigation and intra-uterine devices) cost hundreds or thousands of dollars and are often not an option for women without medical insurance. Although a number of organizations (i.e. Planned Parenthood) offer birth control at more affordable prices, some women are limited by time and transportation (Solinger 5-11; Donovan 11). As adoption research reveals, this means there is more government support (i.e. tax credits, foster care allowances) and societal support for middle- and upper-class women to adopt the children of poor women than there is for poor women to parent their own children. Indeed, Rickie Solinger notes that "[t]hroughout the Reagan-Bush era, adoption was promoted as a cure for child poverty and a way to reduce welfare costs" (198).

It is clear that women of colour have fewer choices in regard to mothering because they are disproportionately represented among the poor on a national and global scale; however, class discrimination against these women is additionally compounded by racial discrimination. Research shows that women of colour, especially African-American women, experience racial and cultural discrimination in the adoptive parent selection process (Patton 157; Day). This can be attributed to negative stereotypes that are prevalent about Black women; they are perceived to be promiscuous welfare queens and drug users who choose to live in a culture of poverty. On the contrary, White women are associated with purity, heroism, safety, and resources (Patton 130-167; Solinger 139-224). Although there are racist stereotypes associated with Asians (i.e. intelligent, hard-working, and opportunistic) and Hispanics (i.e. hot-blooded, criminals, and family-oriented), they are more nuanced with respect to Asian and Latin-American women (Maldonado 1421-1425). These stereotypes are consistent with the patterns associated with opportunities to mother; as potential adoptive parents, women of colour are more likely than White women to experience discrimination in the approval process (Roberts 272-275; Day), and as birthparents, women of colour are more likely than White women to feel societal pressure to surrender a child for adoption as well as a greater likelihood of having a child removed by the child welfare system (Solinger; Arons 10). It is clear that in the adoption market, White women are more likely to end up with a child, whereas women of colour are more likely to go without.

The decision and ability to become a mother is not solely determined by the woman involved—it is also determined by her race and class categorization, as well as by the opportunities and choices afforded to her. Due to the race and class status they enjoy, middle and upper-class White women are considered ideal mothers and are given the social and political support to consider adoption as an additional choice for becoming a mother. The stereotypes and concerns about women of colour as mothers combined with their likelihood to be economically and/or politically disenfranchised makes them more likely to voluntarily or involuntarily relinquish a child for adoption or experience discrimination in the adoptive parent approval process. Since the children of poor women of colour flow disproportionately into the homes of middle and upper-class White American women (Solinger 22-24; Briggs 94-95), the profound influence of race and social class cannot be denied in the context of mothering and adoption.

Who Can be Mothered?

> They says: "If you was white, should be alright,
> If you was brown, stick around,
> But as you's black, hmm, brother, get back, get back, get back."
> —Big Bill Broonzy, 1951

Domestically and internationally, White children are the most likely to be mothered in the context of adoption. Adoption agency specialists report that the number of White women seeking to adopt exceeds the number of White infants available for adoption (Maldonado 1426-1430). Middle and upper-class White women who are unable to adopt White infants domestically can also consider international adoption more easily, which many do in order to adopt infants who are white or are light in skin colour, at the expense of older and/or darker-skinned children at home (Lewin; Banks 951-955; Maldonado 1426-1430).

> Interviewer: *Why did you decide to adopt from another country and race?*
> TRA Mother: *At that time there were not a lot of healthy, White babies. They were reserving them for those who didn't have any kids.*

> Interviewer: *Why did you decide to adopt from another country and race?*
> TRA Mother: *With all of these open adoptions domestically, with birth mothers selecting adoptive parents, once I started looking into that it was kind of really sad.... White couples are competing for healthy, White babies.*

Many potential adoptive mothers work to find children whose appearances are similar to their own in order to avoid being easily identified as a non-biological parent (Ahn-Redding and Simon 3-9; Banks 951-955). Internationally, the Russian Federation (Russia) is favoured by White adoptive mothers because children there are also White (see Table 1 in Appendix). Russia, however, now limits the number of children adopted by U.S. citizens, which has further decreased the number of White children available for adoption by White American women (Simon and Altstein 17-18).

> TRA Mother: *Originally though, we had thought about adopting from Russia though. Mainly just so that when somebody looks at our family it wasn't so obvious they were adopted right off the bat.*

As many White women prefer white children, and women of colour are less likely to enjoy the opportunity to adopt, there are many children of colour who wait extended periods of time for a mother or are never adopted at all. Asia is home to 62 million orphans. Latin America and the Caribbean have eight million children living without mothers. Internationally, there are a multitude of reasons for the relinquishment of children by their birthmothers, including political upheaval (i.e. Korea, Vietnam), extreme poverty (i.e. India, Romania), and gender preference (i.e. China, India).[6] Domestically, women of colour, specifically African-American women, cite fear of living on welfare, elimination of Medicaid-funded abortions, and societal problems, such as poverty and unemployment, as reasons to surrender a child (Atkins; Arons 9).[7] Additionally, adoption agencies consistently report that the demand for White infants exceeds the supply, whereas non-White infants are readily available (Stolley; Maldonado 1423-1434; Bartholet, *Where Do* 1166).

International adoption trends reveal that when White children are not available for adoption, White women's second preference is for Asian and Hispanic children. International adoption rates have increased 183 percent since 1989 with many adoptees coming from countries whose populations are neither predominantly White (i.e. Ukraine), nor Black (i.e. Ethiopia) (see Table 1 in Appendix; Kinder and Hjelm). Latin American countries (i.e. Guatemala, Paraguay) are often selected by White transracially adoptive mothers because facial and body features of children from these countries (i.e. eye shape) are more likely to be similar to their own. So, although children from these countries are often darker in complexion, they are not Black (Maldonado; Bartholet, *Family Bonds* 87).

TRA Mother: *We wanted a girl; an infant. Light skinned.*
Interviewer: *When you knew you were adopting transracially what were your initial thoughts?*
TRA Mother: *Acceptance by others: that's why we wanted her lighter skinned.*
Interviewer: *Were you concerned about the difference between the race of you and your child?*
TRA Mother: *No. Maybe if she was Black or Oriental; more obvious. Some people don't even know [she is adopted] except that she tans up so well.*

Of course, White women who adopt internationally also do so from China and South Korea, which ensures that a child will be identified as an adoptee. Many White mothers attribute their preference for international adoption from these countries, over domestic adoption, to being easier, faster, and safer (Maldonado; Gainey 79-116).

Interviewer: *Why did you decide to adopt from another country and race?*

TRA Mother: *No [domestic] agency would take a look at us because we had children.*

TRA Mother: *In the U.S. adoptions are open and birth mothers select adoptive parents. Could be a quick process, or a long wait, or never. Given our ages we wanted to have a child within a certain length of time.*

A number of the White adoptive mothers I interviewed explained that even though they were willing to adopt a child of colour, they were not comfortable going to the bottom of the racial hierarchy to adopt a Black child.

TRA Mother: *[Explaining her parents' racial opinions] My mother said, "I'd like to see what she'd say if one of those girls brought home a Black man." So I know it's still an issue. And that is one of those things that maybe kept me from pursuing an African American or biracial baby.*

TRA Mother: *We wanted her to be accepted right away and loved. Frankly, with our parents being 80 years old we thought about what would be easy to live with. Chinese was an issue. Can't imagine how it would be with a Black child, especially with our fathers.*

TRA Mother: *Although in brutal honesty we were also aware that it would be much easier to raise a Hispanic baby then it would be to raise an African American baby.*

Consequently, Black children, domestically and internationally, are perceived as the least desirable by White adoptive mothers; it has been estimated that eight percent of adoptions in the United States are transracial, however, only about one percent of adoptions involve White mothers and Black children (Simon and Altstein 5-6). Approximately 50,000 African-American children are in foster care and waiting to be adopted. Africa has 39 million children without mothers, many of whom have been orphaned by the AIDS epidemic (AVERT).[8] Although the *Child Care Act* of 1983 previously made it difficult for Americans to adopt from South Africa, changes in 2000 have made it easier to do so. However, adoption from Africa is much less frequent than adoption from countries such as Russia, China, and Guatemala (International Adoption Stories). Trends in adoption from countries with Black children are very different from Latin American and Asian international adoption trends. For instance, many White American women jumped at the opportunity to adopt girls available in China due to the one-child law (Simon and Altstein 9-12). All of this suggests that there is an adherence to a race/class hierarchy on the part of White adoptive mothers; it is evident not only in the degree of choice they enjoy, but in the choices they make.

In 2006, Solangel Maldonado identified racial preferences in transracial adoption through comments made by domestic adoption representatives. These comments illustrate that White children are the most likely to be adopted, Black children are the least likely to be adopted, and other children of colour fall somewhere between (Maldonado 1422-1423).

> White babies, including Hispanic infants [are] in highest demand among American couples.

> We have families who say I'll take Hispanic, American Indian, anything but black.

> Blond blue-eyed girls are at the top [of the racial hierarchy] and African-American boys are at the bottom.

> There is a racial hierarchy. People prefer Chinese girls to African-American boys.

> Most whites prefer healthy white infants and when they learn that such babies are in short supply, they are more likely to adopt children of Columbian, Korean and American Indian ancestry than to adopt African American children.

Maldonado also included an anonymous telephone interview with an adoption coordinator who explained that 84 families were waiting for a newborn, yet only seven would adopt an African-American child. At the time, the agency was working with at least 15 women who would give birth to African-American or biracial children, which underscores the point that Black children are the least desired by adoptive mothers and, consequently, the least likely to be mothered (Maldonado 1434).

Who can be a mother or be mothered is clearly driven by women that enjoy the privilege and resources to choose the race of the child they wish to adopt. Consequently, amongst all children, White children are the most likely to be mothered. On the contrary, Asian and Hispanic children are more likely than White children to go without being mothered, while Black children, in particular, are the least likely to be mothered.

CONCLUSION

Using a conflict theorist perspective to analyze empirical and ethnographic data on transracial adoption not only reveals that a race/class hierarchy exists in macro-level adoption trends, but also in the micro-level decisions and practices of White adoptive mothers. At the macro-level, domestic and international policies regarding adoption and welfare often decrease the ability of poor women and/or women of colour to mother their children while simultaneously providing incentive for middle- and upper-class White women to adopt these children of colour. At the micro-level, White women who are privileged enough to become mothers through adoption use race and class hierarchies to select children. Correspondingly, it is as a result of these race/class hierarchies that White children, both domestically and internationally, are the most likely to be mothered with respect to adoption. While increasing numbers of Asian and Hispanic children are being welcomed into White homes, a disproportionate number of Black children languish in foster care and orphanages. In the twenty-first century, an understanding of adoption and mothering is incomplete without a consideration of how race and social class increase the ability of White middle- and upper-class women to become mothers through adoption by decreasing the opportunity of women of colour to mother, and of why children who are Black are the least likely to be mothered through transracial adoption.

This chapter explores how a person's place in hierarchies of race and social class play an integral role in determining who can be a mother and who can be mothered. It can be argued, however, that a person's gender is also important as it relates to questions of race and class. Future research and discussion of transracial adoption and mothering could also examine questions of gender with respect to my questions of who gets to be a mother and who gets to be mothered. The literature on gender in regard to mothering and transracial adoption is growing (Twine; Briggs). Still, many feminist scholars who discuss transracial adoption with a focus on women do not exhaustively explore, in conjunction with race and class, the question of how being male or female impacts one's ability to be adopted, to be an adoptive parent, or even to be an involved birthparent. Similarly, current research on the characteristics adoptive parents desire in their adoptive children also raises questions about gender preference, but these questions are not thoroughly investigated either (Zhang and Lee; Brooks, James, & Barth). To further my intersectional analysis of transracial adoption and who gets to be a mother or be mothered in terms of race and class, more research, particularly, as it relates to gender, needs to be pursued in the future.

Table 1: Number of Intercountry Adoptions in 1998

Russian Federation	4,491
China	4,263
Korea	1,829
Guatemala	911
Vietnam	603
India	478
Romania	406
Colombia	351
Caribbean	314
Philippines	200
Ukraine	180
Mexico	168
Bulgaria	151
Brazil	103
Paraguay	7

Source: Simon and Altstein; *Adoption Across Borders: Serving the Children in Transracial and Intercountry Adoptions*

[1] The author recognizes that many factors can play a key role in transracial adoption, particularly gender, however the focus of this work is race and social class. The conclusion considers further research topics in which the relevance of gender is discussed.

[2] Each interviewee voluntarily completed an informed consent form that was approved by the human subjects review board of the associated institution. Identifying information divulged in audio recordings and transcriptions of interviews are confidentially and securely stored by the interviewer.

[3] A recent report listing women's reasons for voluntary relinquishment included being unmarried, poverty, homelessness, domestic violence, physical and mental disabilities, recent immigration especially without documentation, and having a child removed previously by the child

welfare system. Although White women historically were more likely to use a formal adoption agency, their surrender rates decreased from 19% in the early 1970s to about 2 percent in the late 1990s with many choosing single motherhood instead. The surrender rates of White women are slightly higher than women of colour (0.9 percent) who most likely and historically relied more upon informal family networks for adoption (Arons 10; Atkins 1A). Despite these trends, a number of adoption scholars theorize that African-American women have and do turn to formal adoption as government social services that previously sustained many of these families decreases (Atkins 1A). An additional factor to consider is that African-American children are four times as likely as White children to be in the child welfare system. Scholars note that this is partially explained by the disproportionate poverty rates among Blacks, but also that Black mothers are judged more harshly than White mothers by the child welfare system (Arons 10).

[4]Internationally, poverty plays a large role in the surrender of children as is the case in Romania, Guatemala, and many countries in Africa. Disenfranchisement is not limited to economics, however, since the policy that required Chinese families to have only one child, and the cultural preference for boys, resulted in a disproportionately large number of Chinese girls available for adoption (Simon and Altstein 9-18).

[5]Racial scholars note that in the United States some racial groups move up and down within this racial hierarchy insofar as they specialize in and dominate a particular area of economic life. For example, during the development of factory-made clothing in the 1920s, Jewish people who had been tailors in the "old country" quickly adapted to machine production. As they began to flourish in retail industry and move into managerial and ownership positions, many moved out of the working class and began to employ Blacks in poorer-paying manual labor positions. Jews' social class mobility affected their place in the racial hierarchy as they increasingly became subsumed into the "White" category by the mid-1900s. The impact of deindustrialization on the United States in late twentieth century meant a decrease in available jobs, and that some racial groups, particularly, African Americans and Hispanics, lacked the opportunity to move up in social class (Waldinger; Brodkin Sacks). Blacks and Hispanics continue to find themselves at the bottom of racial hierarchies and are disproportionately represented among the poor (Schaefer 228).

[6]*Ibid.*

[7]*Supra* note 2.

[8]In 2005, children living without caregivers in Asia numbered 62 million, 39 million in Africa, and 8 million in Latin America and the Caribbean.

WORKS CITED

Ahn-Redding, Heather, and Rita J. Simon. *Intercountry Adoptees Tell Their Stories*. Lanham, MD: Lexington Books, 2007. Print.

Arons, Jessica. *The Adoption Option: Adoption Won't Reduce Abortion But It Will Expand Women's Choices*. Washington, DC: Center for American Progress, 2010. Print.

Atkins, Elizabeth. "Adoption of Black Babies Increases as Stigma Fades." *The Detroit News* 10 January 1993: 1A. Print.

AVERT. *AIDS Orphans*, 2009. Retrieved July 12, 2012 from http://www.avert.org/aids-orphans.htm.

Banks, R. Richard. "The Color of Desire: Fulfilling Adoptive Parents' Racial Preferences through Discriminatory State Action." *Yale Law Journal* 107 (1998): 875-964. Print.

Bartholet, Elizabeth. *Family Bonds: Adoption, Infertility, and the New World of Child Production*. Boston: Beacon Press, 1999. Print.

Bartholet, Elizabeth. "Where Do Black Children Belong? The Politics of Race Matching in Adoption." *University of Pennsylvania Law Review* 139 (1991): 1163-1256. Print.

Briggs, Laura. "Feminism and Transnational Adoption: Poverty, Precarity, and the Politics of Raising (Other People's?) Children." *Feminist Theory* 13.1 (2012): 81-100. Print.

Brodkin Sacks, Karen. "How Jews Became White." *The Social Construction of Difference and Inequality: Race, Class, Gender, and Sexuality*. Ed. Tracey E. Ore. Mountain View, CA: Mayfield Publishing Company. 2003. Print.

Brooks, Devon, Sigrid James, and Richard P. Barth. "Preferred Characteristics of Children in Need of Adoption: Is There a Demand for Available Foster Children." *The Social Service Review* 76.4 (2002): 575-602. Print.

Broonzy, B. B. "Black, Brown, and White." 1951. Web.

Brush, L. D. "Worthy Widows, Welfare Cheats: Proper Womanhood in Expert Needs Talk about Single Mothers in the United States, 1900 to 1988." *Gender and Society* 11 (6) (1997): 720-746.

Coltrane, Scott. *Gender and Families: The Gender Lens*. Thousand Oaks, CA: Pine Forge Press, 1998.

Day, Dawn. *The Adoption of Black Children: Counteracting Institutional Discrimination*. Lexington: MA: Lexington Books, 1979. Print.

Donovan, Patricia. "When Plans Opt Out: Family Planning Access In Medicaid Managed Care." The Guttmacher Report on Public Policy, 1998. Print.

Farrington, Keith and Ely Chertok. "Social Conflict Theories of the Family." *Sourcebook of Family Theories and Methods: A Contextual Approach*. Eds. Boss, Pauline G., William J. Doherty, Ralph LaRossa, Walter R. Schumm, Suzanne K. Steinmetz. New York: Plenum Press, 1993. 357-384. Print.

Gailey, Christine Ward. *Blue-Ribbon Babies and Labors of Love: Race, Class, and Gender in U.S. Adoption Practice*. Austin, TX: University of Texas Press, 2010. Print.

Gans, Herbert J. "The Possibility of a New Racial Hierarchy in the Twenty-First Century United States." *The Cultural Territories of Race: Black and White Boundaries*. Ed. Michele Lamont. Chicago: The University of Chicago, 1999. 371-390. Print.

International Adoption Stories. *Adoption Africa*, 2006. Web. July 12, 2012.

Kinder, Noel and Rebecca Toni Hjelm. "International Adoption: Trends and Issues." *Child Welfare League of America*, 2007. 1-2. Print.

Lewin, Tamar. "New Families Redraw Racial Boundaries." *New York Times* 27 October 1998: A1. Print.

Maldonado, Solangel. "Discouraging Racial Preferences in Adoptions." *UC Davis Law Review* 39 (2006): 1415-1480. Print.

Omi, Michael, and Howard Winant. "Racial Formations." *Race, Class, and Gender in the United States: An Integrated Study*. Ed. Paula S. Rothenberg. 6th Ed. New York: Worth Publishers, 2003. 12-21. Print.

Patton, Sandra. *Birthmarks: Transracial Adoption in Contemporary America*. New York: New York University Press, 2000.

Roberts, Dorothy. *Killing the Black Body: Race, Reproduction and the Meaning of Liberty*. New York: Panthenon, 1997. Print.

Schaefer, Richard T. *Sociology*. 11th Ed. New York: McGraw-Hill, 2008. Print.

Simon, Rita J., and Howard Altstein. *Adoption Across Borders: Serving the Children in Transracial and Intercountry Adoptions*. Lanham: Rowman and Littlefield Publishers, Inc., 2000. Print.

Solinger, Rickie. *Beggars and Choosers: How the Politics of Choice Shapes Adoption, Abortion, and Welfare in the United States*. New York: Hilt and Wang: A Division of Farrar, Straus, and Giroux, 2001. Print.

Stolley, Kathy S. "Statistics on Adoption in the United States." *The Future of Children: Adoption* 3.1 (1993): 26 - 41.

Strong, Bryan, Christine DeVault, Barbara W. Sayad, and Theodore F. Cohen. *The Marriage and Family Experience: Intimate Relationships in a Changing Society*. 8th Ed. Belmont, CA: Wadsworth/Thomson Learning, 2001.

Twine, France Winddance. "Transgressive Women and Transracial

Mothers White Women and Critical Race Theory." *Meridians* 1.2 (2001): 130-153. Print.

Waldinger, Roger. "When the Melting Pot Boils Over: The Irish, Jews, Blacks, and Koreans of New York." *Rethinking the Color Line: Readings in Race and Ethnicity.* Ed. Charles A. Gallagher. Mountain View: Mayfield Publishing Company. 1999. 287-299. Print.

Waldman, S. and L. Caplan. "The Politics of Adoption." *Newsweek* 21 March 1994: 64-65.

Wynter, Leon E. *American Skin: Pop Culture, Big Business, and the End of White America.* New York: Crown Publishing Group, 2002. Print.

Zhang, Yuanting and Gary R. Lee. "Intercountry Versus Transracial Adoption: Analysis of Adoptive Parents' Motivations and Preferences in Adoption." *Journal of Family Issues* 32.1 (2011): 75-98. Print.

11.

Knowing You Made a Difference

Mothering Adopted Children with Hidden Disabilities

ALICE HOME

ADOPTION HAS BECOME INCREASINGLY COMPLEX in recent years because of the growing diversity of children awaiting permanent homes. Greater numbers of children have a range of special needs that can act as a barrier to placement and affect adoption outcomes (Tan, Marfo and Dedrick). These children have conditions or histories that make them difficult to parent, which can increase the risk of the adoption being disrupted prior to legalization or dissolved thereafter (Forbes and Dziegielewski). While most families avoid adoption breakdown, many parents feel "all alone in the Twilight Zone" in their struggle with high stress, unusual family demands and strained relationships (Smith and Howard). Given these challenges, it is surprising that most research deals only with parental impact on children or factors that affect adoption outcomes. The few studies that seek the parents' perspectives rarely examine the specific experience of adoptive mothers as such, even though they are the ones that predominantly participate in research (Forbes and Dziegielewski). These women's voices are rarely heard and their experience is virtually absent from representations of motherhood. Seen as doubly deviant from the "good Mum" stereotype, these adoptive mothers are often portrayed as either "weird" or as saints (Audet and Home).

Adoptions are classified as "special needs" mainly when children have certain bio-behavioural conditions and/or a past history of multiple placements, abuse or neglect (Wind, Brooks and Barth). This paper focuses on the adoptive mothering of children with a hidden disability, Attention Deficit Hyperactivity Disorder (ADHD), which affects a disproportionate number of adoptees (Simmel et al.). ADHD gives rise to developmentally inappropriate levels of hyperactive/impulsive behaviour and/or inattention, impairing social functioning and learning across settings (Segal; Barkley et al.). As over two-thirds of those affected have another disability, mothering these children can be complex. In addition, the absence of early visible signs in disabilities such as ADHD and Autism Spectrum Disorder delays diagnosis and leads to scrutiny and judgment from the public. The failure of these apparently normal children to meet societal expectations is often interpreted as willful disobedience that is the result of poor mothering (Segal).

Existing literature on raising children with disabilities tends to focus on the negative aspects of this parenting experience with little consideration of mothers' other roles. Conversely, this paper presents the views of adoptive mothers on the rewards and challenges of raising children with ADHD and related disabilities. It does so by using data drawn from a Canadian study of employed mothers caring for children aged 6-17 with this disorder.[1] The literature review includes material on general parenting of children with hidden disabilities because relevant adoption research is scarce. After a summary of the methodology, the key findings are presented and discussed in relation to social work literature and societal myths about mothers raising adopted children with these special needs.

BACKGROUND LITERATURE

There is surprisingly little social work literature on adoptive parenting when children have special needs, despite a substantial increase in this type of adoption (Cumming-Speirs et al.). Special needs children have a condition (medical, disability), history (abuse/neglect, prior moves) and/ or circumstances (older, minority or sibling group) that can complicate adoption placement (Babbs and Lewis). Special needs related to disability can be physical, intellectual, developmental or emotional. The latter can include behavioural and mental health disorders. Existing studies of parents who have adopted special needs children examine the parenting experience, as well as preparation or post-adoption support. This research is often confusing because of varying or incomplete information on methodology, the type of special needs, sample size, child age at placement, and the severity of disability. Although 80 to 98 percent of special needs "parent" samples are comprised of women, many of whom have adopted their children, very few studies specifically look at adoptive mothers. No known study was found that compares adoptive and biological mothers of children with disabilities.

Despite these limitations, some themes about mothering adopted children with special needs did emerge from the preceding body of research. Many adoptive mothers question their competency and feel unprepared for the difficulties confronting them (Forbes and Dziegielewski; Ashbury, Cross and Waggenspack). One reason may be that behavioural and emotional disabilities that emerge after placement can be quite different from the special needs for which many parents had been prepared (Audet and Home). These hidden disorders can impair children as much as a visible disability and no amount of good parenting will *cure* them (Babbs and Lewis). Research also shows the presence of emotional, developmental and behavioural disabilities is accompanied by increased parental stress, a reduced sense of competence and strained parent-child relationships (Eanes and Fletcher). One reason for this may be that aggressive or defiant child behaviour has an immense impact on parents because it subjects them and their children to frequent criticism and alienation from others, including teachers and peers (Podolski and Nigg; Avery). This helps to explain why one study found mothers of children with ADHD felt less competent and received less family and community support than those caring for children with a hidden physical condition (Cronin).

Knowing what to expect can equip parents to make informed, realistic decisions about whether adopting a child with these special needs is right for them (Foti-Gervais). However, social workers may lack specific information or hesitate to share it, while parents can have difficulty understanding the implications prior to placement (Cohen, Coyne and Duvall). Agencies prioritize permanency planning by finding appropriate families, promoting attachment and preventing disruption in the immediate post-placement period (Festinger). Once adoptions have been finalized, support for these families is much more restricted. While this is partly an effort to contain costs (CWLA; Smith and Howard), it also reflects the myth that "once the child is placed…(s/he) magically becomes a different person … and the family does not need any kind of support" (Cohen and Westhues 108).

Families who have adopted special needs children report both growing needs and decreased satisfaction several years after placement (McDonald, Propp and Murphy), yet parents are expected to manage "on their own" unless adoption dissolution looms (Foti-Gervais; CWLA). This abrupt loss of support has been likened to "having your medicine taken away overnight" (Festinger 529). Relationships can become so strained that adoptive parents end up "running on empty" with little energy left for other aspects of their lives (Smith and Howard 64). However, adoptive mothers can hesitate to seek help, as they feel they "should" be able to cope or else fear they will be blamed for bonding issues (Ward-Gailey; Cohen and Westhues; Audet and Home). As society makes women responsible for the family's mental health, adoptive mothers may eventually search for support groups, counselling, adapted in-home child care or respite, but they find limited and fragmented services (Smith and Howard).

As society makes few provisions for children who cannot progress to autonomy at the expected pace, the lack of services limits most families living with child disability (Green). Support that is barely sufficient for average families does not begin to meet the needs of families dealing with special needs children (Greenspan). This affects mothers most, as they are expected to adjust their work lives so that their maternal role can be mobilized at any time needed (Shearn and Todd).

Despite the many challenges, research suggests adoptive parents remain strongly committed to their children with special needs and find satisfaction in their role. Biological, foster and adoptive parents of children with varied disabilities report similar types of rewards, which include the enjoyment of children's special qualities, pleasure in their children's progress despite disability and the reward of learning, especially on the part of the mother (Audet and Home; Segal; Brown). The research on which this paper is based examines both the rewards and challenges of mothering adopted children with hidden disabilities. The following section explains how the research was conducted and describes the characteristics of adoptive mothers who participated.

RESEARCH METHODOLOGY
AND CHARACTERISTICS OF PARTICIPANTS

This bilingual research was carried out in collaboration with a national self-help organization for parents and professionals dealing with ADHD. It featured a qualitative study of 40 mothers in the Ottawa area and a national survey of 197 women. After ethics approval, recruitment for both studies was carried out via self-help networks for parents of children with ADHD or related disabilities. Associations for adoptive parents also publicized the research and pamphlets were distributed to community centres, social agencies, libraries, clinics and relevant professionals in Eastern Ontario. All publicity outlined research goals, procedures, participant rights and how to obtain further information or arrange participation. Semi-structured interviews were used in the qualitative study to allow depth while providing focus for any mothers with attention issues. The pre-tested interview guide covered job and family situations, rewards and challenges of mothering these children while employed, as well as supports used or needed. Content analysis of the full sample revealed key themes, while repeated reading of interviews with five adoptive mothers uncovered similarities and differences with other participants. This paper is based on those interview data and quotes from responses of the 18 adoptive survey respondents (S1, S2...) to open questions on main rewards and challenges. Like other survey participants, most adoptive mothers lived in two-parent families and the majority of their children with ADHD had additional disabilities.

The five mothers who were interviewed are typical of adoptive parents in that they were aged 35 to 55, had completed college or university and had above-average family incomes. Four worked as professionals, the fifth was self-employed. The four in two-parent families were employed 28 to 34 hours weekly, while the single mother held a full-time paid job. Three cared for two children, one for three and one for a single child. Together, these women were caring for seven children with ADHD, six of whom had added disorders. Three were mothering children with disabilities only, while two also had a child who was developing "normally." Adoptive family situations were quite diverse. One was also caring for a child born to her, one was a single parent who had adopted internationally and a third had children from three different birth families. Two mothers had adopted sibling groups, one after fostering an older sibling from infancy. Children were placed as newborns with four mothers, while the fifth adopted a two-year-old. It is striking that only one mother was warned of any potential disability risk prior to placement, while the others discovered their children's disabilities several years later. Mothers began to suspect disability when children's uncontrollable behaviour, excessive energy or severe sleep problems could not be managed by usual parenting methods. Several received a diagnosis only after the child was in first grade. None had received specific information or a detailed family history that might have prepared them for the difficulties they now faced. One finally discovered a strong birth family history of ADHD after she found the adoptive parents of her child's biological sibling.

REWARDS AND CHALLENGES OF MOTHERING
ADOPTED CHILDREN WITH HIDDEN DISABILITIES

This section presents the rewards and challenges reported by adoptive mothers who participated in the survey or in an interview. Adoptive mothers reported the same three main types of rewards as biological mothers but experienced them in subtly different ways. Children's unusual qualities were mentioned most often. The latter included having boundless energy: "he climbed the Eiffel Tower, counted all the steps, 1000 or whatever. The others were kind of dragging their legs ... but he was running along happy as a clam, just not tired and great fun. So his energy is a plus. It can drive you nuts but it is a plus" (E13). These children are resourceful, enthusiastic, very funny and entertaining. When visitors come: "he does the entire acting schtick of playing the piano, doing his gymnastics and telling every joke he has ever known, which is very annoying though pretty funny" (E13). These bright, creative children can also be unusually perceptive, viewing the world in a totally unique way that their adoptive mothers find refreshing: "my child comes out with comments that are so insightful and accurate that others may only think but not say" (S172).

The second reward noted by these adoptive mothers was their child's progress or success despite the disabilities. Mothers are proud of small gains that show all their hard work is finally paying off. They rejoice in "finally having a conversation that feels 'normal' for a mom and a 13-year-old" (S 193) or getting good feedback when they usually receive complaints. One mother, whose child had often been expelled from community activities in the past, worried when she saw her son's ski instructor talking to her husband:

> "Oh no—is Leslie going to be thrown out of the class?" Then I noticed my husband was smiling. He came inside and said "he is doing just fantastically, so much progress since the first time" and I thought "WOW, my kid!" Most parents would not raise the flag over this but I did. So when they do something they couldn't do that other people's kids do easily, and your kid is just hanging in there being like a regular teenager, it's great. (E1)

A few women reported learning or personal growth from having to be resourceful in the face of unexpected disabilities. This type of reward took on special meaning for adoptive mothers: "you can see some potential there and you feel that you may have made a difference in their lives ... I chose to adopt a family group, so the sentiment is more intense – though it doesn't come very often" (E1). Even if some adoptive mothers wondered whether these rewards were worth the difficulties, others reflected: "I very much wanted to experience motherhood... these kids are far more challenging than your average kid but I have enjoyed being a parent" (E14). Another pointed out that mothering her two adopted daughters without special needs prepared her for the challenge of raising her son with ADHD. She concluded:

> Kids of all types are great ... I adore this kid no matter what ... you just do it. I haven't felt driven to say, "I wish we had never adopted you" but I HAVE kicked the wall saying, "what caused you to be like this?" He is my third child and you get better as

you go ... if this had been my first child at 25 I would have been a nut case. (E13)

Like other research respondents, adoptive mothers found rewards hard to identify because of the many challenges they faced. Difficult behaviour was mentioned twice as often as any other category. This was sometimes merely annoying silliness more appropriate for someone half the child's age. However, it often involved picking up the pieces after a child's ADHD led to acting before thinking: "her impulsivity and inability to think things through causes problems, inconveniences, messes, minor catastrophes, creating continual chaos—and a huge amount of effort is needed to keep boundaries and structures in place to minimize it" (S117). These children make constant demands without sensing that the request or timing is inappropriate. However, oppositional behaviour was what mothers found most disruptive, as "power struggles erupt over absolutely everything. We cannot even get him to choir practice without half an hour of shrieking" (E13). Along with this comes provocation and insensitivity to the effects of their actions on others:

> We don't want to argue but she starts arguments. She says "I want to give my brother a hug before I get my teeth done," which all sounds very nice but he doesn't want anything to do with her at that time of the morning. He just puts his hands up and says "No thanks," yet she keeps on coming. And coming, and coming and coming. And so what's going to happen next? Pow! And so I have to cope with this big thing.... She doesn't read anybody. She doesn't read gestures. She's always in forward mode. (E11)

Not surprisingly, all this makes for a tense family climate. The daily wear and tear of hyperactivity means these children "move too quickly—often spilling, dropping or breaking things" (S14) and are "...always pushing to go somewhere, do something with a strong sense of urgency, upsetting the whole house" (S155). As emotional maturity develops more slowly in children with ADHD, their activities must be structured for years longer than expected:

> At six, my son was able to do some things on his own and enjoy them. Never this whole questioning all the time ... but for her, I have to make sure the event she is going to is okay. I don't want her to stay at a friend's for more than an hour because I know she gets arguing. Like I have to be always thinking ahead for

her and I find it's not parenting at all. It's like running the army. You know, this is Private So and So and I'm the Sergeant, and I have to be in charge of Private all the time so she doesn't get into trouble. (E14)

Adoptive mothers find they have to change the way they parent these children because they "don't respond to the ordinary parental things. You have to be more forceful. You have to be more persistent. He is very stubborn, he is highly demanding and he doesn't give back much" (E14). Adapting to the adopted child's special needs can lead to resentment from siblings who do not have special needs: "I parent him quite differently from the way I parented them ... you cannot do it the same way. They think he is a spoiled brat. They will say 'Why don't you punish him? You should put him in his room for two hours!' but it is not going to work.... They think they were given a much more raw deal" (E13).

Two situations make mothering children with these disabilities especially difficult. Being a single parent is tiring for anyone, but solo-mothering a demanding child who "sucks energy out of you" can be overwhelming. It means "you've got to have respite but it is just not available ... they will not take difficult kids so I have nowhere to send my son overnight.... You are on 24/7. There is never a break" (E14). While single adoptive mothers need someone who can take over occasionally, having two strongly involved parents is critical when several children have behaviour problems. A mother whose adopted sibling group had complex behaviour problems noted that one parent must always be on guard to mediate conflict and prevent dangerous actions like "jumping off the second floor of the house, climbing trees way to the top and climbing out onto hydro poles from the trees" (E28). In another family whose two adopted children required similar high levels of vigilance, the mother stated: "the kids take over your life and ADHD takes over your family" (E1). Even mothers who know prior to placement that the child may have special needs can experience the grief of losing their "normal" child once the disability becomes obvious. Despite knowing the risks of adopting a child who may have behavioural challenges, mothers can be disappointed that family life is not as expected: "Home is supposed to be a place where you unwind, where you're supposed to feel safe.... Other families are at home relaxing, talking with their kids and doing things together.... Our home is not that way" (E28).

Challenges from these disabilities extend beyond the family into the community. Even if schools know children's special needs, they often lack the understanding and resources to educate them differently. Mothers are expected to intervene immediately when something "inappropriate" happens, such as arguing with teachers or overreacting to peers. After school, homework is a battleground because ADHD makes it difficult for these children to remember or concentrate on their homework, and they resist needed help. Uninformed teachers interpret lost books or forgotten or incomplete assignments as poor motivation or inadequate supervision at home. In the community, mothers often face negative attitudes regarding their children and their parenting, which can be more devastating for adoptive mothers who may be subjected to scrutiny prior to legalization. They can end up walking a tightrope between advocating for the child's rights and encouraging him or her to change:

> You have to go through such a huge performance giving everyone the heads up beforehand. Then if things still go wrong, and they often do, you have to be prepared to go in there and try to advocate, while also letting your kid know that what he was doing was clearly not appropriate and he needs to face the consequences. You also have to help him avoid feeling like a failure, as he is constantly getting thrown out of programs by people who don't understand his disability. (E1)

There is also peer exclusion as children with these behavioural and social disabilities don't fit in. They rarely have close friends or anyone to play with and don't get invited to birthday parties. Neighbours often exclude the whole family from get-togethers and parents "get dirty looks and rude comments from strangers because of his behaviour" (E28). Raising very difficult children in a community that doesn't understand can be the hardest part, according to one mother who had adopted a family group: "Colleagues say 'What are you complaining about? When my kid was that age he was difficult too'. I understand why they don't get it but I feel like saying 'Give me a break - just getting through the day is hard enough'" (E1). This is why adoptive mothers who have strong informal support feel fortunate, such as one whose "very supportive community of friends all accept him and see what is good about him" (E13). Another, whose family had difficulty accepting her children's disabilities, finally felt understood when a relative whose grandson had ADHD said: "I know you're raising them the way you have to and not the way you want to" (E1).

Another reason such support is essential is that timely access to formal services is very limited for any mother whose child has hidden disabilities. Most participants in the survey had difficulty getting their children assessed and treated in the public system and many lacked benefits to cover private services. Adoptive mothers have the added difficulty that professionals can be insensitive to adoption or disability issues, as neither of these subjects receives much attention during professional education. Many adoptive mothers need help with both issues yet are unable to find knowledgeable professionals. Obtaining respite is a survival issue for both biological and adoptive mothers who are single and those with two or more children with behaviour disorders. However, competent sitters are scarce and relatives are rarely able or willing to help: "I have been unable to find anything and trust me, I've looked. Every informal arrangement I set up in the past has fallen apart because of my son's behaviour – people just don't want him" (S46). Adoptive mothers who turn to child welfare agencies feel particularly let down when they are denied help: "After having made us promises for support before the adoption, we were left stranded after it was finalized. 'He's yours now – good luck!'" (S177). Even when they express concern about child protection, it is not always enough to get action: "You say 'Please help me—I don't know—I might hit my kid'. They are supposed to respond to that, okay? That's their mandate. They didn't. They didn't" (E14). Adoptive mothers were unequivocal that "these kids and families don't deserve to be dumped ... agencies should offer respite to families struggling with challenging children adopted through them" (S14).

In an effort to reduce stress, gain flexibility or be available for emergencies, mothers diverted time and energy from their careers. They made the "choice" to switch jobs, cut hours or work at home, sometimes because no after-school programs were available for adolescents who are unable to stay home alone safely. Some mothers stayed in unsatisfying jobs, turned down promotions or new positions to avoid upsetting the balance at home. Only a few seemed aware of the sacrifices they had made: "My career is definitely on the line, with a huge promotion and financial benefits impossible as a result of my son" (S104). Mothers in less privileged situations may not have the choice of reducing work commitments, unless they have access to rare adoption subsidies. These mothers simply do not have the same options as adoptive mothers whose children do not need expensive professional or special services or unusual parental time investment. Increasing access to subsidies would make it possible for potential adoptive mothers to consider a special needs placement.

Several mothers noted that the fact their children were adopted made dealing with these disabilities more complicated. The lack of medical and birth history meant they had "no connections to help us with the road map" (E13), which made an accurate diagnosis more elusive, further

172

delaying access to appropriate treatment. Furthermore, several mothers were told they were overprotective and had unrealistic expectations precisely *because* they had adopted. To some extent, learning to reduce their expectations can be helpful, according to one mother: "this is not a kid that can swim on his own. He is always going to need support...I have learnt to make fewer demands and to appreciate what is good" (E13). However, they felt they were no different from any other parent who discovers belatedly that her child has disabilities. According to these adoptive mothers, typical adoption issues and concerns did not come up much, perhaps because concerns over disability issues are so overwhelming on their own. These mothers nevertheless craved contact with others in similar situations, participating in support groups for adoptive parents or in ADHD self-help groups. While both of these resources provided support, neither met their dual needs as adoptive mothers of children with this disorder.

None felt that adoption preparation was complete or specific enough to equip them to manage. Some even questioned whether the child might have done better with more experienced parents or in a different family setting: "perhaps a farm family where he could run around more...I may have tried to fit a square peg into a round hole" (E13). Finally, these mothers sometimes felt guilty "even though we probably feel it less than if our kids had inherited their disorders from us." This mother dealt with it by "trying to imagine how their young, single birth mother would have coped with so few resources. That's when I think we have made a difference" (E1).

DISCUSSION AND CONCLUSIONS

These findings suggest that in many ways, adoptive mothers share similar rewards and challenges with other women caring for children with hidden disabilities. Celebrating the child's qualities and progress, resisting comparisons with peers and feeling confident about raising him or her differently seem key to satisfaction. It is easy to lose sight of rewards and feel incompetent, however, when behaviour problems shade all aspects of family life and severely impinge on mothers' time, energy and options (Fox, Vaughn and Dunlap). As society takes such sacrifices for granted while failing to understand this difficult mothering role, these women are blamed for their children's problems and must constantly fight for resources. This research also revealed some unique features of mothering adopted children with these disabilities. The advantage of feeling less guilt for disorders that are mainly genetic can be offset by greater difficulty identifying disabilities without family medical history. Raising a special needs child can bring special satisfaction when an informed choice is made, but only one mother was aware of disability risk prior to placement. As pointed out by Smith and Howard, there is a huge difference between choosing to adopt a child with a known disorder and discovering "years later that the 'normal' child adopted is in fact limited by significant disabilities" (202). In some ways, these adoptive mothers face similar experiences to biological mothers whose children unexpectedly develop signs of an unknown inherited disability.

This mismatch between adoptive mothers' expectations and children's intense needs is compounded by some persistent societal myths. The public still holds all mothers responsible for the mental health of their children and may attribute any problems to a "bad seed" or question why a stable home does not "cure" them (Ward-Gailey). Professional assumptions can impede acceptance of a disability and delay dealing with it effectively (CWLA). Adoptive mothers in this study put off seeking help through fear of being labeled incompetent and they approached the agency only when it was clear they could not meet a child's special needs without added support. As reported in other studies, agencies failed to recognize the seriousness of the situation and were reluctant to help (Forbes and Dziegielewski). Feeling abandoned by the supports they had counted on, these mothers had to fight to get the counselling, support groups and respite needed to keep their families intact. These same frustrations were reported more often than any other parental need in another study of special needs adoptions, which found children were seen as having a more positive family impact when these frustrations were absent (Reilly and Platz).

These adoptive mothers were highly motivated to keep their families intact and help their children thrive despite disability. Maintaining that commitment involves providing adoptive mothers with adequate pre-placement information and preparation for predictable adjustment issues (Foti-Gervais). Agencies also have to be there over the long haul to respond to unexpected needs as they arise with counselling, in-home services and subsidies (Wind, Brooks and Barth). However, this formal support is not enough. Even mothers who have not chosen to adopt a child with hidden disabilities rise to the unexpected challenges and do what needs to be done (Ward-Gailey). They should receive acceptance, understanding and support instead of criticism from extended families, neighbours, professionals and the broader community (Brown). These adoptive mothers are committed to making a difference in a child's life. They deserve to be recognized for their contribution.

[1]The author wishes to thank CHADD, Canada (Children and Adults with Attention Deficit Disorders) for collaborating in this research, in particular, Greg Trepanier and Joel Kanisberg as advisory committee. The financial support of Social Sciences and Humanities Research Council of Canada is gratefully acknowledged.

WORKS CITED

Asbury, E., D. Cross, and B. Waggenspack. "Biological, Adoptive and Mixed Families: Special Needs and the Impact of the International Adoption." *Adoption Quarterly* 7.1 (2003): 53-72. Print.

Audet, M. and A. Home. "Adopting Special Needs Children: Parents' Perception of their Role Quality and Social Support." *Child Welfare: Connecting Research, Policy and Practice*. Eds. K. Kufeldt, K and B. McKenzie. Waterloo, ON: Wilfrid Laurier Press, 2003. 157-166. Print.

Avery, C. *Well Being of Parents Raising Children with Learning and Behaviour Disorders*. Diss. University of Delaware, 2000. Print.

Babbs, L. and R. Lewis. *Adopting and Advocating for the Special Needs Child*. Westport, CO: Bergin & Garvey, 1997. Print.

Barkley, R., G. Edwards, M. Haneil, K. Fletcher and L. Metevia. "The Efficacy of Problem-Solving Communication Training Alone, Behaviour Management Training Alone, and Their Combination for Parent-Adolescent Conflict in Teenagers with ADHD and ODD." *Journal of Consulting and Clinical Psychology* 69.6 (2001): 926-941. Print.

Brown, J. "Rewards of Fostering Children with Disabilities." *Journal of Family Social Work* 11.1 (2008): 36-49. Print.

Child Welfare League of America. *Standards of Excellence for Adoption Services*. Washington, DC, 2000.

Cohen, J., and A. Westhues. *Well-Functioning Families for Adoptive and Foster Children*. Toronto: University of Toronto Press, 1990. Print.

Cohen, N., J. Coyne and J. Duvall. *Characteristics of Post-Adoptive Families Presenting for Mental Health Service (Final Report)*. Newmarket, Ontario: Children's Aid Society of York Region, 1994.

Cronin, A. "Mothering a Child with Hidden Impairments." *The American Journal of Occupational Therapy* 58.1 (2004): 83-92. Print.

Cumming-Speirs, C., S. Duder, J. Grove, and R. Sullivan. "Adoptable But Still in Limbo: The Forgotten Children in Canada." *Child & Youth Case Forum* 32.2 (2003): 75-87. Print.

Eanes, A. and A. Fletcher. "Factors Associated with Perceived Parental Competence Among Special Needs Adoptive Mothers." *Families in Society* 87.2 (2006): 249-258. Print.

Festinger, T. "After Adoption: Dissolution or Permanence?" *Child Welfare League of America* 8.3 (2002): 515-533. Print.

Forbes, H. and S. Dziegielewski. "Issues Facing Adoptive Mothers of Children with Special Needs." *Journal of Social Work* 3.3 (2003): 301-320. Print.

Foti-Gervais, L. *Adopting Children with Developmental Disabilities: A Qualitative Approach to Understanding Adoptive Parents' Experiences.* Diss. University of Alberta, Edmonton, 2005. Print.

Fox, L., H. Vaughn, and G. Dunlap. "We Can't Expect Other People to Understand: Family Perspectives on Problem Behaviour." *Exceptional Children* 68.4 (2002): 437-450. Print.

Green, S. "We're Tired, Not Sad: Benefits and Burdens of Mothering a Child with a Disability." *Social Science & Medicine* 64 (2007): 150-163. Print.

Greenspan. "Exceptional Mothering in a 'Normal' World." *Mothering Against the Odds.* Eds. C. Garcia Coll, J. Surrey and K. Weingarten. New York Guilford, 1998. 37-60. Print.

Johnson, H., D. Cournoyer, G. Fisher, B. McQuillan, S. Moriarty, A. Richert, E. Stanek, C. Stockford, and B. Yirigian. "Children's Emotional and Behavioral Disorders: Attributions of Parental Responsibility by Professionals." *American Journal of Orthopsychiatry* 70.3 (2000): 327-339. Print.

McDonald, T., J. Propp, and K. Murphy. "The Post Adoption Experience: Child, Parent, and Family Predictors of Family Adjustment to Adoption." *Child Welfare* 80.1 (2001): 71-94. Print.

Podolski, L. and J. Nigg. "Parent Stress and Coping in Relation to Child ADHD Severity and Associated Child Disruptive Behavior Problems." *Journal of Clinical Child Psychology* 30.4 (2001): 503-513. Print.

Reilly, T. and L. Platz. "Post-Adoption Service Needs of Families with special Needs Children: Use, Helpfulness and Unmet Needs." *Journal of Social Service Research* 30.4 (2004): 51-67. Print.

Segal, E. "Learned Mothering: Raising a Child with ADHD." *Child and Adolescent Social Work Journal* 18.4 (2001): 263-279.

Shearn, J. and S. Todd. "Maternal Employment and Family Responsibilities: The Perspective of Mothers of Children with Intellectual Disabilities." *Journal of Applied Research in Intellectual Disabilities* 13 (2000): 109-131. Print.

Simmel, C., D. Brooks, R. Barth and S. Hinshaw. "Externalizing Symptomatology Among Adoptive Youth: Prevalence and Pre-adoption Risk Factors." *Journal of Abnormal Child Psychology* 29.1 (2001): 57-69. Print.

Smith, S. and J. Howard. *Promoting Successful Adoptions*. Thousand Oaks: Sage, 1999. Print.

Smith, B., J. Surrey and M. Watkins. "'Real Mothers': Adoptive Mothers Resisting Marginalization and Re-creating Motherhood." *Mothering Against the Odds*. Eds. C. Garcia Coll, J. Surrey, and K. Weingarten. New York: Guilford, 1998. 194-214. Print.

Tan, T., K. Marfo, and R. Dedrick. "Special Needs Adoption from China: Exploring Child-Level Indicators, Adoptive Family Characteristics and Correlates of Behavioural Adjustment." *Children and Youth Services Review* 29 (2007): 1269-1285. Print.

Ward-Gailey, C. "Ideologies of Motherhood and Kinship in U.S. Adoption." *Ideologies and Technologies of Motherhood*. Eds. H. Ragoné and F. Winddance Twin. London: Routledge, 2000. 11-55. Print.

Wind, L., D. Brooks, and R. Barth. "Adoption Preparation: Differences Between Adoptive Families of Children With and Without Special Needs." *Adoption Quarterly* 8.4 (2005): 45-74. Print.

12.
Lesbian Adoption

Transcending the Boundaries of Motherhood

APRIL SHARKEY

L ESBIAN FAMILIES, in all of their manifestations, have grown in numbers and visibility in the past three decades. In Toronto, and in every major city in Canada and the United States, annual pride celebrations include a spectrum of lesbian family formations. While diverse family forms have always existed historically, new possibilities for Canadian lesbian families emerged in the 1990s, when the combination of greater access to reproductive science and later the passing of Bill C-38 (2005) offered new choices when building families.[1] With increased medical access to New Reproductive Technologies (NRTs) and marital rights, it is true that Canadian lesbians are better able to create families more freely and openly. Still, in spite of these advances, lesbian couples have different obstacles to navigate in the creation of family because, as lesbians, they are unlike heterosexuals who can rely more simply and often on biological ties as a basis for establishing socially and legally recognizable family. Even in the case of NRTs, for example, a man in a heterosexual partnership that uses donor sperm has automatic rights to the child, whereas a lesbian couple that uses donor sperm to become pregnant must still negotiate the legal system in order for the non-biological mother to gain rights. So, while lesbians in Canada can marry, they must still depend upon the legal system to establish their co-parent-to-child connections, responsibilities, and rights. Lesbians remain distinct from heterosexuals to the extent that the use of formal and/or informal ties of adoption must be assumed from the outset of family planning. While one lesbian mother may give birth to a child with the use of NRTs, her partner must choose to become a formal or informal adoptive mother of the child. The fact that lesbian couples must always traverse some constellation of family ties that includes in/formal adoption is twofold in effect: on the one hand, it continues to marginalize lesbian couples even as they have acquired new same-sex rights with respect to both marriage and adoption in Canada; and, on the other, it ensures that lesbian families continue to be transgressive as a site that contests the heteronormative family model.

This essay examines the critical implications of the novel ways in which lesbians, particularly lesbian couples, use adoption to form their families either to supplement the biological tie or in place of it altogether. It argues that the construction of lesbian families directly challenges and transforms traditional, patriarchal constructs of the meaning and makeup of family. It explores how lesbian mothers' in/formal adoption practices provide us with a unique opportunity to challenge heteronormative family models that many lesbians reject even as they have acquired many new same-sex rights.

While lesbian mothers do enjoy new and increasing same-sex rights in the heteronormative Canadian context, their families continue to be situated in the margins. The result is that their families can also be understood as sites of transgression. *Lesbian* mothers problematize hetero-dominant constructs of family. They do so because the limits of the same-sex couple's reproductive biology means parental rights and relationships can never be secured initially or solely on the basis of biological ties that are mutually shared with the child. In the absence of any hetero-reproductive malfunction, therefore, a mutual biological bond with the child is the heterosexual couple's prerogative, and not that of the lesbian couple. What this means ultimately is that, whether or not they enjoy same-sex rights, and whether or not they want to reinvent the family, both would-be and active lesbian mothers must and will continue to create new models of family, because their adoptive and/or bio-adoptive family ties are already in question and contrary to the mainstream.

There are a number of adoption practices in which lesbian mothers can and do engage as couples, which enlists them in the reinvention of the family. These practices can involve mutually formal adoptive ties on the part of both mothers, the use of a sperm donor and/or NRTs by one mother and in/formal adoption by the other, the use of one mother's contribution of an egg to the other who becomes the birthmother, and/ or the mutual use of a sperm donor and/or NRTs and in/formal adoption by both mothers. Before I explore these practices, however, I would like to note that this paper focuses, specifically, on the adoption practices of lesbian *couples*. Apart from the demands of space that curtail a broader discussion, the main reason is that with the advent of same-sex marriage and adoption rights in Canada, lesbian co-mothers represent a perceived threat from the perspective of the queer left: with same-sex rights in hand, lesbian couples and their families are thought to capitulate to heteronormativity because they are more easily subsumed and/or integrated into heteronormative society than, for instance, other queer families. The reason I focus on lesbian couples who mother, therefore, is that I want to explore how these mothers' adoption practices, when coupled with their sexual identities, continue to place their families in opposition to heteronormativity, even as their newly acquired rights have been read to imply this is not the case.

In this paper, I argue that lesbian couples that mother are and remain transgressive because of their adoptive mothering practices. To put it another way, adoption can be understood to both queer lesbian couples' families and, thereby, challenge the heteronormative family model, even as lesbian couples have experienced an increase in same-sex rights. As I will show, this is because the heteronormative family model is also a bio-normative model, one that inherently marginalizes families that found themselves on the basis of adoption. Finally, I will show how the marginality associated with adoption intersects with the marginality of lesbianism in such a way that it also continues to render transgressive and queer the mothering practices in which lesbian couples engage to form their families.

Adoption, as a social institution, can pertain to any number of non-biological parent-child relationships that are either formal or informal (i.e. ranging from legal adoption, step-ties, to informal ties between a common law parent and child). Due to the heteronormative idealization of biological ties, however, adoption of any kind is a suspect family form. As Myrna Friedlander notes, this is evident in the fact that "[b]irth parents, adoptive parents, and their children struggle for self-acceptance against stigma and marginalization" (751). Adoption can lead to feelings of shame, guilt, and alienation due to its association with failure in terms of bio-normativity. These feelings can affect all members of the adoption triad because they contravene normative notions of family (i.e. birthmothers, because they relinquish; adoptees, because they lack a biological tie; and adoptive parents, who are read as infertile), all of which contributes to both the historical and contemporary marginalization of families impacted by adoption. According to Sally Haslanger and Charlotte Witt, for instance, "during most of the 20th century, adoption was largely hidden because it was a source of shame for all those involved: the birth parents for what was often an 'out of wedlock' pregnancy, the adoptive parents for their presumed infertility, and the child for being 'unwanted' or 'rejected'" (4). Today, the shame and guilt might be less about marital status, and more about the inability to care for children and infertility. Regardless of one's position in the adoption triad, however, the failure, guilt and/

or sense of marginalization to which adoption can give rise is ultimately a testament to the social and historical value that our culture places on families realized through biological connectedness.

The experiences of shame and guilt associated with adoption indicate that adoptive families are not easily awarded the privileges enjoyed by bio-families in a bio-normative context. The unequal distribution of privileges between adoptive and biological families is evidenced by Jacqueline Stevens, who observes that "when it comes to adoption law, the state favors the genetic family, treating it as a norm," whereas the adoptive family is treated as "deviant" because it is "demanding of special government regulation and scrutiny" (73). For Stevens, families not bound by biology exist in separate spaces, ones that are delimited by the boundaries of biological family constructs that dominate our culture. Indeed, this is one reason she argues "it is imperative to question the dichotomy between adoptive and genetic families;" because, ultimately, this "division marginalizes and stigmatizes those families, relations, and relatives called 'adoptive'" (71). An important effect of this "taxonomic" division is that it sets up a hierarchy wherein adoptive ties are socially perceived as second-best, or as a consolation, for what is typically assumed to be the adoptive parents' inability to biologically [re]produce children. Friedlander, who is critical of systemic bias against adoptive families, also illustrates this dichotomy, somewhat surprisingly, when she writes "[a]doption is about attachments to family, broken and constructed" (747). Her use of the word "broken," its negative connotation, inadvertently privileges the value of bio-normativity, which she intends to critique; it is also an example of the way in which the language of adoption too easily devolves into a notion of inadequacy, failure, or lack.

Prior to drawing parallels between the marginalization of adoptive and lesbian families, I will identify some unique ways in which lesbian mothers are socially scrutinized and disenfranchised. Cheryl Muzio provides the most obvious ways in which lesbian mothers are marginalized: "[t]he experience of lesbian mothering blends the roles of two groups that have been alternately ignored and oppressed in Western society: women who care for and raise children and women who choose to love other women" (215). In effect, as mothers, lesbians are oppressed through an intersection between sexism and heterosexism; lesbian identity, and really lesbian sexuality, troubles the lesbian mother's ability to be or be read as either a "woman" or "mother" in heteronormative contexts. As Carol Anderson Boyer observes, this is because "lesbian sexual orientation is often perceived as incompatible with childrearing"

(230); their deviant sexual status effectively undermines their identities as mothers in that their sexuality is socially perceived as a threat to the wellbeing of children. Their sexuality is also an obstacle to their ability to reproduce independently of a third party, which, for obvious reasons, means that lesbian mothering is more precarious and unpredictable with respect to autonomy. While heterosexual couples must sometimes rely on a third party for reproduction, lesbians must always depend on an intermediary, for instance, a private sperm donor, sperm bank, and/or fertility clinic.

While lesbians can access NRTs more freely today, the medical institutions that accommodate their needs remain prone to heterosexism in the delivery of these services. The impact of systemic heterosexism manifests in many subtle ways, ranging from the rejection of would-be gay male sperm donors, to the visible lack of parenting literature in waiting rooms that directly addresses lesbian mothers. Unilateral HIV testing of lesbian mothers is another example of how NRT services remain steeped in heterosexism; for example, a condition of my own fertility treatments was that both my partner and I take HIV tests, even as my partner was not going to biologically participate in our attempt to produce a child.[2] While this requirement makes sense with respect to heterosexuals seeking some forms of assisted reproduction, it also illustrates these institutions' fundamental inability to grasp the ways in which lesbians create families.

Aviva Rubin discusses further obstacles faced by lesbians who remain in the margins, even as they enjoy new access to same sex marital and adoption rights. She observes "our insecurities at the deepest level are still profoundly triggered by not having a clear role to play as defined by traditional, heterosexual, normative models" (122). In spite of newly acquired rights, lesbian mothers' marginalization is sustained through their ongoing exclusion from traditional models of mothering. At the same time that lesbian mothers lack traditional role models, their situation within a heteronormative sphere can also intensify their insecurities to such a degree that they become susceptible to internalized homophobia. As Boyer notes, many lesbians might be deterred from having and/or adopting children, because "the level of internalized homophobia experienced by some gay and lesbian individuals may be so intense that they feel themselves unfit to parent or undeserving of having a child" (230). Taken together, Rubin and Boyer's observations further imply that even lesbians who do opt to mother may not entirely free themselves from the effects of homophobia, which can compound their experiences of marginalization.

Clearly, adoptive and lesbian families are marginalized in unique ways. Nonetheless, there are important respects in which the bio-normativity that impacts adoptive families and the heteronormativity that impacts lesbian families converge. In particular, the marginalization of adoption helps to secure, not only the biological family's centrality, but also the centrality of the heterosexual family, because our culture's idealization of biological ties is simultaneously an idealization of heterosexual reproduction. Conversely, the social denigration of lesbian sexuality helps to secure the centrality of the biological tie because embedded in the social rejection of homosexuality is an affirmation of bio-hetero-normative[3] reproduction. As a result, biological and heterosexual family models map onto each other, and in such a way that both models have implications for the marginalization of adoptive and lesbian families. For instance, as Sarah Tobias notes, "[t]he pervasiveness of heteronormativity accounts for the fact that gay and lesbian families are constantly marginalized" and "[b]oth aspects of heteronormativity—that is, heteronormativity as normal and heteronormativity as normatively desirable—are apparent in dominant discourses about the family and the politics of adoption" (106). In other words, the forces that lead to adoption being labeled as "other" are not entirely unlike those that *other* lesbian, gay and queer families; that is, like adoption, lesbian sexuality implies an inability to reproduce bio-normatively.

To the extent that adoptive and lesbian families threaten bio-heteronormativity, the convergence of adoption with lesbian mothering functions as a unique site of transgression with respect to dominant notions of family. I will examine three methods lesbians use to form their families within a bio-heteronormative context. One way lesbians create family is through joint adoption. When lesbians adopt as a couple, they not only provide a home for a child, they change the landscapes of adoption, motherhood, and even lesbianism. Another way in which lesbians engage adoption to form a family is to combine adoptive and biological ties, wherein one woman gives birth to a child that the other adopts formally or informally. In this case, one mother is biologically connected to her child while the other assumes the social role of mother through any number of identities. The multiple identities to which this approach gives rise acts to expand the meaning of mother and allow for new possibilities in constituting families. The third way lesbian mothers trouble mainstream ideals of family with adoption occurs when both mothers assume a simultaneous biological and adoptive tie to their children. This occurs when both mothers give birth and both adopt the other's child (in/formally). It also occurs when lesbians use NRTs and adoption in ways that completely confuse the meaning of both adoptive and biological ties, for instance, when one mother donates her egg to her partner who then carries the child they will mutually mother to term.

When lesbian mothers adopt jointly, they challenge mainstream notions of family. In doing so they eliminate the possibility that biological ties will define their family, and, thus pose challenges to the bio-normative model. They also reject bio-heteronormativity, because as women who choose adoption over pregnancy, they refuse to succumb to the expectation that they should enlist their sexual organs in reproduction. In addition, lesbians who mutually opt for adoption transgress sex and gender norms insofar as they are better situated to achieve a more egalitarian approach to parenting. In a Canadian study, Michael Woodford et al. found that lesbian couples that adopt are more likely to experience a sense of equality and "a higher sense of worth when it [comes] to their roles within the family" (283). Woodford et al. also concluded that the lack of bio-hierarchy in joint adoptions allowed both women to form more autonomous parenting styles, in that "participants described how adopting as a couple enabled both partners to feel legitimately empowered as parents in ways that biological parenting could not have" (283). Another way in which lesbian co-adoption destabilizes the trappings of bio-heteronormativity is that it sidesteps power imbalances rooted in bio-favouritism and/or competition that can occur in families that are constituted on the basis of biological and adoptive ties.

Lesbian mothers that choose adoption over biological reproduction of any sort, when the latter is an option, contravene socio-cultural stigma that surrounds adoption. When lesbian partners who are biologically able to conceive choose to adopt, they thwart two assumptions about adoption; they thwart the assumption that infertile women turn to adoption, and the assumption that adoption is a second choice. Lesbian mothers who adopt may also do so because they want to transgress bio-heteronormative boundaries of race, ethnicity and geography. Moreover, many politicized lesbians who are committed to principles of social justice may also be more inclined to adopt children who are marginalized within the adoption system itself (i.e. children deemed "hard to place" because they are of colour, older, or disabled), which further serves as a rejection of bio-heteronormativity. All of these adoption practices can be understood to challenge normative assumptions about family or the idea that family members should be and look alike.

Lesbian co-mothers who form families through adoption simultaneously exceed and transgress the expectations of bio-heteronormativity through their approach to creating family. For instance, adoptive lesbian mothers in Suzanne Pelka's study were deemed to have challenged heteronormative institutions in "that they too had created a baby *together*, albeit through piles of legal paperwork and adoption hearings" (211). In effect, lesbians who choose to adopt, even though they are able to reproduce, destabilize bio-heteronormative constructions of family because they both reject the biological tie outright and force the institution of adoption to acknowledge lesbians as mothers.

A common avenue lesbians use to create families involves the use of biological and adoptive ties, wherein one woman acts as the biological mother and the other adopts in/formally. While this strategy in the formation of family can lend itself to bio-favouritism and competition among lesbian co-parents, there are still important ways in which it challenges mainstream notions of the family. Pelka's study, which examines jealousy between lesbian co-mothers, reveals the bio-normative pitfalls lesbian couples that reproduce *and* adopt may face. She notes, when feelings of competition between lesbian co-mothers "surfaced it was in the context of a non-birth mother feeling jealous of the physical relationship that her partner, the birth mother, and her children shared" (201). Despite this, lesbian couples that do create families with biological and adoptive ties question bio-heteronormativity in much the same way as lesbians that co-adopt, simply because their sexuality always puts them at odds with heterosexual modes of motherhood. Rachel Epstein articulates a similar idea, more broadly speaking, when she writes "the existence of queer families, in all our diversity, cannot help but disrupt the heterosexual matrix"(22). For instance, the fact that lesbian families are headed by two (or more) moms fundamentally muddles heterosexual meanings of family that turn on a mother/father dyad; they effectively challenge popular patriarchal beliefs that male role models within the family are a necessity at all, regardless of whether their children are either male or female. What I would add to Epstein's insight, however, is that lesbian couples' *adoption practices* cannot help but disrupt the *bio*-heterosexual matrix, because adoption is as much a disruption of bio-heteronormativity as lesbianism or queerness is with respect to heterosexuality alone. Specifically, it is not merely or necessarily lesbianism (or women's lesbian identities) that allows for the possibility of a family being headed by two women—it is also adoption, because one lesbian mother, or both, must ultimately rely on adoption to create their families.

The last method lesbian couples use to create families that I will discuss mutually confuses normative concepts of biological and adoptive ties. In this instance, lesbian couples, although they enlist adoption, actually attempt to mimic mutual biological connection to their children with the use of NRTs. To better illustrate this idea, consider that two women both produce an egg that is fertilized with the same donor sperm, and that each woman's fertilized egg is implanted in her partner's womb where it is carried to term. As Pelka observes in her study, this approach to lesbian mothering can be understood solely to reinforce bio-normativity because, as she explains, when "one partner is the gestational/birth mother and the other is the genetic mother, both partners feel equitable biological ties to children conceived this way" (195). Nonetheless, lesbians who intentionally set out to construct what may initially appear to be "equal" biological relationships can also be said to construct ties that really are equally adoptive; the difference here in terms of adoption is only that it occurs *in utero*, and not *extra utero*. Where practices such as these begin to be recognized through the lens of adoption, and not solely biology, the effect of this lesbian adoption practice is that it blurs the boundaries between meanings of adoption *and* biology, in that, the use of adoption is biological at the same time that the use of biology is adoptive, all of which troubles the bio-normativity some lesbian mothers intend to reproduce.

Through a diverse range of adoption practices, lesbian mothers and their families demonstrate that there is a need to expand our notions and definitions of kinship. The methods lesbians use to create their families show us not only that bio-heteronormativity is a force that dominates our everyday ideas about family, but that these ideas are challenged directly and indirectly through a convergence of lesbian identity and adoption. Whether lesbians' ties to their children are adoptive or biological *and* adoptive, their families remain a site of transgression that illustrates the degree to which the meaning of family ties is genuinely malleable. And while lesbians' approaches to family can sometimes be read to reproduce bio-heteronormativity, they can also be read to produce new and more provocative modes of adoption that destabilize bio-heteronormativity. As greater numbers of lesbians become mothers, and the visibility of their adoption practices increases, their families stimulate change within our institutions and among people that must increasingly acknowledge, as they encounter, lesbians' unique family forms, for instance, in schools, the local gym, or at neighbourhood coffee shops, where, strollers in tow, lesbian moms meet other mothers, with whom they discuss their children and parenting strategies. While lesbian mothers already challenge traditional family forms wherever they insert themselves in social spaces by virtue of their sexual identities, they also challenge these constructs through their reliance on adoption in the creation of their families. Where lesbian identities converge with adoption, they give rise to new family forms that create unique sites of resistance to bio-heteronormativity.

¹The Canadian Parliament passed *The Civil Marriage Act* in 2005 to recognize same-sex marriage.

²When I questioned the need for this test, my fertility doctor told me that both parents are always tested, regardless of sexuality. When I pressed the doctor as to why, I was told that this "puts you on an "equal' footing with heterosexual couples. "

³My use of the terms bio-heteronormativity and bio-normativity originates from discussions with Frances Latchford about this chapter. She uses these terms to signify the dominant discourses of family that prioritize biological kinship ties in conjunction with heterosexuality.

WORKS CITED

Boyer, Carol Anderson. "Double Stigma: The Impact of Adoption Issues on Lesbian and Gay Adoptive Parents." *Handbook of Adoption: Implications for Researchers, Practitioners, and Families*. Ed. Rafael Javier et al. Thousand Oaks, CA: Sage, 2007. 228-241. Web.

Epstein, Rachel. "Introduction." *Who's Your Daddy? And Other Writings on Queer Parenting*. Ed. Rachel Epstein. Toronto: Sumach Press, 2009. 13-22. Print.

Friedlander, Myrna L. "Adoption: Misunderstood, Mythologized, Marginalized." *The Counseling Psychologist* 31.6 (2003): 745-752. Web.

Haslanger, Sally and Charlotte Witt. *Adoption Matters: Philosophical and Feminist Essays*. Ithaca: Cornell University Press, 2005. Print.

Muzio, Cheryl. "Lesbian Co-Parenting: On Being/Being with the Invisible (M)other." *Smith College Studies in Social Work* 63.3 (1993): 215-229. Print.

Parliament of Canada. Bill C-38: *The Civil Marriage Act*, 14 Sept. 2005, Web. 30 August 2011.

Pelka, Suzanne. "Sharing Motherhood: Maternal Jealousy Among Lesbian Co-Mothers." *Journal of Homosexuality* 56.2 (2003): 195-217. Print.

Rubin, Aviva. "My Co-world and Welcome to It: Adventures in Non-Conjugal Parenting." *Who's Your Daddy?: And Other Writings on Queer Parenting*. Ed. Rachel Epstein. Toronto: Sumach Press, 2009. 117-123. Print.

Stevens, Jacqueline. "Methods of Adoption: Eliminating Genetic Privilege." *Adoption Matters: Philosophical and Feminist Essays*. Haslanger, Sally and Charlotte Witt, eds. Ithaca and London: Cornell University Press, 2005. 68-94. Print.

Tobias, Sarah. "Several Steps Behind: Gay and Lesbian Adoption." *Adoption Matters: Philosophical and Feminist Essays*. Eds. Sally Haslanger,

and Charlotte Witt. Ithaca: Cornell University Press, 2005. 95-111. Print.
Woodford, Michael R., Katherine Sheets, Kristin Scherrer, Roxanne d'Eon-Blemings, Ingrid Tenkate, and Blair Addams. "Lesbian Adoptive Couples: Responding to Shifting Identities and Social Relationships." *Affilia: Journal of Women and Social Work* 25.3 (2010): 278-290. Web. 12 July 2011.

13.
Culture, Law and Language

Adversarial Motherhood in Adoption

RICHARD UHRLAUB AND NIKKI MCCASLIN

For me, a real mother is one who recognizes and respects the whole identity of her child and does not ask him to deny any part of himself. This is difficult to do in a closed adoption system that requires the child to be cut off from his heritage, and that pits the original mother against the replacement mother. If one mother is real, the other must be unreal.
— Betty Jean Lifton, in *Journey of the Adopted Self*

SINCE THE DAYS OF KING SOLOMON'S famous judgment, a maternal tug of war has been underway, wherein women who have borne children find themselves in adversarial relationships with persons who wish to parent those children. In modern adoption philosophy and practice, adversarial motherhood has been shaped by cultural factors, which in turn have created laws and language that perpetuate adversarial beliefs and practices. Passionately contested laws and imprecise, often offensive language have arisen from what Rickie Solinger describes as "the reciprocal relationship between ideology and public policy—how the former infuses the latter, and how, in turn, public policies create outcomes that strengthen the bases of ideology" (13). The result was a eugenics-driven philosophy from 1900 to 1940 (Herman 1) followed by a post-war era in which the resultant ideology and public policies harmed mothers and adopted children in unprecedented, though often well-intended, ways.

Though many adoption professionals now recognize the benefits of openness, honesty and cooperation among all parties in an adoption, the residual effects from the earlier adversarial philosophies and practices remain entrenched in the form of antiquated laws and unsatisfactory language. Just as in the story of Solomon, laws and language that confer the title of "real" mother exclusively upon either the birthmother or adoptive mother inevitably threatens to split the child both women claim to love. This chapter examines four topics from the points of view of two adoptees: cultural influences that place mothers through birth and adoption at odds with each other; historical factors in American adoption law; examples of adversarial language; and some suggestions toward a more collaborative culture for mothers involved in adoption and in turn toward a healthier environment for children raised in adoptive families.

CULTURAL INFLUENCES

Modern American adoption was designed "to meet the needs of couples whose dreams of a family were shattered by infertility and to provide a solution for birth parents who found themselves facing an unintended and untimely pregnancy" (Schooler 40). However, adoption is never that simple because with it comes a mixture of motives, interests and assumptions about how it is supposed to work. Miriam Reitz and Ken Watson state that, historically, adoption as a social institution not only provided homes for children, but also served parental needs ranging from securing an heir to indentured labor and satisfied various social agendas aimed at reducing costly orphan care (3). They describe a fantasy-based arrangement that has evolved:

> Adoptive families and adoption agencies collaborated to pres-
> ent adoption as what it can never really be—a chance for birth
> parents to go on happily with their lives, for children to grow
> up in trouble free families, and for adoptive parents to fulfill
> themselves and find immortality through children to whom they
> have sole claim by virtue of adoption. (4)

Such an idealized view fails to take into account (or chooses to ignore) many of the following distinct and divisive cultural realities that are elicited in adoption and mothering.

Mothers versus Not-Mothers

Social anthropologist Sheila Kitzinger describes motherhood as something that women view as a right in Western civilization: "[t]o deny that right is to take away her freedom. Coupled with this, there is a sense that a woman who has never had a baby must be emotionally unfulfilled and is therefore less than a woman" (39). Although child bearing and rearing are generally viewed as good things, even blessings, Kitzinger notes that birth "is not just a matter of biology and primordial urges, but of cultural values ... the woman's identity changes too: she becomes a different kind of person—a mother" (95).

In a woman's quest for identity as a mother, therefore, a lost child or the inability to bear one can have serious emotional consequences. Symptoms that now meet diagnostic criteria ranging from Mood Disorders to Generalized Anxiety, Acute Stress and even Post Traumatic Stress Disorder (DSM-IV 345-428, 463-476) were previously lumped into a neurosis dubbed "Momism" by psychologist Hans Sebald in the 1970s. He used the controversial term (which was particularly offensive to feminists) to describe a situation in which "the child becomes an irreplaceable figure, who is needed by the mother so that she can deduce her identity as Mother" (34). Sebald observed that this condition or its symptoms can arise from the trauma or experiences of extreme powerlessness faced by women who fail at this quest, for instance because they are infertile or have, willingly or unwillingly, relinquished their parental rights. For the birthmother (a term which has become controversial), these experiences could be the effect of her abandonment by the baby's father and/or her own parents, or her exile during pregnancy to a maternity home or to live with relatives. For the adoptive mother, infertility or miscarriage and unfulfilled desires to be a parent likewise create trauma and a deep sense of powerlessness. For both mothers, a resultant excessive identification with—and the tendency to cling to—their children can create a difficult environment for those children. These parallel maternal identity crises often meet in adoption, positioning these grieving or traumatized mothers as rivals.

Good versus Bad Mothers

Images of motherhood can range from idealized pictures of someone who is life-giving and nurturing, like Isis, the Virgin Mary or Mother Theresa, to an opposite image, such as the Balinese witch-goddess, Rangda, who steals children from their mothers (Neumann 3-4). In the adoption milieu, such images are visceral and are derived from beliefs about fertility and infertility, norms and *mores* regarding sexual behaviour, emotional maturity, financial stability, optimal family configuration and consequent implications in light of the best interests of the child. In relinquishment and adoption, birthmothers and adoptive mothers are often labeled as "good or bad," and "fit or unfit" based on their qualifications. Ann Fessler notes that:

> as early as the 1940s, [psychiatrists and social workers] began to classify middle class girls who became pregnant as neurotic: the

unwed mother was a neurotic woman who had a subconscious desire to become pregnant.... One of the outcomes of this new professional diagnosis was the justification of the separation of mother and child: a neurotic woman was seen as unfit to be a mother. (147-148)

For example, Patricia Taylor, who at the age of seventeen unwillingly relinquished her daughter in 1961, recalls, "At some point during one of our many arguments about me keeping my baby, my mother told me that, if I refused to sign the relinquishment papers, the agency would take legal action to have me declared an unfit mother" (61-62). Even today, some agencies ignore future uncertainties implicit in current divorce and unemployment rates and perpetuate the mantra that, in order to be a "fit" mother, a woman must be married, financially secure and therefore able to provide a stable, loving home. As a result, some women are honored while others are shamed over the circumstances under which they become a mother.

Fertile versus Infertile Mothers

In a discussion of the research of Frances Clothier, Donald Winnicott and Joseph Pearce, adoptive mother Nancy Verrier concludes, "There is something special which happens to prepare a mother for the birth of her baby, a sequence of events which begins at conception and which cannot be learned or acquired 'by even the best of substitute mothers'" (53). Consequently, a woman's inability to bear children might act as a powerful catalyst for tension or even resentment between herself and a woman who lacks the resources, ability or desire to parent her baby. A modern understanding of adoption holds that all members of the adoption triad (adoptive parents, birthparents and adopted persons) experience losses during the process of relinquishment and adoption. It is understandable that many triad members tend to focus primarily on their own losses, and adoptive mother Kay Halverson offers a contrast to the assumption that only unwed mothers suffer heartbreak and stigma. She reflects on her own grief over infertility in *The Wedded Unmother*. Grace Ketterman, M.D., cautions adoptive parents, often viewed as "superior" by first parents, that "You may believe that you are inferior to the child's biological parents [due to infertility] and unconsciously set up competition with them for your child's respect and loyalty" (107).

Especially during the years following World War II, social workers commonly matched babies with adoptive parents of similar hair and eye coloring, so that they could pass as their biological children. While this may have helped to conceal the shame of both infertility and sexual indiscretion, the shared secret usually got out. Adoptees of this era were often traumatized by the secrets and lies.

Adoptive parent Adam Pertman acknowledges that, even in today's open adoptions wherein birthparents and adoptive parents know each other's identities, adoptive parents pay an emotional price for their infertility. "Our sensitivities about raising a family usually have been heightened by fertility problems that prevented us from producing biological children, then our self-confidence has been shaken by the emotionally turbulent voyage that adoption invariably entails" (16). It is, therefore, no surprise that some adoptive parents, whether consciously or subconsciously, are tempted to minimize the significance of biological parents in order to validate themselves as the child's "real" parents.

Married versus Unmarried Mothers

Historically, North American women who became pregnant out of wedlock faced difficult options. These included stigmatized single motherhood, relying on relatives to help raise the child, a hastily arranged marriage, or entering a maternity home, which would provide obstetric care and other pregnancy-related services. Many of these homes were established in the 1800s by churches. They "housed them [birth mothers] and their babies for as long as two years, during which the mothers were instructed in childcare, a trade, and religions" (Raymond 103).

While the Judeo-Christian view of adoption is compassionate as it regards the protection of orphans, as early as 1918, Percy Gamble Kammerer described attitudes toward unwed mothers as divided into two camps: society either viewed them as those who had "sinned and who should be made to feel the full burden of [their] behavior," or those "to whom the problem of illegitimacy represent[ed] an unfortunate indication of social and biological maladjustment" (308).

Sir Francis Galton, father of the eugenics movement, is alleged to have invented the nineteenth-century idea that "[s]ome particularly prolific breeders were among those considered most 'abnormal'—single mothers" (Raymond 71). Conversely, Kammerer's later work (1918), which was originally part of a series of criminal science monographs, was one of the first U.S. sociological studies to examine the social relation between illegitimacy and criminality, even as he was sympathetic to eugenics. He evaluated 500 women and concluded, "eugenicists cannot yet speak with precision" despite "a tendency on the part of some social workers to solve the complexities of human motivation by throwing the responsibility upon the ancestors" (182). So although Kammerer did conclude, "the relationship between feeblemindedness in particular, and mental abnormality in general to illegitimacy should be evident" (263), he also acknowledged that his study was both flawed and biased because his subjects were limited to indigent unmarried mothers whose information was gathered, not by researchers, but by hospitals, police or public welfare workers. And contrary to strict eugenic views, which made many couples hesitant to adopt illegitimate children, he also gave considerable weight to the impact of social factors (including alcoholic fathers, bad home environment, companions, and educational disadvantages). Indeed, he stated that "the illegitimate child grows up no better and no worse than the legitimate children of its own class" (309).

From the 1920s to the 1950s, a slow shift began in the form of a marketing campaign to make "bastards" and "street urchins" more adoptable. Driven by people like the influential, but corrupt, adoption "pioneer" Georgia Tann, the expectation that all single white women surrender their babies became woven into American culture (Raymond 108, 137). Especially after World War II, therefore, "'mother' was an honorific that could be bestowed or denied by the judgments of professionals" (Solinger 95). As a result, "unwed mothers were defined by psychological theory as not-mothers," an idea that retains popular currency and which many birthmothers have "internalized" (95). For instance, today, the highly-conservative pundit Ann Coulter traces "almost any societal problem" (36) back to single motherhood. She castigates single mothers for their irresponsible sexual behavior, and praises those "unwed mothers who care enough to give their children up for adoption" as those who "come overwhelmingly from responsible backgrounds" (43).

Search and Reunion

Many adoptive parents labor under the illusion that, if they are good enough parents, their children will never feel the need to contact birth family. Verrier sympathizes with fellow adoptive parents, who are considered possessive "bad guys" if they express apprehension or discomfort when their children make contact with their families of origin. It is not uncommon for those who adopt to wish that their well-loved adoptees would never feel the need to search. But, when it comes to matters of identity formation or grief resolution for the adoptee, love is rarely an acceptable substitute for heritage (Verrier 28-45, 100). For instance, Jane Schooler recounts the situation of Jill Gardner, who overheard her mother talking on the phone. "Cognitively, my mom and dad were very supportive of my reunion.... However, emotionally my mom had a hard time.... Her worst nightmare was that I would leave her for my biological mother" (38-39).

Adversarial Systemic Factors

One of the most perplexing aspects of adoption has been the assumption that arose in the last half of the twentieth century that legislators, adoption agencies, courts, and even records clerks have a fundamental mission to separate and protect members of the adoption triad from one another. For those who operated from the assumption that mothers who surrendered their babies for adoption were, by definition, "neurotic" or "unfit," it would logically follow that these women could also pose a threat to the stability of adoptive families and should be presumed incapable of sorting out the messy, complicated relationships often encountered through search and reunion. While there are cases, particularly those involving abuse or neglect, in which it is possible that one party might pose a threat to another, they comprise a small minority. Though states with unrestricted access to records for adult adoptees have reported no serious problems, some legislators and agency workers still allege the necessity of laws requiring paid third parties to act as buffers to "protect" first mothers from the children they lost and adoptive mothers from the potential family complications they may dread.

Rich Mom, Poor Mom

Pulitzer Prize nominee Adam Pertman devotes an entire chapter in *Adoption Nation* to the subject of money. In it, he quotes Bill Pierce, former spokesman for the National Council for Adoption, who compared adopting a child to an automobile purchase: "This is a capitalist system...People don't seem to believe that $16,000 or $17,000 is too much for a new car. If we're going to have quality service, you're going to have to pay for it" (266). In particular, Pertman suggests, private infant adoption has transitioned from a charitable social service into a profitable business. As a result, different triad roles are commercialized. For example, birthparents are now the "manufacturers," adoptable babies the "product," agencies and attorneys are the "brokers," and adoptive parents are necessarily positioned as "the buyers" who, as such, often assert, along with some agencies and politicians, that adoption laws should be tilted in their favour (Pertman 246-278).

The exchange of cash for children invariably appalls adopted persons, though adoptive parents may more readily squelch any discomfort over financial arrangements as a necessary part of the process. Financial hardship can place undue pressure upon women to relinquish their babies, which clouds the question of choice. At the same time, as fewer American women relinquish babies, the market has shifted and led to an increase in compensation for many birthmothers. As New York adoption attorney Benjamin Rosen observes, "I'm not saying it's baby selling, but the empowerment of birth mothers is making it more of a sellers' market" (Pertman 250). In states that allow prospective adoptive parents to pay housing and medical costs related to the last trimester of a pregnancy, the idea of investment or down payment can develop, particularly if such states also allow pre-birth relinquishment agreements. Substantial up-front emotional and financial investments place agencies in a position, if necessary, to dissuade either party from changing their minds about the transaction. Unlike "parenthood," therefore, the mindset of "ownership," replete with signed contracts and the exchange of currency, can foster the illusion of a permanent and exclusive claim to the child.

Money, power and secrecy often go hand in hand. Law professor Elizabeth Samuels observes that adoption agencies and attorneys may have "financial and institutional incentives to conduct adoption arrangements with a minimal possibility of future scrutiny" (15). Savvy adoption agencies and attorneys wield considerable influence at state legislatures, often through lobbyists retained to promote their interests. It is not uncommon for agencies that promote closed adoptions to pit the interests of the parties to the adoption against each other in order to position themselves as "protectors of privacy." Doing so allows them to retain control of the process and capitalize on the opportunity to generate revenue from adoptive parents on the front of the adoption and searching birthparents and adoptees on the back end.

ADVERSARIAL FACTORS IN ADOPTION LAW

In many states, adoptions began as contractual arrangements between the parties, formalized by a deed that transferred custody of a child from one set of parents to another. For example, Colorado's initial statute, concurrent with statehood in 1876, required that the deed be "executed, acknowledged and recorded ... as in the case of conveyance of real estate" (Pike 10). The document was then filed in a designated place and open for public inspection as proof of legal status, similar to records for marriage or property. In such states there were no court hearings, though judicial officers primarily approved these deeds with a signature (9). Courts only began to step in as cases involving unscrupulous deals between parents increased.

Utopian Influences

In a quest to cure an assortment of social ills, a number of "utopian societies" sprang up in the nineteenth century. Among them was a group called the Perfectionists, who as early as 1848 embraced the idea that mothers were interchangeable and an illegitimate child's ancestry and identity was easily erased and reassigned. The group discouraged women from bonding with their children and "based their organization on communism and what later became known as free love" (Kitzinger 64). Even more influential among American and European biologists, psychologists, and sociologists was Albert E. Wiggam, who further built upon Galton's ideas in his widely acclaimed 1922 book *The New Decalogue of Science*. He proclaimed the laboratory "The new Mount Sinai" (79) and called eugenics the "first commandment of science to statesmanship"(99). He also labeled "the duty of preferential reproduction" as the new sixth commandment, invoking Hebrew law, Plato's political philosophy, and Jesus in support of the idea (99, 110). He scolded politicians for failing to "socialize and politicalize science" (128). Such thinking ultimately enhanced the tensions between mothers of different socioeconomic classes. For instance, intelligence testing expert Henry Goddard and Albert H. Stoneman, the General Secretary of the Michigan Children's Aid Society, cautioned potential adoptive parents to carefully research children's histories before adopting. Renowned pediatrician Henry Chapin, husband of the founder of New York's Spence-Chapin adoption agency, believed that "citizens with better genetic endowment were more likely to suffer from infertility" and that "eugenic factors mattered in adoption." Thus, Chapin asserted that "not babies merely, but better babies, are wanted" (Herman 1). As a result, birthmothers whose genetic endowment was already in question due to class, and additionally, to relinquishment were, by definition opposed against middle and upper class adoptive mothers. And, although post-war America has distanced itself from the terminology of eugenics, "blood and biology remain[ed] central themes in adoption history" (Herman 3) as policy makers created laws that required increasingly thorough background information about birthmothers (Pike 6).

As Solinger asserts, U.S. policy makers had definite "postwar population goals. These goals constituted a mid-century variant of traditional eugenics: vitalize the white, middle-class family and, at the same time, curb childbearing among minorities" (26). The American belief that married couples who are upper class are worthier and better parents financially, morally, and genetically remains intact. It also continues to pit mothers against each other, in part, because these families are so much better equipped to influence the legalities of relinquishment and adoption in their own, as opposed to the birthmother's, favour.

Shifts in Adoption Law

Before infant formula was invented in the late 1800s, early American adoption laws often required mothers to breastfeed their babies for a period before relinquishment. By the late 1930s, however, single mothers were commonly prevented from even seeing their babies (Raymond 136). The rationale was supported by the 1937 findings of ethologist Konrad Lorenz, whose observations led to his theory of "imprinting." Lorenz demonstrated that, as a survival mechanism, chicks, ducks and goslings will "follow and become attached to a moving object during a critical period early in life" (Sigelman and Ryder 386). Indeed, his theory is cited still in modern psychology textbooks that examine attachment theory. John Bowlby's finding that "by the end of a half-year the elements of attachment behavior are clearly established" (322) have also been interpreted by some to mean that just like goslings, if switched early enough in life, a baby would be "none the wiser" (Verrier 19). One way in which this can be understood to impact the dynamics between mothers is that, as it blurs the distinction between "mother" and "primary caregiver" (Verrier 19), it implies that human mothers are interchangeable. The effect is that the erasure of the birthmother following adoption is justified further, despite the fact that more recent research[1] done on infants up to seven months old indicates that the infant is "far from being the passive protohuman of early developmental studies," and "has a direct experience of relationships and subsequently of the self" (Balswick 125-130).

The child's birth certificate has become pivotal in adversarial adoption, especially as it concerns the birthmother. Samuels notes that the practice of amending an adopted child's original birth certificate began in the United States during the 1930s (1-2). When a pregnant mother cooperated with a "redemptive" series of steps, ones which usually included counselling, internment in a maternity home, and the surrender of her child for adoption, the state became complicit in a denial that she had ever given birth, and sealed away the original birth certificate (Solinger 25). The amended birth certificate symbolically severed ties with the adoptee's family of origin and, along with the adoption decree, legally established the child as a member of the new family. The implication of the signatures of doctors and state officials on the new birth certificate is that the adoptive mother has given birth to the child she has adopted. As the child's true origins are hidden, and a new relationship and identity is formed by what can be likened to legalized perjury, so too is the birthmother's part in motherhood eradicated. While the baby's new legal name on an amended birth certificate makes the adoptive mother a "real" mother, the court's sealing of the original birth certificate symbolically renders the first mother a "not-mother."

After the postwar baby boom of the late 1940s, '50s and early '60s, more state legislatures began to impose greater secrecy, partly in response to sensational news stories of women seeking to recover the children they had lost to adoption. A now widening chasm between adoptive and birth parents during the 1960s and '70s led to calls for greater protections for adoptive families (Samuels 5-6). In 1967, Colorado's House Bill 1001, sponsored by an adoptive uncle, required for the first time that the parties in an adoption remain anonymous to one another. Contrary to the idea that adoption secrecy laws were designed to protect birthparent privacy, the stated intent of the law was to make the adoptive family more stable and immune from unwanted disruption by a birthparent (Kyle 117). The new law codified the adoptive parents' preeminent social status and has culminated in the further denigration of birthmothers.

Similar changes took place nationwide between 1945 and 1975, a time that has been dubbed the "Baby Scoop Era" by members of Origins-USA, an activist first-mothers' group whose mission is to replace adoption with legal guardianship whenever possible, as a means of eliminating amended birth certificates. They, along with adoptee groups like Bastard Nation and cross-triad organizations like the American Adoption Congress, are raising their voices, gaining political clout, and demanding that lost rights to information and equal treatment under the law be reinstated. As Kenneth Karst argues, "When law is seen as an instrument of status dominance in a conflict of cultures, no one should be surprised when the losers of the legislative battle refuse to accept the law's legitimacy" (51). As legal changes purported to protect the adoptive family have forced birthmothers and adoptees to fight for these rights denied to them, is it any wonder that birthmothers and adoptive mothers too often experience each other as adversaries?

THE LANGUAGE OF ADOPTION

It was not until the sexual revolution of the 1960s that adoption language began to change, as ideas about marriage were questioned and the moral and genetic taint of illegitimacy began to lift. Children previously viewed as "bad seeds" or "born in sin" became acknowledged as innocent. Furthermore, as better educated, better paid single women acquired resources that enabled them to keep and provide for their children, the line between never-married and divorced women with children also began to blur, and especially because the latter also defined themselves as "single mothers."

In 1979, Marietta Spencer, program director of Post-legal Adoption Services at the Children's Home Society of Minnesota, published an article entitled "The Terminology of Adoption." In it, she called for reform in adoption language and discussed the emotional impact of the existing usage on members of the adoption triad. Notably, Spencer minimized the birthmother's ties to her child, and even her humanity as a mother: "The mother is the vehicle through which the child's genetic endowment through a long line of ancestors has passed" (452). She also favoured using "birthmother" because it "differentiat[ed] the biological process" from "the childrearing process" (456). She discouraged using terms such as "given up," "relinquished," or "surrendered" because they "imply that children were torn out of the arms of their mothers by an unfeeling state or social agency" and "may encourage adopted children to fantasy*(sic)* about being reunited with their biological parents" (454). She even rejected the use of the legal term "natural mother" because it implies that the adoptive mother is somehow "unnatural" or "artificial" (454). She opposed using the term "adoptive parent" outside professional discussions of adoption, asserting that it left these parents "permanently labeled by the process by which they acquire[d] a child;" she felt it denoted a "conditional parenthood, a qualification of allegiance, a suggestion that the family relationship is tentative and temporary," and "places in doubt the authenticity of the family tie" (458). Despite the value of her acknowledgement that words "evoke feelings" and "can become labels" (451), her underlying assumptions about adoptive mothers and birthmothers were clearly competitive, if not adversarial. More recent efforts toward respectful adoption language do not appear to have remedied the problem satisfactorily either. For example, the terms "birthmother" and "biological mother" are offensive to many first mothers, and many adoptive mothers object to terms such as "adopter," "real mother" and "natural mother," although all are widely used.

It is often assumed that Spencer coined the term "birth mother" in her 1979 article, "The Terminology of Adoption," but it was first used by the adoptive mother and Nobel Prize winning author, Pearl S. Buck. The term is implied in Buck's writing as early as 1956, when she writes: "Let us remember that the child is and must be the first consideration—not the parents either by birth or adoption..." (38). In 1972, Buck wrote regarding her own adopted daughter "[h]er birth mother was a girl in a small town in Germany..." (21). In contrast, Buck only qualifies mothers and not fathers—she simply says "her father" or "their fathers" instead.

Lee Campbell and other members of Concerned United Birthparents (CUB) had also begun to call for the replacement of "biological" mother with "birthmother" in 1976, asserting that "biological" was too clinical and impersonal, with no genuine maternal connotations.

Current descriptors used by many adoptees, which include "a-mom," "b-mom," and "bio-mom," often confuse the public and offend mothers by birth and adoption. To complicate the issue further, the same terms which designate parents who voluntarily relinquished a baby also apply to persons whose parental rights are terminated by the state as a result of Dependency and Neglect actions, often due to substance or physical abuse. Today, Origins-USA members, who call themselves "mothers of adoption loss," object to the term "birthmother" (or "the b-word" as they call it) and claim that it portrays them as promiscuous, second-class and not real. They also adamantly deny that they ever "relinquished" anyone, since the term implies a choice, when many who lost their children did so under duress. On their website, Origins-USA asserts, "no prefix or modifier is needed to describe our role in our children's lives...." As adopted persons, however, the authors respectfully disagree and believe that the adoption triad does need precise terminology to maintain respect for the parties involved, distinguish identities, help define relationships and experiences, and to prevent adversarial motherhood.

Effects of Adversarial Language

In the 42 states that have yet to restore adult adoptees' unqualified access to their original birth certificates and adoption records, adopted persons must appear in court (often a juvenile court) in order to demonstrate "good cause" for opening their "sealed" files. The caption in a 2009 Colorado Court of Appeals ruling in the adoptee's favour describes the 45-year-old plaintiff as "*In the matter of the Petition of J.N.H. and Concerning B.B.M., a Child.*"[2] Such language sends a strong message that, even as adults, adoptees retain the perpetual legal status of children who are the product of a "secret" mother who must have been someone (or done something) very bad. Where adoptive mothers are systemically rendered "good" and birthmothers "bad," or at least suspect, as a result of the implicit meaning of secrecy, any attempt to integrate the reality of the "secret" mother into the adoptee's life is likely to evoke the idea that s/he is ungrateful, selfish, unpredictable, disruptive, ill-advised and/ or intrusive.

Some first mothers want to be called "Mom" by the children with whom they reconnect. This can pose emotional difficulties for many adoptees, since "Mom" is the person who fed, held, clothed, housed, nurtured and educated them. As a consequence, the adoptee becomes implicated in the process of adversarial motherhood too, insofar as s/he can easily feel torn between two mothers who identify and want to be identified as "Mom." This is why many adoptees, especially at first reunion, can only refer to their natal mothers by their first names. Sometimes the colliding realities are simply too overwhelming to assign the same emotionally loaded term to two different women. Betty Jean Lifton explains that "[t]he task of adopted children is to reconcile these two mothers within them—the birth mother who made them motherless, and the psychological mother who mothered them" (14). Some adoptees manage this reasonably well, while others never manage it at all.

As children who were transferred from one mother to another, adopted persons need words to help navigate what, in important respects, is a dual reality. She or he is simultaneously: a social problem and a precious gift; a symbol of shame and normative family; a source of grief and joy; a human being and a commodity; the answer to one mother's prayers and an alleged threat to another mother's privacy. As Rafael Javier puts it, "[a] central challenge to clinicians is how to help adoptees come to terms with transference material that incorporates two sets of self/parent representations" (12).

In reunion, the adoptee's emotional ambiguity intensifies further, because s/he is faced with both mothers in the flesh. This can leave the adoptee as though s/he is walking a tightrope, for instance, because s/he does not want to hurt or diminish either mother. The adopted have lifelong, but different, ties to both mothers, each of whom are *real*, but there is no contemporary language which adequately reflects this reality.

SUGGESTIONS FOR REDUCING
ADVERSARIAL MOTHERHOOD IN ADOPTION

Joyce Maguire Pavao encapsulates the dilemma of adversarial motherhood: "it looks like neither set of parents can do what's in the best interest of the child" (1). The emotional tug of war inherent in adoption language, law and practice only enhances an adoptee's sense of commoditization, already made strong by sealed records which necessarily position parents as legal adversaries. We offer the following suggestions toward healthier adoption practice and outcomes:

Embrace a healthier cultural view of motherhood by structuring genuine open adoptions whenever possible. In legal rearrangements of custody other than closed infant adoption, all involved must quickly come to terms with the fact of shared parenthood (Hunt 131). North American parents might take a lesson in attitude from the Inuit Eskimos who, according to Kitzinger, exercise a form of collaborative motherhood, wherein, if one family encounters hard times, another one will adopt their baby and name it for one of the child's ancestors in order to preserve its heritage (34). Mary Jo Rillera and Sharon Roszia (nee Kaplan) are among several authors who offer useful models for cooperative adoption.

Restore the unrestricted rights of adult adopted persons to their original birth records. We also recommend that states institute the use of more truthful birth certificates for adoptees who choose them; a new legal document which would list both natal and custodial parents using language which recognizes and honors the significance of both in the adoptee's life. Another option might be the combined use of both the original birth certificate and adoption decree for legal and identification purposes.

Engage members of the adoption triad to develop mutually acceptable adoption terminology. Neither Spencer's model nor efforts toward respectful adoption language are satisfactory, as of yet, and probably because they were generated by social workers and government officials rather than triad members.

Policy makers should exercise great caution when considering the implications of the language of psychosocial theories that are allowed to influence the law. The meanings of such language, when embraced in legislation, can reinforce adversarial motherhood, as well as adoption pathology, long after such theories have been eclipsed or disproven.

Remove profit-based incentives from adoption to the greatest degree possible, because they, too, pit mothers against one another, as producers and consumers. The need for this is urgent, given the decrease of available American babies, and the related increase of international adoption.

Past adversarial adoption culture, laws and language leave a legacy that is, at best, mixed. However, it is our conviction that the adoption triad and those professionals who dedicate themselves to the well-being of its members need not be limited to or defined by the past. We hold forth great hope that those who look back and reflect on adoption in the twenty-first century will strive toward a healthier culture, humane laws based on truth, and authentic, compassionate language that does not oppose mothers or parents against one another, and thereby, honors the children they love.

[1]Balswick, King and Reimer (125-130) cite the following: Vygotsky, *Thought and Language* (Cambridge: MIT Press, 1986); Stern, *The Interpersonal World of the Infant: A View from Psychoanalysis and Developmental*

Psychology (New York: Basic, 2000); Meltzoff and Borton, "Intermodal Matching by Human Neonates," *Nature* 282.5737 (1979):403-4; Mac-Farlane, *The Psychology of Childbirth*, (Harvard University Press, 1975); and Siqueland and DeLucia, "Visual Reinforcement of Non-nutritive Sucking in Human Infants," *Science* 165 (1969):1144-46.

[2] Jeff Hannasch, the Petitioner-Appellant, prevailed on the arguments that: (1) for adoptions finalized prior to July 1, 1967, Colorado law contained no provision for anonymity between the parties to the adoption; and (2) adoption records were therefore confidential from the public but not the parties. The Court of Appeals overturned a ruling from the El Paso County Court, which sought to force Hannasch to hire Colorado Confidential Intermediary Services to perform a search to obtain consent from his birthparent(s), despite the fact that he already had a copy of his adoption decree which included his birth name and mother's maiden name. The higher court unanimously agreed that the notion that someone could know the name(s) of his or her birthparent(s) but could not have access to the records containing those names was "an absurd result." Hannasch was able to obtain a copy of his original birth certificate, which contained the name of his father who had died in 1973 [*In the Matter of the Petition of J.N.H. and Concerning B.B.M., a Child*, 209 P. 3d 1221 (Colo. App. 08CA1235, 2009)].

WORKS CITED

Balswick, Jack O., Pamela E. King, and Kevin S. Reimer. *The Reciprocating Self: Human Development in Theological Perspective*. Downers Grove, IL: InterVarsity, 2005. Print.

Bowlby, John. *Attachment and Loss*. New York: Basic Books, 1980. Print.

Buck, Pearl S. "I am the Better Woman for Having My Two Black Children." *Today's Health* 50 (Jan. 1972): 20+. Print.

Buck, Pearl S. "We Can Free the Children." *Woman's Home Companion* 83 (June 1956): 38 Print.

Clothier, Florence. "The Psychology of the Adopted Child." *Mental Hygiene* (1943): 222-230. Print.

Coulter, Ann. *Guilty: Liberal "Victims" and Their Assault on America*. New York: Crown Forum, 2008. Print.

Diagnostic and Statistical Manual of Mental Disorders. 4th ed. Arlington, VA: American Psychiatric Association, 2000. Print.

Fessler, Ann. *The Girls Who Went Away*. New York: Penguin, 2006. Print.

Goddard, Henry H. "Wanted: A Child to Adopt." *Survey* 27 (October 14, 1911): 1003-1006. Print.

Halverson, Kay. *The Wedded Unmother: The Personal Story of a Woman Who Struggles to Understand and Accept Infertility*. Minneapolis: Augsburg, 1980. Print.

Herman, Ellen. "Eugenics." *The Adoption History Project*. Dept. of History, University of Oregon, n. d. Web. 17 Jan. 2009.

Hunt, Angela E. *Loving Someone Else's Child*. Wheaton, IL: Tyndale, 1992. Print.

"In the Matter of the Petition of J.N.H. and Concerning B.B.M., a Child." Colorado Court of Appeals, 08CA1235, April 2009. Print.

Javier, Rafael, et al., eds. *Handbook of Adoption: Implications for Researchers, Practitioners and Families*. Thousand Oaks, CA: Sage, 2006. Print.

Kammerer, Percy Gamble. *The Unmarried Mother: A Study of Five Hundred Cases*. 1918. Montclair, NJ: Patterson Smith, 1969. Print.

Karst, Kenneth. *Law's Promise, Law's Expression*. Yale University Press, 1993. Print.

Ketterman, Grace. *Mothering: The Complete Guide for Mothers of All Ages*. Nashville: Oliver-Nelson, 1991. Print.

Kitzinger, Sheila. *Ourselves as Mothers: the Universal Experience of Motherhood*. New York: Addison-Wesley, 1994. Print.

Kyle, Lyle. "Report to the Colorado General Assembly: Proposed Colorado Children's Code." Colorado Legislative Council Research Publication no. 111, December 1966. Print.

Lifton, Betty Jean. *Journey of the Adopted Self: A Quest for Wholeness*. New York: Basic Books, 1994. Print.

MacFarlane, J. *The Psychology of Childbirth*. Cambridge: Harvard University Press, 1975. Print.

Meltzoff, A. N. and Borton, R.W. "Intermodal Matching by Human Neonates." *Nature* 282.5737 (1979): 403-4. Print.

Neumann, Erich. *The Great Mother: An Analysis of the Archetype*. New York: Pantheon, 1955. Print.

Nydam, Ron. *Adoptees Come of Age: Living Within Two Families*. Louisville, KY: Westminster John Knox, 1999. Print.

Origins-USA.org, n. d. Web. 8 August 2008.

Pavao, Joyce Maguire. "Psychoeducation for Pre-Adoptive Families." *Child Welfare Report*, Feb. 1996, N. pag. Web. 21 Aug. 2008.

Pearce, Joseph. *Magical Child*. New York: Bantam Books, 1977. Print.

Pertman, Adam. *Adoption Nation: How the Adoption Revolution is Transforming America*. New York: Basic Books, 2000. Print.

Pike, Ruth. "Colorado's Laws Affecting Children: Report of Findings. Unit I – Adoption. Prepared for the Subcommittee on Courts, Procedures and Statutory Revision of the Interim Committee of the Thirty-Fifth General Assembly of the State of Colorado." December, 1946. Print.

Raymond, Barbara. *The Baby Thief: The Untold Story of Georgia Tann, the Baby Seller Who Corrupted Adoption*. New York: Carroll and Graf, 2007. Print.

Reitz, Miriam and Watson, Ken. *Adoption and the Family System*. New York: Guilford, 1993. Print.

Rillera, Mary Jo, and Sharon Kaplan. *Cooperative Adoption*. 2nd Ed. Westminister, CA: Triadoption, 1985. Print.

Samuels, Elizabeth. "The Idea of Adoption: An Inquiry into the History of Adult Adoptee Access to Birth Records." 53 *Rutgers Law Review* (2001): 367-427. Print.

Schooler, Jane. *Searching for a Past*. Colorado Springs: Pinon, 1995. Print.

Sebald, Hans. *Momism: the Silent Disease of America*. Chicago: Nelson Hall, 1976. Print.

Sigelman, Carol, and Elizabeth Ryder. *Life-Span Human Development*. 5TH ed. Belmont, CA: Thomson-Wadsworth, 2006. Print.

Siqueland, E. and C. DeLucia. "Visual Reinforcement of Non-nutritive Sucking in Human Infants." *Science* 165 (1969): 1144-46. Print.

Solinger, Rickie. *Wake Up Little Susie: Single Pregnancy and Race Before Roe v. Wade*. New York: Routledge, 1992. Print.

Spencer, Marietta. "The Terminology of Adoption." *Child Welfare* 58.7 (July-Aug. 1979): 451-459. Print.

Stern, D. *The Interpersonal World of the Infant: A View From Psycho-analysis and Developmental Psychology*. (Rev. ed.) New York: Basic Books, 2000. Print.

Stoneman, Albert H. "Adoption of Illegitimate Children: The Peril of Ignorance." *Child Welfare League of America Bulletin* 5 (February 15, 1926): 8. Print.

Taylor, Patricia E. *Shadow Train: A Journey Between Relinquishment and Reunion*. Baltimore: Gateway, 1995. Print.

Verrier, Nancy. *The Primal Wound: Understanding the Adopted Child*. Baltimore: Gateway, 1993. Print.

Vygotsky, Lev. *Thought and Language*. (E. Hanfman and G. Vakar, ed. and trans.) 1937. Cambridge: MIT Press, 1986. Print.

Wiggam, Albert E. *The New Decalogue of Science*. Indianapolis: Bobbs-Merrill, 1923. Print.

Winnicott, Donald. *The Family and Individual Development*. New York: Basic Books, 1966. Print.

Contributor Notes

Alice Home is a Professor Emeritus of social work at the University of Ottawa. Her current research explores Canadian stakeholders' views on the experiences and needs of parents whose adopted children have special needs. Her previous research focuses on employed mothers of children with hidden disabilities and groups for parents of children with ADHD, FASD or ASD. She is an adoptive mother of two adult children with ADHD.

Frances Latchford is an Associate Professor in the School of Women's Studies at York University in Toronto. Her adoption research utilizes feminist, continental and poststructuralist philosophies, as well as postcolonial, psychoanalytic, and queer theories of subjectivity. She is currently completing a monograph, *Steeped In Blood: Crimes against the Family under the Tyranny of a Bio-genealogical Imperative,* which considers the production of "family" experiences through discourses of family, adoption, sexuality and incest. She has also published articles examining drag and transsexuality in theatrical performance, queer identity, subjectivity, rights, and ethical knowledge.

Kate Livingston is a Ph.D. candidate in the Department of Women's, Gender and Sexuality Studies at The Ohio State University. Her research examines the politics of birthmotherhood in U.S. adoption law, policy and practice. Her current projects explore feminist theory and activism in open adoption and post-adoption support for birth parents. A native of Columbus, Ohio, she received her B.A. from Smith College in Government and her M.A. from the University of Cincinnati in Women's, Gender and Sexuality Studies. She is one of three birthmothers in her extended family.

Karen March is an Associate Professor in Sociology and Anthropology at Carleton University. Her book, *The Stranger Who Bore Me:*

Adoptee-Birth Mother Relations (University of Toronto Press, 1995), is among the first academic publications on adoption search and contact. She and Dr. Charlene Miall, at McMaster University, conducted a Canada-wide survey of attitudes toward adoption, the significance of biological parenting for child outcome, open adoption and gendered parenting stereotypes. Karen is writing a book on biological mothers and how the loss of children to adoption affects women's self-perception. She has served on *Adoption Quarterly*'s editorial board and was the *Canadian Sociology Association Newsletter* Society/Societe's Editor in 2002-2005.

Elisha Marr is an Assistant Professor of Sociology at Calvin College. Her current research and publications focus on transracial adoption. Her teaching and research interests also extend to families, the intersection of race, class, and gender, policy, and media/popular culture. She uses micro and macro-level research on transracial adoption to contribute to sociological scholarship on motherhood, structural racial inequality, and the relationship between media, public opinion, and public policy.

Judith Martin is an adoptive mother of three and grandmother of five, a professor and a writer on child welfare, foster care and adoption. She currently teaches at the University of Wisconsin Green Bay Social Work Professional Program, where she encourages students to strengthen research skills that will help better meet the needs of children and their mothers and fathers.

Nikki McCaslin is a senior instructor and humanities librarian at the University of Colorado; she has an M.A. in English Literature and an M.A. in Librarianship. She discovered when she was twenty-years-old that she had been adopted as an infant. She was later able to locate and form relationships with her first mother and five siblings. McCaslin is the mother of three adopted children and is the author of the book *Finding Our Place: One Hundred Memorable Adoptees, Fostered Persons, and Orphanage Alumni* (Greenwood Press, 2010).

Nicole Pietsch is Coordinator of the Ontario Coalition of Rape Crisis Centres. Since 1998, Nicole has assisted women and youth living with violence, including immigrant and refugee women, youth who are incarcerated or living in an institutional setting, and Deaf youth. Nicole's written work has appeared in *Canadian Woman Studies* and the University of Toronto's *Women's Health and Urban Life*. In 2010, her review of how the legal system interpreted race and gender within British Columbia's Reena Virk case appeared in *Reena Virk: Critical Perspectives on a Canadian Murder*, a collection published by Canadian Scholars' Press.

April Sharkey is a doctoral candidate in Women's Studies and Course Director at York University in Toronto. Her interest in motherhood and adoption stems from her own experiences with 'heteronormative' fertility clinics and NRTs. Her main interests include lesbian and queer geographies and children's studies. Her dissertation research focuses on the possibilities of positive narratives from queer youth in Toronto given the different places and spaces they inhabit.

Katherine Sieger is a doctoral candidate in the Cultural Foundations of Education Department at Syracuse University and has a Masters Degree in Women's Studies from the University of Cincinnati. Her research interests include: non-traditional identities of motherhood, unplanned pregnancy, pregnancy choice, heteronormativity in sex education and youth sexual identities. She is a Research Fellow with the Queering Education Research Institute (QuERI). She develops sex education and STI curriculum workshops for health teachers and works with youth on issues of sexual health, agency, and sexuality.

Amy E. Traver, Ph.D., is an Assistant Professor of Sociology at the City University of New York, Queensborough, U.S. She has published articles on adoption from China in *The International Journal of the Sociology of the Family*, *Qualitative Sociology*, and *Sociological Focus* and entries on adoption topics in *The Encyclopedia of Social Problems* and *The Praeger Handbook of Adoption*. Traver is the editor (with Michael Kimmel) of *Women, Family, and Class: The Lillian Rubin Reader* and the author of articles on education published in *The Journal of Education Policy* and *The Irish Journal of Sociology*.

Gail Trimberger, MSSW, LCSW, is an Assistant Professor at the University of Wisconsin-Green Bay Social Work Professional Program. She has direct practice and administrative experience in medical, long-term care, and end-of-life settings. She is particularly interested in issues related to grief and loss, and ethical decision-making.

Rich Uhrlaub, M.Ed., serves as Co-Director of Adoptees in Search - Colorado's Triad Connection. He is the President of the Colorado Adoption Intermediary Commission, and a member of the Legislative Committee of the American Adoption Congress. He is a contributing author of *Finding Our Place: One Hundred Memorable Adoptees, Fostered Persons and Orphanage Alumni* (Greenwood, 2010). He is currently working on a creative non-fiction novel based on the story of his origins.

Sarah Wall has a Ph.D. in Sociology from the University of Alberta, where she teaches courses in both gender and family. Her research interests include adoption and family, organizational ethics, and nursing professionalism. Sarah's work experience as a registered nurse prompted her research in nurses' work and the organizational, professional, and sociological factors that influence it. While taking her master's in health services administration, Sarah and her husband expanded their family of two daughters to include their internationally adopted son. As an adoptive mother, Sarah developed her current interest in analyzing discourses that circulate in the adoption community.

Jenny Heijun Wills is Assistant Professor of American text and culture in the English Department at the University of Winnipeg. Her research interests include Asian American literature, African American literature, adoption narratives, and interethnic approaches to race and ethnic studies.